Holy Wow!

Holy Wow!

The Patience Olympics

Volume IV

Dana St. Claire

ISBN Paperback: 978-1-7331059-9-6
ISBN eBook: 978-1-7376220-1-7
ISBN Audio: 978-1-7376220-0-0

Cover artwork: Miladinka Milic
Interior design: Creative Publishing Book Design

I dedicate this book to
my good friend, Debbie Barsotti… Nonna Extraordinaire.
This woman knows what family and friendship,
Love, and laughter are all about.

And

"Here's to the bridge-builders, the hand-holders,
the light-bringers,
those extraordinary souls wrapped in ordinary lives
who quietly weave threads of humanity
into an inhumane world.
They are the unsung heroes in a world at war with itself.
They are the whisperers of hope that peace is possible.
Look for them in this present darkness.
Light your candle with their flame.
And then go. Build bridges. Hold hands.
Bring light to a dark and desperate world.
Be the hero you are looking for.
Peace is possible.
It begins with us."

~ The Wisdom of L.R. Knost

Appetizers

Dana's Savory Hors d'œuvres of Volume IV Insight

Welcome to Volume IV of the *Holy Wow! Quartet.* Wowzariffic! Who knew there would be 4 volumes?

If this is your first journey into The Land of *Holy Wow!...* I'm glad you're here. If you've read other volumes of *Holy Wow!* then you know the first 3 volumes are really 1 big book. This volume... *The Patience Olympics...* is a book unto itself. Whereas the original *Holy Wow!* is a book I have been on the verge of writing for over 40 years, *The Patience Olympics* has only been tumbling around inside me for the last 20 years.

This volume took me longer to write than the first book... the one that ended up being divided into 3 volumes... i.e., many more words. I had a general idea of what I wanted *The Patience Olympics* to be... how I wanted it to show up. But let me tell you! I have been schooled! This volume had very distinct ideas of what it wanted to be and what it needed to say. I felt like I was "along for the ride." As in… "hang onto your hat!"

The Patience Olympics is a book about relationship. And patience. Tolerance. Kindness. Moving thru the vast and wide Realm of Humans Relating with a degree of grace. And gratitude.

We are called upon to meet each day with a good attitude… a positive outlook. Both offer their own quantum effects amidst the dither and miscellany of human interaction.

I have always found relationship fascinating. I'm intrigued by the ways different people interact with their fellow humans. Intrigued by the ways different people interact with themselves.

In *The Patience Olympics* I write about The Big 3: parenting, loving connexions and elders. The relationships and caring human interactions at both ends of the incarnant journey… and the vast in between. Parents and children… nurturing younglings to become healthy, contributing adults. Human to human in loving collaboration… "I care about you." Adult children caring for their parents… as their elders come to the end of their Earthtone Life.

In no way is this the end-all, be-all book about any of these vast, dimensional subjects. This is me… writing about my fascinations with my fellow humans and our mutual interactions. Who we each get to be as we show up for The Dance. Playing The Game. Riding the Rodeo of Life.

I'm sharing with you my fascinations with kindness, compassion, and communication.

The Path *Is* The Goal.

As with the other volumes of *Holy Wow!...* the chapters here in *Volume IV* alternate between "my" chapters... and chapters with insight, input, and suggestions from The Interpretorium Tour Guide. The Interpretorium is a place where beings who are about to Incarnate: Human On Planet Earth attend their Orientation Moment... their standard refresher course in Incarnate Embodiment.

The Interpretorium presents pre-incarnant beings with useful information and helpful updates on current planetary customs, circumstances, and conditions. These current updates are punctuated with insights from a Recent Returnee... arriving back from her latest incarnation in the region known as the West Coast of the United States. She brings her own tips, pointers and considerations... in the context of up-to-date Earthtone affairs.

These Interpretorium chapters also include realistic, human-Life dioramas and the actual experiencing of human emotional elements… complements of Realizmotron… our state-of-the-art Authentic Scenario Generator.

In this volume… mention of "your original Orientation Moment" refers to insights and Interpretorium data shared in the even-numbered chapters in *Holy Wow!* Volumes I, II, and III.

Volume IV is The Interpretorium's "Enhancement Upgrade Seminar"… building upon Orientation insights and understandings regarding the complicated and wide-ranging realms of human patience and relationship.

A new addition in Volume IV… I begin each of the odd-numbered chapters… "my" chapters… with an evocative quote. From, among others… Maya Angelou… Oscar Wilde… Albert Einstein.

As in all volumes of *Holy Wow!*… here in *The Patience Olympics*, I capitalize the word Life. Out of respect… for Life.

Cruising around on Planet Earth for more than 7 decades… I've made note of a few things. Experienced a taste… my Life's version… of the broad smorgasbord of all that is imaginable as we humans relate to one another. Ups and downs. Ins and outs. From sour to sublime.

Relating to one another is where it's at on Planet Earth. Anyone who thinks we're here for anything else… amassing great power, wealth, fame, status, ponies… is not taking into consideration the wealth of Life's many subtle, sterling qualities. The merry-go-round of all that "amassing" whirls and twirls within the amusement park of relationship. And how we treat each other. Revealing who we each are as we play within the roller coasters, hot dog stands, and tilt-a-whirls of Life.

In *Holy Wow! Volume I…* the Interpretorium Tour Guide suggested… on your way into incarnation… stand in line 3 times at the "Install Your Patience Here" kiosk. Maximum dosage. Recommending, "Don't leave home without it." She makes a good point.

Patience and tolerance… calm perseverance and acceptance… lubricate human interaction. Embracing this triple treat of your suggested 3 doses of patience… equips you with the stamina you'll need as you deal with… the trials and frustrations… the crazed and the stupid… awaiting you on that blue-green Planet of Paradox.

Thinking about it… where has impatience and vexation ever really gotten you?

Note to self: Annoyance and irritation… all judgey and grudgey… are not the allies they want you to believe they are.

As you are busy being human… this tendency to look for and focus on what's wrong is brought to you by toxic habit thought and all it does… to keep you thinking about it. Picking at it. Making everything worse than it needs to be. Seeing everything as worse than it is comes from habit.

A mindless, Life-sucking habit. Toxic habit thought keeps your wheels a'spinnin' in the noxious mud flats of Life.

As we are all busy being human… it takes some reorganizing of realization to recognize… *you* are not your thoughts. Your human instrument is equipt with a mental body… it thinks. It perceives. It ideates. This mental activity equipment is yours to use. It does not use you.

This is an even bigger, fatter deal when it comes to your emotional apparatus. We each come appointed with razzamatazz emotional paraphernalia. Your emotions feel sooo real. You believe… "I am my anger." "I am my frustration." "I am my self-doubt." "I am my anxiety and confusion." "I can't help the way I am." Yes… you can. This emotional nature is for you to operate and utilize… not for you to be gaslighted and victimized by its distressed gyrations.

You are not your physical body… even tho it sure "looks like" you are. *You* are not your physical fitness… nor your flab. Your physical body is the state-of-the-art vehicle… the neato-keen ambulatory equipment… you get to use as you navigate physical-plane reality. It is not who you *are*.

Each human being is animated by the spark of Spirit. This essence of conscious awareness enlivens your vehicles. Your physical, emotional, mental instrument is yours to utilize… as you cruise around being human in the physical, emotional, and mental environments of Planet Earth.

Earth is not called The Planet of Paradox because that has a snazzy ring to it. Paradox… absurdity… contradiction and conundrum… rock the very core of human existence.

Another person I quote in The Patience Olympics is Mark Twain… a towering figure in American literature. With much to say and saying it often with humor and flair, Twain was considered the first worldwide celebrity. "Known to everyone ~ Liked by all." He offers this nugget of clear observation, which touches me deeply:

> "Do not complain about growing old.
> It is a privilege denied to many."

"A privilege denied to many." A privilege, indeed… yet not always easy living within. The habits and tendencies of your Life… as well as genetics and practices… accumulate, showing up in significant and meaningful ways. Many of them leading to uneasy decline.

My husband, Scott, and I lived with and cared for my parents in their declining years. As with my children being miraculous and wonder-full… here I am also thankful for "the material" we worked with as we cared for my folks. All in all… they were an easygoing pair. Yet, picking up the reins of their Life and being present with them in the day-to-day could be challenging. Difficult. Trying. It definitely "had its moments."

One day, in the midst of it all, I said to Scott... "*This is the patience Olympics!*" And here we are.

"A#1" consideration for families caring for declining elders:

Don't burn out the caregiver.

Even more clearly stated:

Take good care of the caregiver.

With this in mind... as you come to the close of this book, after the end of chapter 9... you will find 2 "Afters." One "Afters" contains resources and suggestions for the ever-important health and well-being of caregivers. The other "Afters" tells you about documents and affairs to have in order to facilitate the legal aspects of caring for the elders in your Life. Both contain useful... hopefully, helpful... information.

If you have read other volumes of *Holy Wow!*... sprinkled thru-out *The Patience Olympics* you may recognize familiar insights and stories woven amidst the threads of this current tapestry. This is intentional. Pertinent Orientation Material from earlier volumes interweaves here.

The Patience Olympics is The Interpretorium's Enhancement Upgrade Seminar... in response to interest expressed by cognent beings after their Orientation Moment. This volume addresses the interests of those who anticipate incarnating as engaged, loving parents… or to help ailing elders. *The Patience Olympics* develops and enhances the flow of perceptive realization in these areas.

In this Enhancement Seminar… points and insights are repeated and revisited. Repetition is a robust human learning strategy. Practice. Rehearsal. The human instrument's way to anchor and develop comprehension. Becoming fluent in another language takes practice and repetition. A person learning to play the piano… practices… over and over. A play, a concert, a dance recital = lots of rehearsals.

At times, coming across repeated information… can bring a hasty, knee-jerk shutdown… an automatic "I've heard this before." To be considered… when you encountered said information before… you were who you were then. This is now.

> "We cannot step into the same river twice."
> ~ Pre-Socratic Greek philosopher, Heraclitus
> (540-480 B.C.E.)

We change. The river changes. Just because you heard something before doesn't mean you won't hear it differently… gain new insight… as you hear or read it now. You are not *now* who you were *then*.

Be open to concepts you may have heard before. Allow yourself to hear these matters fresh. As you are open to new possibilities… insight may enter your awareness in new and different ways.

Repetition builds acuity. Insight. Perception. Skills. Understanding.

Also consider: You may have heard or read an insightful passage 147 times. And on #148… Aha!! This happened to me with the declaration … "God is love." I can't even tell you the multitude of times I heard or read "God is love." Yeah, yeah… ok. Then in 1 fateful instant… it hit me:

God *Is* Love!

Holy Glockenspiel! I got it! All those other times… I'd heard the words. Yet, clarity eluded me. The enormity of it did not land. Until it did!

Yes… I "heard it all before." And then I Got It!

This realization landing has had an incredible effect on me… in vast and dimensional ways. It has certainly given me unerring insight into repetition as a tool to greater awareness.

The Life-changing effects of mantra, chanting and using affirmations comes to mind.

Make yourself available to receive new nuggets of realization. Look at… be in… *this* moment. With fresh eyes. Wisdom and understanding may arrive when you least expect it. (That's always fun.)

You may have noticed… *Holy Wow!* Volumes I, II, and III are each dedicated to my amazing daughter, Lyla. As you know, Volumes I, II, and III were written as one large book, which I dedicated to her. This Volume IV is a completely other, freshly written book. I am delighted to dedicate it to and acknowledge my dear… also amazing… friend, Debbie Barsotti. Truly an extraordinary human being. A kind, fun, gracious *artiste*… spry and dexterous at the art of being human. Go, Deb!

The Patience Olympics' dedication page also includes an inspiring suggestion from the vast and wide wisdom of L.R. Knost.

Now and then I have chided myself for "taking so long" to write *Holy Wow!* You and I both know… had I written it at any other time in my Life… it would be a different book. Altho, you know what? A few years back I watched episodes of my cable-access TV show, *Meditation with Dana St Claire*, preparing to add it to our YouTube channel. I had to smile… there I was 25 years ago, sharing many of the same insights and awarenesses I include in *Holy Wow!* Now interwoven with new bits and realizations I had not yet come to even a few years ago.

Writing *Holy Wow!*... and now *The Patience Olympics*… has been an incredible process. As I mentioned… all along, and particularly with this volume… interweavings, topics, and realizations pop up of their own accord. "Now you're writing about *this!*" Okay.

I particularly like… I'm beavering away on a certain phrase, passage, or conundrum… lo and behold! In a stunningly timely manner… an illuminating tidbit shows up in a conversation or a movie or a news article… dimensionalizing the very concepts I'm currently pondering and writing about. Wow! Thanks! That's fun. And definitely appreciated.

A Coda to Volume IV Appetizers: Remember how I wrote earlier "I have been schooled!"? About how *The Patience Olympics* had very distinct ideas of what it wanted to be and what it needed to say. And I was "along for the ride." Welllll… it turns out… just like the original *Holy Wow!* was divided into 3 volumes… because Volume IV has so many words… it, too, is being divided. Into 2 volumes. This Volume IV you hold in your hand is the first 9 chapters of *The Patience Olympics*. Volume V… soon to follow… will contain chapters 10-13. And obviously whatever else it wants to say.

We humans are on quite a ride … drawing in the Sweet Breath of Life… claiming our space… creating a Life… as this blue-green orb spins around the sun. We are each doing the very best we can. Yes, I know. In some cases, it does not look or feel that way. Yet here we all are.

We each made the choice to incarnate human on Planet Earth. The clever part of being here is making this all do-able. Maybe even pleasant. Possibly fulfilling. More bliss than blisters.

We, each and all, are fighting a great battle. A battle within ourselves. Bubbling within the cauldron of external circumstances and affiliations. We react and respond. We learn and grow. Or hibernate. Stagnate. Aimless. Idle. Motivated. Engaged. Inspired. Inspiring.

Top of the list to making it thru… Be Kind To Yourself. Be Kind To Others.

Don't allow toxic habit thought… harmful emotional fixations… be in charge of your precious human Life.

Stand up for yourself… inside yourself. Encourage yourself to become the person you want to be. Encourage others to be themselves. Choose to learn from setbacks and annoyances. Don't let frustrations and disappointments win.

Grow your self.

Grow your soul.

An acknowledging salute to Meher Baba (1894-1969)… who knew what he was talking about. Or in his case… not talking about:

"Don't worry. Be happy."

Table of Contents

Thanks for Riding Along with Me

O kay, so right here at the get-go, I am going to tell you something about my writing style. I like words. And I like playing with them. I don't want you to think my wonderful book editor didn't catch my stylistic tendencies. Rather, she chose to let my writing be my writing. Which I hugely appreciate.

Let's start with "…". You will learn as you read *Holy Wow!* that this book had an incredibly long gestation period. As it finally started tumbling out, it came with "…". A breath, a beat, a moment. If using "…" was finally how things were going to get going… who was I to resist? This "…" worked well for me. And it kept working. Naturally, I hope it works well for you, too.

Over the 4 decades as *Holy Wow!* gestated, I did, of course, write other things. When I wrote, I used "tho" for "though" and "thru" for "through"… which quite naturally led to "altho" and "thru-out." When my editor, Pam, first read my *Holy Wow!* manuscript, she pointed out that I was using "texting language." She expressed concern that some readers might criticize my choices and think less of my work because of such abbreviations… such casual language. As I have used these spellings my entire adult Life… I pointed out that texting just finally caught up with me. I don't mean to be vexing… this is just the way I write.

I totally understand the proper and professional… and I want you to know that Pam is both. It's me who feels odd seeing "tho" and "thru" completely spelled out in my writing. That doesn't look like me. I realize those spellings are considered by some to be text shorthand. To me… they are just the more sensible way to spell those words.

On to another thing or 2. Did you know that humans devised and used numbers centuries before letters were invented? This development of numbers, counting, and recording systems was humanity's first long-distance communication tool, having a profound effect on the ability to share knowledge, transmit information, and thrive. I am intrigued by this historical significance of numbers. Giving a shout out to numbers… in my writing, I use the actual numeral to indicate numbers. (Except in the rare case when a number starts a sentence… then, I spell the word rather than using the number symbol.)

I use the word "grok" to mean "deeply understand." I also use the word "connexion" to indicate ever-so-much more connected that a mere connection. Here and there I use "yeah" as an informal "yes"… not to mean "yay." You will also find the occasional unique spelling of a word, and capitalizations that indicate certain Orientation Programs and Certifications. Now and again, in the midst of a sentence, you will come across an " = " sign. As in… "This ability to have a chuckle = a most sanity-producing maneuver as you are busy being human."

There is additional creative spelling and word usage… "intellecting" or "thinkery," for instance… which, to me, are self-explanatory. The words "equipt" or "spoilt" you may recognize as the British spelling. I've always liked them spelled that way.

Words are tricky little comprehension packets. You will come across "cognent," which can be seen as a blend of "cogent" and "cognitive." I use "cognent" to describe the beings who are not in incarnation, yet. And "incarnant" to describe the beings who are.

I share this with you, Dear Reader, to say… these writing nuances are neither mistakes nor oddities. They are the creative choices that make *Holy Wow!* the experience it is. I write this to thank you for riding along with me and for easing into my stylistic ways. Now, let's have some fun!

CHAPTER ONE

Don't Make
The Hard Stuff Harder

"This vast and wide opening of your heart."

"I hope my children look back on today
and see a parent who had time to play.
There will be years for cleaning and cooking,
but children grow up when we are not looking."
~ Unknown

Ah, yes... patience. Friend or foe?
Along with its sidekicks... tolerance, calm, fortitude... riding the range of human interaction.

Like Batman and Robin. Tonto and the Lone Ranger. Partners. A posse of peaceful possibility.

Applying a moment of personal observation… you gotta ask yourself… "Where has being impatient ever gotten me?" Irritated? Frustrated? Annoyed? Angry? Has that leap to impatience helped the situation? Made everybody feel better?

Life regales us with situations a'plenty. And, with us humans being social creatures, plenty of interactions, too. So many choices to make as we hoof it thru Life's circumstances and relationships. Some choices we make are helpful… doing right by the moment. Some… not so much.

Any parent or teacher will tell you… kids are always ready to give you a whole lot of opportunities to exercise your patience muscles. Like having a personal trainer! Only different.

When my kids were little, people would say to me, "You should write a book!" About being a parent. I would think, "What in the world would I say?" Even when they were little, my 2 kids were pretty miraculous. They had their little trips amazingly together. They were charming and cooperative. We had great times together. I always figured I had lucked out. I just got good material to work with. What could I possibly say about the way I parented?

Like every young parent… I was flying by the seat of my pants.

I did what came naturally. What felt right. Believe me… I wasn't "intellectualizing" this whole parenting thing. Who has time for that? I couldn't put what I was doing… and the way I was doing it… into words and concepts.

Standing in awe of these 2 young beings… I was just humming along. Enjoying being a mom. Enjoying my time with my 2 funny, bright, delightful little bunnies… Lyla and Isaiah.

Over 30 years later… all of a sudden… it became clear to me what I was "doing."

When Isaiah and Lyla were young… because of where I was at in my Life… I saw them as my gurus. My teachers. They were *so* that. So much insight came from just being with them. I was in admiration of who these 2 miraculous little humans were.

This is one of the many aspects we parents get to decide… am I impatient? Consumed by what a pain in the patoot all this parenting stuff is? Such a bother. So hard. Overwhelming. Relentless. Too much.

Or am I enjoying this ride? In awe. Taking it all in… the complications… the crazies. The cuteness. The ongoing, continual continuousness. Determined… choosing… to be having a good time. For my own sake. For the sake of these remarkable young humans.

Here's something that doesn't occur to you when you're deep in the thick of Universe Baby: It's all over in a blink! That sure didn't occur to me as I was changing diapers…

schlepping the bag(s) of gear… comforting in the wee, dark hours of the morning. This sure *feels like* it will go on forever.

Then Zoop! All of a sudden… Isaiah is in first grade(!). Then they're both in grammar school! A whole other way of being. The school schedule takes over Life. Next thing you know… they've graduated from high school. What? It's over already?

Yup. It's over.

Up to your elbows in the thick of it… so consumed… it doesn't even cross your mind… this *isn't* forever. This isn't the whole book. It's only the first chapter. A precious, never-to-be- experienced-again chapter. Yes, you're a parent for the rest of your Life. Yes, there are many variants… demands… nuances. Nuisances. But there isn't *anything* that compares to the intensity of those first several years. And the preciousness.

Parenting your kids into adulthood is a different kind of intense. Variations on the theme of intense. Older children bring different challenges and negotiations. You are still present. Participating. Always the parent.

When Isaiah was about a year old… as I was still reeling from the onslaught of being a new mom… I met a woman with 5 kids. "Stair-step" kids. Her youngest was 4 and her oldest was 11. I was agog. I blurted out, "It must have been so intense when they were babies!" Their mother replied…

"Are you kidding? That's the easiest time." Whoa. That was a major perspective shift for my young mommy self. This is the *easy* part?

The Wonder Wheel of parenting is all intense. Rewarding. Aggravating. Continuous. The "intense" just gets different as the kids get older.

What kind of parent do you want to be? What kind are you? What kind of parent were you? Were you loving and engaged? Authoritarian and distant? Hands on? Hands off? Memorable… for all the sweet things? Memorable… for all the harshness? There for me? Gone without a trace? You *are* the parent. It's yours to choose.

This is the miraculous, meaningful measure of all things… you get to choose. It's all up to you. Whew!

During my first pregnancy, with Isaiah… I read a lot of books about both pregnancy and parenting. I got a chuckle out of how the pregnancy books all sound like once you give birth… it's "all over." Yes, in terms of the actual pregnancy… this is true. But in terms of now I'm a parent and Life is careening on and on… ooowee, Baby! The fun has just begun!

The best advice I read in any parenting book… "It all washes off."

I was given a copy of Dr. Spock's *The Common Sense Book of Baby and Child Care* during my first pregnancy.

I'd heard the name "Dr. Spock" my whole Life. In 2016, doing research for *Holy Wow!,* I was surprised to discover how controversial Spock's book was when it first appeared in 1946. Wildly radical. Advice unheard-of. Just in time for the post-World War II baby boom.

Dr. Spock encouraged parents to be flexible and affectionate. Show your love. Encourage your children to express their individuality. This = "wildly radical?" From the '50s on… many young childhood specialists… like T. Berry Brazelton and Rudolf Dreikurs… continued guiding young parents to be encouraging. Show your affection.

Earlier generations parented with a heavy hand… strict rules and discipline. Harsh correction and inflicting punishment were the rules of the road. "This is the way it's done." Rigid adherence to schedules… concern about appearances ruled the day. There are parents today who still believe this is what being a parent is all about.

My personal take? This heavy-handed approach shows a distinct lack of imagination. Where's healthy engaging with your kids? Where's the insightful creativity? Thanks to Dr. Spock and other child-rearing professionals… at least in our current world, there's more wiggle room. Good for parent. Good for child. Heaven knows, kids like to wiggle.

Full disclosure… the only part of *Baby and Child Care* I actually made time to read was the Introduction. Then

Life careened off in many directions… as it is so prone to do. One comment from Dr. Spock's Introduction leapt out at me… and has stayed with me all these years.

"Unless a person has gone thru a major change in their own consciousness, they will parent exactly the way they were parented." Hmmm. Interesting.

By the time Isaiah was born, I had been meditating for 8 years. Reading Dr. Spock's words… I could easily acknowledge… I had definitely gone thru a major change in my consciousness. Altho I'm here to tell you… there were times my mother's voice came right out of my mouth. Southern accent and all.

In my mid-20s, I had a lovely friend named Mary. She and her husband, Richard, had a daughter and 2 sons… all young teenagers at the time. These 3 kids were splendid people… remarkably angst-free. They carried on conversations with adults… looking you in the eye… laughing at your jokes. The first time I went to dinner at their house… my mind was significantly blown. As the meal finished, these 3 kids… without a word from their parents… got up and cleared the table(!). With no grousing or grumbling… chatting and joking amongst themselves… they went into the kitchen and did the dishes! Then 1 of the boys came out and swept the floor! They just *did* it. No griping. No fuss. Just doing the needful.

Well, I'm here to tell you... this did not slip past me. I took notice.

When my first pregnancy was confirmed... I went straight to Mary. "How did you do *that*?" She chuckled. "A lot of it was dumb luck and the rest of it was this book." She gave me a copy of *Children: The Challenge*.

"This book" became a significant component of my Life... parenting and otherwise. Truly an insight-full blessing.

Children: The Challenge was first published by Rudolf Dreikurs in 1964. Dreikurs (1897-1972) was one of America's foremost child psychiatrists. He created this warm, reassuring guide to help parents better understand their children's behavior. His intention was to evolve parenting awareness. Giving parents tools to cope with common child-rearing problems. I appreciate the way he includes many real-world examples thru-out the book. Showing actual ways to stimulate cooperative behavior... without heavily relying on punishment or reward.

One of his ideas really stood out for me... sidestep "Because I told you to!" Being all authoritarian... telling the child what to do... is not a parenting requirement. Instead... within reason... allow the child to make their own choices. Allow them to be part of the solution. As a child is encouraged to make their own decisions, they begin to understand... "This is how you do Life."

So, you're in a tussle with your kid about wearing a coat when they go outside. You *can* sidestep the tussle. Your only option is not a testy "You have to wear a coat because I say so! Do it!" Here's a possibility... engage the child by offering 2 different coats... "Do you want to wear your blue one or your orange one?"

There is great benefit... for both parent and child... when the child is allowed to make choices. This helps a child realize Life offers several possibilities. It also fosters understanding of taking responsibility for the outcome. Let's have a learning moment rather than an overbearing... punishing... moment.

Another option... "It's chilly outside, it would be good for you to wear a jacket. If you don't want to... go ahead and go out, but if you get cold, come back in and grab your jacket." You are saying, "You choose what to do. I trust you will know if you're warm or cold. You make the decision." When the kid does come back in to put their jacket on... avoid the tendency to snark or say, "I *told* you so." Truly... resist. Instead, be present with your child... "It *is* cold out there, isn't it? You're making a good choice to put your jacket on."

A good friend of mine recounts... his father had to be Totally In Control of Everything his wife and children did. My friend was in his 30s before he realized... "I can make my own decisions and act on them." For him, at that time... truly a revelation.

As a parent... or teacher, or employer... you do not need to default to anger, blame, or lecturing. These are not your only choices. You can be more creative. More aware and attuned. More in this moment. Here. Now.

Let's say I'm looking to move beyond knee-jerk lecturing, anger or blame... what does *this* moment call for? How do I get to *be...* here... now? I'm sure I have options. What would they be? Looking to grab a handle on the moment? Draw a deep, centering breath (even more helpful than it sounds). Put a little thought-juice into it. How will I respond? What other possibilities are there? Stretching those brain cells... those heart cells. Present and creative... rather than rigid and authoritarian. Meeting the requirements of *this* moment. *This* child. *This* interaction.

As you read *Children: The Challenge*, parts of it will seem outdated. You'll think, "I've heard this before." Which is true... you have. Much of Dreikurs work has become part of the childrearing lexicon. Every parent educator in the country has been influenced by his work and this book. Choose to look with fresh eyes. Even in the midst of "I've heard this before"... you will come upon helpful suggestions and information. The examples of actual child-parent interaction are revealing and insightful. Even if parts of it you've "heard before"... this is definitely a worthwhile read.

In *Children: The Challenge*, Dreikurs emphasizes the importance of encouragement. His viewpoint clearly stated:

> "Encouragement is more important
> than any other aspect of child-raising.
> It is so important that the lack of it
> can be considered the basic cause for misbehavior."

Dreikurs' key parenting concepts are:

Encouragement

Respect... the child to the parent... the parent to the child

Kind and firm parenting

The family council... promoting effective communication, individual responsibility, and family harmony. Mutually respectful engagement in problem-solving... democratic leadership. Fostering family camaraderie in living the day-to-day of Life

Understanding the goals of misbehavior... seeking attention, power, or revenge... coming from a sense of inadequacy

Basically... maintain a casual, friendly attitude... stay calm in the midst of the kids' sometimes wild and crazy behaviors

Many, many times… I've given or suggested *Children: The Challenge* to new parents I meet. Yes, it's true… even random strangers on the street. I'm all about sharing what works. Lyla recently texted me… "I just ordered *Children: The Challenge* for my mentee at the Embassy. He and his husband are in the process of adopting a baby. *Children: The Challenge* is the most consistent baby present I give."

Dreikurs' sensibilities and recommendations are a helpful lubricant for happy parenting and a fulfilling homelife. Both of my children were raised with encouragement and respect… largely influenced by *Children: The Challenge*. It's a beautiful thing to see them each raising their children with similar kind regard.

The generational aspects of gentle, encouraging parenting are profound. It only takes one generation to break long-held cycles of abuse and neglect.

If you grew up in a painful home environment… you can be the one to change it. You can be the generation to make different choices. To show up for your kids in a kind and loving way. You can be the change you always wanted to come and rescue you.

I also give a grateful shout out to T. Berry Brazelton… a smiley, delightful man… a celebrated baby doctor who revolutionized our understanding of how each child uniquely develops.

"He put the baby at the center of the universe"… observes his colleague Dr. Barry Lester, who is also a pediatrician.

Dr. Brazelton is widely known for developing this "child-oriented" approach. He guided families to lay the foundation vital for children's early learning and healthy development. He was intent upon helping folks build strong family-child relationships… stating clearly, "Parents need as much support as their babies do."

As I mentioned a moment ago… in the conventional wisdom of previous generations… child-rearing was strict and authoritarian. It was believed infants did not feel pain. When children were hospitalized, parents were allowed few, if any, visits. Parents were instructed to follow strict schedules… demand obedience… and refrain from kissing or cuddling. Babies were to be fed every 4 hours, by the clock, preferably from a bottle.

My mother completely followed that last decree. Even when baby me was ready to sleep thru the night… she woke me up every 4 hours to give me a bottle. Because that's what she was "supposed to do."

Dr. Brazelton… confirming Dr. Spock's viewpoint… rejected rigid, authoritarian practices as senseless and cruel. His colleague, Dr. Lester, goes on to say… "We take for granted all the changes he helped bring about. Dr. Brazelton more than anyone is responsible for the return to natural childbirth, breast feeding and the ability of parents to stay with a hospitalized child."

Writing close to 40 books... Dr. Brazelton also had a column in Family Circle magazine. He hosted an Emmy Award-winning TV show, "What Every Baby Knows"... which ran for 12 years on the Lifetime channel. I read his books. And delighted in the photos of his smiling, engaged presence. I did not know about his TV show or his magazine column. I do know... thru each of these venues, he was a kind, compassionate guide for many parents.

It seems to me... his most powerful contribution to healthy parenting = he *liked* babies and kids. His pleasure and enthusiasm for who each child *is*... conveys to parents the possibilities for a greater degree of congenial, gratifying interaction with their kids.

A person whose Life was touched by his work wrote... "Dr. Brazelton broke the cycle of violence in my family. I never hit my children and learned from him that as I am the adult, I can think of more effective, non-violent ways of raising my children. The payoff for me is to see my grown, well-adjusted, adult children using the same effective, loving techniques I used as they raise their children."

Dr. Brazelton emphasizes... from birth... infants are individuals with their own unique qualities. They are social organisms... ready to shape... as well as be shaped by... their caregiving environment. His emphasis?

Babies each learn and develop at their own pace.

Awareness of this helps parents recognize not only are there different stages of development... there are different types of babies. Each with their own inborn characteristics... their own temperament and qualities. Their own "nature" component of "nature via nurture."

"Temperament" describes a child's personal style... the way she or he experiences their world. Is your child highly social? Is she slow-to-warm-up? Is your child flexible when faced with change... or troubled by unexpected transitions? Does he prefer the routine and predictable? Or is he just fine with anything goes?

Obviously... even children born in the same family have very different temperaments. Each with their own distinct personal style and way of being.

The three major types of temperament are: easy... slow-to-warm-up... and difficult. Understanding a child's temperament is a vital part of parenting. Dr. Brazelton uses the term "goodness of fit" to describe how well a baby's temperament fits with the expectations and demands of their home environment... from challenging to sublime.

Some may read these calm, engaged, encouraging suggestions and think, "These parenting guidelines are too hard. I can't do that! It takes too much patience" Yes, conscious, aware parenting calls you to your best. It can be hard. Parenting without conscious awareness is hard. With the effects riding hard on a child... and thru-out their adult Life. As they say... "choose your hard."

We each parent the way we were parented. Unless, as adults, we make the conscious choice to be different. To be better. To do this momentous endeavor with kindness and style. A bit of flair. Just like we're having a good time.

One person who parents with a bit of flair and sure seems to be having a good time is actor, producer, acclaimed professional wrestler and enthusiastic girl-daddy... Dwayne "The Rock" Johnson. He wears many hats in his accomplished, multi-faceted Life. The hat he is proudest to wear is his daddy hat. He says, "Being a father is the greatest job I have ever had and the greatest job I will ever have."

He also offers this sincere advice: "To all you young men out there who will be fathers one day, the goal of 'being better' will never steer you wrong."

Some people hear the suggestion to "be better" and leap to the touchy interpretation that they are seen as a failure. Bristling. "What... you sayin' I'm doing something wrong?" Nope. That's not the case. We can all do better.

Receive this recommendation as it is delivered… not that you're doing something wrong… but that Life presents us all with opportunities to wake up. Open our eyes… look around… find ways to develop and proceed. There's always room to improve. Always ways to learn to live a happier, healthier, more centered and fulfilling Life. For yourself. For your family and friends. For the innocent bystanders your Life touches.

Within yourself… learn to be aware of that knee jerk defensiveness bully. Always ready to snarl and feel insulted. Don't allow a defensive attitude cloud your vision… or sidetrack your heartfelt intentions. Don't let hostility and mistrust distract you from your inborn ability to succeed as a well-rounded, contributing human being.

In the first several months of our relationship… Scott and I were astounded to realize… to see… how defensive we each were. At even a twinge of conflict… there it was… that hot leap to defensiveness. Whoa. Well look at that! Where are we going with this? Fortunately, it wasn't like one of us was saying… "You're so defensive!" We each could see and feel our own defensiveness. Not even once did it improve the situation. Defensiveness never helps a thing.

Being defensive is never the Life ally it pretends to be. If anything… it's just the opposite. A defensive reaction may feel like it's taking care of you. However, look closely… the leap to hostility is a thoughtless reflex… a hasty impulse. A mindless contraction which immediately narrows your vision, distorting how you see yourself and your world. Rather than being your ally… being defensive impacts who you show up as. Tangling your resolve. Baffling your best intentions.

Your intention is to be a good parent… with a bit of fun and flair. Having a good time as you interact with your kids. This is totally possible. And has mostly to do with *you*.

You know how you can feel… you can tell… if someone is not having a good time? Kids feel that, too. They know. It kinda sucks to feel like your parent is unhappy while they're hanging out with you. When you're upset… your kid's feel bad whether it's their "fault," or not.

One of the best ways I ever heard the strategies of parenting described:

Treat your children as if they are
diplomats from a foreign country.

You would want a person visiting your country from afar to have a good time while they're in your land. You'd want them to feel welcome and at ease. You make time to talk with them… about expectations and what's what. You equip them with information which steers them toward having a good time... a successful venture. You discuss local customs and conduct. Not every country thinks it's a compliment to belch after dinner.

When you're taking your kids out to a restaurant or to a friend's house... have a conversation with them beforehand about behavior and expectations. "Remember, Aunt Lucy doesn't like you touching her glass figurines." Plan ahead... take something to occupy their hands and attention. "Which toy or book do you want to take to Aunt Lucy's to play with?"

"Remember, we use our inside voice when we're at a restaurant. Sometimes you can play at restaurants. At the place we're going to for dinner tonight... the expectation is you will stay in your chair. Which coloring book do you want to take with you? Crayons? Or colored markers?"

You would happily educate a diplomat or foreign visitor to the ways and customs of your particular country. To the way Life works. Recognizing them as your special guest... you would inform them of expectations.

With your kids... make them aware of "protocol" in Adultotopia. Not in a rude way, but talking to them like they're someone you like. Usually, ahead of time. Doing what you can... so they (and you) will have a positive experience while navigating in your world.

In parenting, the "Golden Rule" applies:

Do unto your children
as you would like your children to do unto you.

A fitting variation could be:

Do unto your children
As you would have liked your parents to do unto you.

Being a parent is *absolutely* A Lot of Work. Having 2 functional, engaged parents does = A Perfect World. Emphasis here on "functional and engaged." Too many times… Life does not turn out that way. There may be 2 parents… but there is no guarantee either or both parents will be "functional" or "engaged." Unfortunate for the child(ren). Unfortunate for the parent(s).

There are oh-so-many variations on the theme of 2 engaged and functional parents. So many variations on the assorted likelihoods to be considered. Even when 2 parents are married, or in a committed relationship… that doesn't mean they are both engaged in constructive parenting. I have spent time both as a single parent and co-parenting without much of a "co-." I'm not sure which is harder. Having to do it all myself 'cause nobody else is around. Or having to do it all myself while somebody else is sitting right there.

Up until the 1940s… the most common scenario had a family's adult male component working out in the world…

hunting, farming, going to the office, the factory, the university. The female unit was found at home. Raising the children... making the meals... keeping the house. Making enough for dinner so there were leftovers for Dad's lunch. Packing said lunch.

In the United States and many other countries... the profound requirements of the World War II era substantially changed this who-does-what configuration. Many women moved from homelife into factories, offices, and teaching positions. Filling the jobs of men, as the men went off to war. Of course, the assumption was... when the war is over, women will return to their place... their housework. Everything will just go back to "the way it was." Right?

Well, that didn't happen. Many women continued to work out in the world. The notions of "this is men's work" and "this is women's work" began to change and evolve. Thru-out society... one could find varying degrees of being okay with that.

An interesting observation on "the way things were"... have you ever noticed... the "male jobs" outside the home usually come equipt with some sort of "completion factor?" The report is finished. The skyscraper, shed or ship is built. "My work is done." Others can admire this job well done. There is a sense of accomplishment. Achievement. Completion. Occasionally there are accolades.

On the other hand… just how "done" is the "woman's work" inside the home? Not very. *Nada.* All is repetitive and continual. No "final product" to admire. No done and done. Make the bed… the bed is slept in… make the bed again. Wash the dishes… a meal is served… wash the dishes again. Do the laundry… the clothes are worn… here we are doing laundry again. Folding it. Putting it away. Again. Sigh.

Okay, maybe she gets 5 minutes of "Ahhhh… done." Then Life scurries on. There is little true sense of achievement. Each completed task gets undone and must be done again. Household chores are never "over." There is no *finito.* Any sense of accomplishment? Fleeting.

In the realm of general sanity… there's a lot to be said for a functional adult being at home. This does not have to be the female adult. Just a caring person present. Kissing boo-boos. Keeping a degree of order within the home. Attending to the ever-present "What's for dinner?"

The menu doesn't just plan itself. "Someone" is coming up with those dinner ideas. "Someone" is grocery shopping… for specific ingredients and keeping the staples stocked. Sous cheffing… chop, chop, chop. Prep, prep, prep. Cooking. Setting the table. Serving. When small children are present… feeding. Clearing the table. Putting away leftovers and condiments. Washing the dishes… or loading the dishwasher. As they are dry… putting dishes and utensils back in cupboards and drawers.

Et voila!

Here we go… ready to do it all over again.

When you are not the one actually engaged in the continuousness of housekeeping procedures … this process seems like magic! If noticed at all. Look! My underwear… sweaters… pajamas… are all clean and folded in my drawer. Food is on the table… in the cupboard… in the fridge. Fresh towels in the bathroom. Magically… the toys are all picked up. Again. When you're not the one doing these ongoing processes… it's easy to be unaware of… to overlook… the amount of labor involved.

When you are not the "house keeper" everything is just where it's supposed to be. The way it's supposed to be. Again. Any person who thinks the "keeping" part of household reality is "easy" is the person who has not done it. Over and over and over again.

Of course, there are those stay-at-home folks who just let it all pile up… dirty dishes in the sink… laundry on the floor… smelly diapers in the pail. Those are choices, too. Creating their own particular household environment.

"Smelly diapers in the pail." Ha ha. Cloth diapers… back in the day. Yes, it's true… I parented small children 40 years ago. I washed, dried, and folded many a diaper. The year Isaiah was 1-2 years old we lived in Tucson, Arizona. Acknowledging the hot temperatures… locals would say, "But it's a dry heat." I'll say! And it is true… "wet heat" has its own ways of being significantly unpleasant. Sticky. And bugs. And more sticky. And more bugs.

In Tucson… I would take a load of washed diapers out to hang on the lines stretched between 2 poles in the backyard. Hot and dry indeed. As I hung the last washed diaper… I'd head right back to the first diaper I hung… like, 7 minutes ago. Starting with the first diaper hung… I proceeded to take each one down. They were totally dry. Like putting them in a clothes dryer. Only different.

Disposable diapers were just arriving on the scene. To be used for emergencies. Or if you go camping. In those days… it didn't occur to folks those disposables would become the diapers used all the time. Well, let's just say… it didn't occur to *me*.

What struck me the most in those days was, indeed, the unceasing continuousness of it all. There it is… The Major Adjustment to being the stay-at-home person. The demands of daily maintenance. Laundry. Meals. Picking up. Keeping track of the kids. Keeping track of *all the stuff*. "24/7" doesn't even sum it up.

Ongoing. Continuous. Round the clock. And round again.

Patience definitely required. Patience and a good attitude.

About your kids and chores. When it comes to the many components of housekeeping… you don't do your kids any favors by doing everything for them. By not including their participation in simply what needs to be done. Every day. As your kids continue their journey thru Life… housekeeping skills are simply a real-world requirement. Unless, of course, their Life sets them up with a housekeeper… a nanny… a personal assistant. That does happen for some. Not for many.

At a young age kids want to help. Involve them in doing the laundry. Even if they just sit on the edge of the washer and drop clothes in. Help them be aware of the steps in the process… put clothes in the washer… add soap. Are clothes even sorted into lights and darks anymore? When the washer is done… put the wet clothes in the dryer. Shake each one out first… so they don't dry in a tight wad. Start the dryer. (Pro points there.) Take the dry clothes out of the dryer. Fold them. Return the clean, folded clothes to the drawers and closets where they belong.

Boy! If *that* isn't the tricky part! Getting those clean, folded clothes put away. Sounds so easy… and it should be. I can't even tell you how many times I would get the clothes all folded… then uh-oh… "something would happen" and I'd be off attending to myriad other persistent Life details. Holy smokes! Somehow those folded clothes would end up all jumbled together again. "How'd the clean clothes end up on the floor?!" Needing to be folded and sorted again. Argh! Sigh.

Hey… jump on over that angst and frustration. Don't even bother being bent. Grab those dried clothes. Have at it. Fold 'em again. Maybe they'll even make it thru the "put away" stage this time. (Good luck.)

Kids can be included in grocery shopping and making meals. Yes, more patience is essential here. Ask their opinion. What should we make for dinner? Should we have mashed potatoes or fried rice? Green beans or corn? When you can… follow thru on their choices and suggestions.

"Come and help me fix the salad." "Let's make cupcakes." "Help me set the table."

Asking your kid's opinion about Life matters. What color shall we paint your bedroom? Which kind of shoes do you want this time? Where would you like to go on our little vacay? Would you like to go to the beach or the mountains? It did not occur to my parents to ask my opinion about anything. I can tell you for sure… when they were children… nobody asked their opinion, either.

"Hey Honey… what do you think should happen here?" Help your kids learn useful skills and worthwhile Life parameters. Ways and means. Strictures and structures. These daily negotiations and maintenance chores are requirements for the successful living of a human Life. Skills they will be performing for the rest of their incarnation. They may as well ease on into these upcoming Life fundamentals.

And, yes... including kids in household chores requires... more patience. More than a few times you may meet with resistance. Imagine that. "I don't want to put my toys away!" "I don't want to set the table." "I don't want to help." There are many ways to work around this resistance. Insisting... yelling... punishing are not your only choices. Arm yourself with creative solutions. Here's where parenting skills... successful negotiating... a bit of calm creativity... come in really handy. We're all in this together, right?

This should go without saying... but I'll say it anyway... all the keeping house chores should not fall to just one family member.

While we're here... let's take a moment to give a shout out to the multi-faceted difference between housekeeping and home-making. As demanding as it is keeping house... making a home calls for even more resourcefulness. A whole other quality of care. Attentiveness. Creativity. A house is where you hang your hat. Home is where your heart is.

Since raising my kids... as I cross paths with a young couple, pregnant for the first time... I can't help but think, "You have *no* idea." No idea the Mt. Vesuvius of activity, minutiae... constant engagement... concern... overload... about to erupt in your Life. Utterly transformative.

31

Truly... there is no way to effectively convey to another person how becoming a parent is going to explode their whole known reality.

You might as well try to describe the ocean... the *totality* of the ocean... to someone who has never seen it. Is there really any way to tell them? How do you convey the ocean's magnitude with mere words? Even with photographs? There is no way they could grasp the huge magnificence... the vast spaciousness. The *experience* of it. Waves crashing. Seagulls calling. The tang of the ocean air. The breezes. Sand and more sand. Immense ocean to the horizon... and beyond. It has to be experienced. You just gotta be there.

Ditto parenting. It is not possible to wrap your brain... wrap you heart... around how vast... how totally engaging... consuming... it all is. You just gotta be there.

It's not like you're trying to keep it a secret. Like you don't *want* to share with these parents-to-be. Without the *experience*... the vastness of it all simply cannot be conveyed.

Yes, new parenting is an onslaught of way too much busy. And... there is another onslaught a new parent cannot *even* be prepared for. The onslaught of explode-your-heart LOVE you feel for this miraculous little being.

I didn't know my heart could even feel this way! So huge. Vast. And vulnerable. It seems this vast feeling of vulnerable... "What if something bad happens?" "What if

I don't do it right?" "What if I'm not good at this?"… leads some people to think they might feel safer if they just shut their heart down. "No way I'm gonna feel so tender and exposed." Even if they're not consciously aware of why… emotionally, they keep their children "at arm's length."

This is no solution at all.

Please believe me when I say… shutting down because you don't want to feel so vulnerable… so not in control… is not the direction you want to travel. And nowhere you want to take your child.

> The greatest gift your child will ever give you
> is this vast and wide opening of your heart.

> The greatest gift you will ever give your child
> is this vast and wide opening of your heart.

Some parents seem to resent how being present for their child calls them… continually… to their highest. To be their best. Yes… this degree of awareness and presence can be overwhelming. Exhausting.

> Parenting Reality #1: Your children
> deserve your very best. No less.

> Parenting Reality #2: *You* deserve your very best.

Yes… being so good… has its strenuous moments. So present. So engaged. So patient. But… truth be told…

many times, the "strain" you may be feeling is self-created. The "woe is me"... the "this is too hard"... you are making up inside yourself. Creating your own inner conflict... which spills out into your world. And sprays on your kids. They're the innocents here.

Yes, many times being a parent is H-A-R-D. However... there is no requirement saying this should snag you and get you twisted. "So hard"... whine, kvetch... does not have to win. Be aware of what you're doing to yourself. What you're telling yourself. Don't blame your child for your inner difficulties.

Don't make the hard stuff harder.

Stretch yourself. Draw several deep breaths. I know... sounds so simple. Turns out to be more helpful than you can imagine. Lean in to your capabilities. Lean in to here, now. You can still be awake and aware... loving and kind... in this challenging moment. And in the next moment, too.

You can.

This is no easy-peasy lemon-squeezy Life venture. There is A LOT to being a parent. To being a kind, loving, engaged parent. A parent who grows healthy, happy, contributing children.

In the movie Parenthood, Tod Higgins, the teenage guy played by Keanu Reeves, says it so well... "You need a license to buy a dog, to drive a car… hell, you even need a license to catch a fish. But they'll let any butt-reaming asshole be a father." Bluntly spoke. Deeply true.

Just because you can plant a seed, that does not lead you to becoming a successful gardener. Every seed needs attentive care and nutrients. To grow. To blossom. To become all it is destined to be.

Parents run the gamut… an immense range of possibilities and options. Just as so many aspects of Life on Planet Earth operate within a spectrum… here we have the huge spectrum of parenting reality. Vast. Wide. The actuality of parenting offers an immense spectrum. From engaged, caring and loving guidance. To toxic and neglectful. Inflicting pain… which can last lifelong.

With this vast array of choices within the parenting spectrum… it would be interesting to know… how many folks are parenting exactly the way they were parented?

I write this in the Spring of 2021… after one full year of Covid-19 lockdown. Amidst the numerous and sometimes numbing ways our world has changed… families have been affected as never before. Everyone at home together. Adults working from home. Kids schooling from home. Money becoming even more of an issue. Food insecurity. Possible eviction. Astounding uncertainty. In the pressure cooker of family Life… The Pressure has been turned Way UP.

Traveling thru this chaotic year… I believe every parent now looks at their kids' teachers with A Lot More Respect. Admiration. Gratitude. (Whew!) Let's get these teachers A Big Pay Raise! It didn't take long to become glaringly obvious… they deserve it.

For some families in lockdown… all of this forced time together has been like winning the lottery. The glory of *time* together. Marvelous connexion. Creativity. Fun. Treasuring our time.

In unhappy families… this concentrated time together is most unfortunate. Distressing. Sadly… all we can figure out to do is make each other even more miserable.

This intense concentration of togetherness only amplifies the family dynamic already in play.

Some parents may emerge from this time realizing the value of growth and change. Let's learn to do this better. Make a happier, more fulfilling home Life. Improve parenting skills. Take a class. Meet with other parents. Stretch. Grow capabilities.

I grew up in a home environment I often describe as "even to a fault." No great highs. No great lows. No yelling and hitting. No spontaneous fun and play.

I didn't know family abuse existed until my late teens when I read an article in Ladies Home Journal. I was shocked. Floored. Husbands and wives hit each other?

They beat their children? I knew other kids got spanked. My young mind never took it beyond those few unpleasant minutes as parents let out their frustrations with a few solid whacks. I had zero frame of reference to even consider serious abuse taking place in families.

I have a clear memory of going to a birthday party at the home of my grammar school friend, Lexie. Her mother was young and beautiful. Amidst the swirl of lively birthday party kids… to this day, I clearly see this young mother sitting in a living room chair looking miserable. Defeated. Sad. The image of Lexie's mother sticks with me. I had never been close to a person who was so sad. Despondent. Near the end of the party… Lexie's father came into the room. He, too, was young and unhappy. He vibed angry… mean. Little explosive puffs of energy came off him. At 8 years old, I had no framework to process what I was seeing… and feeling. But that scenario sticks with me to this day. In my mind I see the 2 of them clearly. As I got older… I understood more of the dynamic I witnessed that day. An unhappy family. A volatile father. An anguished mother… curled up inside herself. Their home environment one of distress.

Children are like little plants. Their home environment is the soil they grow in. When that soil is lacking essential nutrients… encouragement… acceptance… love… children grow up stunted. Impeded. Not able to blossom. Not able to grow into the best version of themselves.

Turns out… a lot of us are those stunted plants.

As an only child… I've always been a fascinated observer of family dynamics. By my early 20s, I'd noticed… the demeanor of the oldest child sets the tone for the family… strongly influencing the family dynamic. Younger children look to the older… "Oh, that's how you do it." Or, in some cases… in reaction… "That is so *not* how to do it." An oldest child who is selfish and demanding creates tense, anxious drama within the family. A home where the nature of the oldest child is expansive and loving has a more settled atmosphere… generous, inclusive. Naturally, the parents' ways of being strongly play into the overall family dynamic. But one cannot deny the part the disposition of the oldest child plays as family members jockey for position and participation.

I was not keen on being an only child. My inner self remembered being with sisters and brothers. I sometimes ached for that camaraderie in my Life. Of course, this part of me was only remembering the good stuff. As a child, I never imagined the family bickering siblings can generate.

I also find fascinating how children of the same family can see their parents and their family Life so differently. I have a very dear friend, Julie, whom I've known for 40 years. Julie is the oldest of 4 sisters. In the early years of our friendship… many times I heard about her wonderful mother. Julie's eyes shone bright as she shared with me about her mother's talents. She was a consummate homemaker… ultra-talented at creating a loving home. Her father was a dear man… warm and loving. An accomplished businessman… well-regarded by his peers. Julie's sisters were precious to her.

Years later, I spent time with her next oldest sister, Joni. Joni's family story was vastly different. Her mother was a slave. Oblivious to her entrapment. At the mercy of her family's whims. Trapped in the kitchen. Suffering under the burden of household chores and family meals. Pathetic. Saddled with the load of creating all those holiday parties and festivities. The very celebrations Julie told me her mother loved orchestrating. As you can imagine… Joni's version of their dad was completely different, too. He was controlling. Manipulative. More beholden to his job than to his family. A real stinker. If I didn't know these 2 women were sisters… I would have been sure they were talking about 2 completely different families.

Their personalities offer a clue to these dissimilar interpretations of their family's Life. Julie was sunny and bright. Laughing at Life's quirks and nuances. Enjoying her Life even thru the difficulties. Joni had a grey and grumpy personality. "You want to know what's wrong? I'll tell you what's wrong." A melancholy rain cloud accompanied her thru Life. Nature or nurture? In this case, I'm going for nature. Sometimes you're just born "that way." (Choose from a long list of "that way"... personality options and temperamental approaches to Life.)

Fascinating... the interactions each person has with and within themselves. For example... there's a new activity or circumstance unfolding in your Life. You have the initial realization... this occurrence is going to happen. Inside yourself... your thoughts and attitudes... your feelings, doubts, and certainties... are stimulated. You immediately begin "talking to yourself" about what's about to happen. Anticipation. Perhaps dread. Or delight. All the internal goings-on slosh about. This upcoming event or situation might include some degree of physical plane preparation. "What am I going to wear?" "Now I really have to finish that report!" "How many people will be there?" "How much food or drink should we plan for them?"

All of a sudden... the day is here! It's happening! You're in it! And in the midst of it all... there you are... thinking, feeling, doing... as the anticipated event actually unfolds.

Then... it's over. Which bits and pieces of the whole shebang do you remember? And how about your feelings in the aftermath? How do you talk to yourself about your experience? Were your pre-event thoughts and anticipations spot-on... or off in left field somewhere? What are you telling others when you share about it? What does this Life moment become for you as time goes by?

Have you noticed this human tendency? A friend returns from vacation… you ask, "How was it?" "Oh, you know… it was great. Except this one bad… strange… uncomfortable thing happened." And that's what they tell you about. The "one bad thing." Kinda kooky.

All this before-during-and-after leads directly to… what you see is what you get. Nowhere is this more true than our interpretation of family interaction. As well as the *memories* of family interaction. It's intriguing how each person has their own remembering of their childhood and family Life. If you remember you had a pleasant childhood… you did. If you remember you had a lousy childhood… you did. No matter what anyone else from your childhood has to say about how good or crummy Life was… you get to call it.

Misery or merriment… your call.

I can hear some people say… "*My* call? *My* call that my father was mentally ill, violent and abusive? *My* call that my mother drank more than she parented? My call she left us? My call that my parents' addictions were priority one in our family Life?" I sincerely apologize to you. You did not deserve to grow up in neglect, violence, and abuse.

Now, as an adult, your best response to these personal violations… figure out ways to heal yourself. Figure out ways to bring yourself relief. Comfort. Therapy. Treatment. Meditation. There are tools and techniques you can learn to use to release your inner Life from the debilitating beliefs and constrictions your childhood homelife inflicted upon you.

Building your wellness is a Lifelong endeavor.
You and your Life are *so* worth that effort.

I've noticed another intriguing family dynamic which offers widely different interpretations of parents and family Life. This is when siblings are born many years apart. I've seen this play out in 2 different ways.

1) Sometimes it seems the older kids got the fuzzy end of the lollipop... growing up as their young parents struggled to put food on the table... making their way thru Life and the rigors of parenting. Maybe making their way thru a master's program... while working full-time. Perhaps nervousness prevailed and they were overly strict. Treats were few and far between. Who could afford them?

For the kids born later in the same family's Life... the parents have relaxed a bit. The financial situation isn't such a consuming struggle. The older parents may be more aware of what a treasure their young children are. There is more time… and money… to engage. To play.

2) Or a situation where the older kids had the younger, more energetic parents… playful… eager to enjoy their kids. Years later when the younger kids come along… the parents are spent. Done. Had enough of all that parenting business. Disinterested. Finito. "You're on your own, kid."

If anything can be counted on… it's that every family is *different*. And unique. Each with their own cast of captivating characters. Their own clowns. Their own monkeys. Each with their own circumstances and surroundings. Their own dynamics and style. Tolerant. Turbulent. Touchy. Eccentric. Encouraging. Complicated.

With characters, dynamics and style in mind… I'd like to share with you some insightful parenting wisdom from L.R. Knost. Ms. Knost is a highly respected child development researcher and mother of 6. "Mother of 6" says a lot right there. Definitely gives her cred.

In her work and parenting suggestions… Ms. Knost is an obvious philosophical descendent of Dr. Spock and Dr. Brazelton. Ms. Knost founded the advocacy and consulting group, Little Hearts/Gentle Parenting Resources, which offers... "humorous and engaging tools to help parents, teachers, and caregivers develop a kinder, more peaceful, and instinctive approach to growing our most precious natural resource... our children!"

HooRay for humorous and engaging tools!

I came upon the work of L.R. Knost a few years back. I admire her articulate compassion... her kind awareness. A winning combo!

I am touched by her uncanny ability to verbalize the way I chose to raise Isaiah and Lyla 40 years ago.

She says:

"Our job is not to toughen our children up
to face a cruel and heartless world.
Our job is to raise children
who will make the world a little less cruel and heartless."

"Discipline is helping a child solve a problem.
Punishment is making a child suffer
for having a problem.
To raise problem-solvers, focus on
solutions, not retribution."

"Instead of raising children
who turn out okay despite their childhood,
let's raise children
who turn out extraordinary because of their childhood."

"Let's raise children who turn out extraordinary because of their childhood." Let's do that! A#1 Good Plan.

I always knew I would be a mom. When I was little, I practiced a lot. My amusement of choice was playing with my dolls. Dressing them… cuddling and conversing with them… arranging their doll furniture around my bedroom. I also knew I would be a different kind of mom than the way my mom was. I knew I would be more fun and engaged. More loving. More like I was having a good time.

When I was 11… my "training" continued. I began babysitting. I was a "mature" 11. As the oldest in a neighborhood with lots of kids… I babysat plenty.

I like kids. I attended Kilgore Kiddie Kamp from age 2 to 12. In many ways, Kilgore's saved my bacon. At age 9, I was made a junior counselor… helping staff attend to the multitudes… herding the kittens… when we'd go on outings and assorted fieldtrips.

Ahhh… Kilgore Kiddie Kamp.

When I was growing up in the '50s and '60s, having a mother who worked full-time was not all that common. On weekday mornings, my mom dropped me off at Kilgore Kiddie Kamp on her way to work. Kilgore's took me to school and picked me up after. I hung out there until my mom picked me up in the evening as she drove home from work. In the summer… I was at Kilgore's full-time.

When I was a kid, this was not my favorite thing. I thought I wanted a mom like everybody else had. A mom who was at home. What did I fantasize that would be like? I really didn't even think beyond wanting what "everybody else had." Wanting what I perceived as the "rightness"… the "comfort"… of a stay-at-home mom.

As I got older… I came to realize how lucky I was.

Kilgore's had all sorts of engaging kid things to do… tables with Lincoln Logs, blocks, and Tinker Toys. A "kitchen" with a wooden stove and refrigerator, a pretend sink. Empty soup cans and frozen food boxes… so we could feel we were "really" playing house. In one large room was a big table where kids could draw… and smaller tables where we played board games. Kilgore's had a large, sandy yard… with a "stagecoach" and 4 wooden horses. Swings. Tether ball. A pile of gigantic truck tires to climb around on. There was group singing and story time. And the call of "Treat!"… cookies and juice in the afternoon. Thanks to much practice at Kilgore Kiddie Kamp… I became a hot-shot jacks player.

During the long days of summer… Kilgore's took us to swimming lessons… and stables for horseback riding. We went on field trips to Firestone to see how tires were made… which smelled really bad. And to Lever Brothers to watch soap being made… which smelled even worse.

In my late teens... I realized in a whole other way how lucky I had been. My mom did not want to stay at home. She wanted a career. She was not a cookies-and-cocoa mom. She was not inclined to make things fun and creative. If I had been at home with her... as the "stay-at-home mom" I thought I longed for... I would have been bored out of my tree. She would not have been happy. We would have both been miserable.

I never thought about being a career woman. I wanted to be a mom. I always felt I had "a work"... whatever that meant. I did not think in terms of "my career." It was always "my work." Looking to my future self... it seemed to me I would be a teacher. It never once occur to me I would be a meditation teacher.

Now... as a longtime meditation teacher and one who has meditated for over 50 years... I've noticed there are more than a few sub-species within our human family. I'm not talking about race, heritage, or culture... but rather, more subtle nuances. One category or "sub-species" I notice is humans who meditate and humans who don't. No judgment. Merely observation.

Humans whose lives include meditating regularly... experience their living of this Life differently... than those who don't meditate.

Another sub-species category within our human family... adults whose lives are directly involved with children... and adults whose lives are not. Again... no judgment. Just very different. I'm sure you agree.

Involvement with children... as a teacher or coach... certainly as a parent... breaks down all sorts of walls and habitual limitations within oneself. Those disassembled calcifications are then adjusted, rebuilt, repurposed into transformed psychological awareness. Well, let's say that possibility exists. "I'm leaving it all up to you... ou... ou" as the song goes. The degree you tussle with this inner transformation is completely your call.

As I mentioned... a lot of parents get their panties in a twist because it's all just too hard. Especially that part about continually being called to your highest and best... a.k.a... the level of engagement a child deserves.

I recently read an interview with child psychologist, Dr. Mona Delahooke, PhD. Her book, *Brain-Body Parenting: How to Stop Managing Behavior and Start Raising Joyful, Resilient Kids* was published in early 2022. You can imagine her subtitle grabbed me... "Raising Joyful, Resilient Kids."

Also, well-put... "stop managing behavior." Dr. Delahooke challenges the conventions of habitual, punishment-based parenting. This traditional attitude assumes... kids act up to get attention (negative or otherwise)...

provoking and whining to get what they want. Or, they make a big fuss for no reason at all. Hold your horses! Dr. Delahooke suggests we take a different look at these assumptions.

Traditional parenting uses threats and punishment to manage children's behavior and secure compliance.

Children want to please their parents. A child having a meltdown in a store because they aren't getting something they want... is not them being ungrateful or difficult. A young child simply has not yet developed the emotional tools to deal with being let down and disappointed. I imagine you've observed... there are adults who have not developed these skills either.

In building self-awareness and developing these tools... Dr. Delahooke points out... children "haven't gotten the circuitry of self-regulation built yet. The ability to accept disappointment and unpredictability and talk yourself down... that's a very long developmental process that most children don't have until they are older."

Her approach to positive, supportive parenting is based on decades of research in pediatric neuroscience. She skillfully translates what her research reveals into practical, compassionate tools and strategies. Biologically, it is proven... there is a better way to parent... to guide our children to become resilient, healthy adults.

Yes, this is a call... another opportunity... for responsive, engaged parenting.

Children have their own unique interpretations of Life's events and interactions. Adults are mistaken to suppose what the adult sees, feels or understands about a situation is the same way the child experiences it. Many times... not even close.

Dr. Delahooke's decades of research show "actually children behave well when they can and when they can't there's a reason."

In traditional parenting... in a store, if a child gets upset for not getting a toy or a snack... they are yelled at or punished. Rarely is there acknowledgment for what is going on for the child. "Not only do you get mad at them, you blame them for being rude or you assign a motive that is negative to a very normal process of a child seeing something at the store and wanting to get it."

In Dr. Delahooke's responsive parenting... acknowledge how the child is feeling. Validate their disappointment. Her research shows... approaching your child's upset or tantrum with empathy instead of punishment has a constructive effect within their brain chemistry.

Here's the kicker... children learn to be flexible and resilient as they're given moments to experience building their own inner flexibility and resilience. Instead of yelling at your child for being upset… responding with empathy and understanding to your child's distress gives them an opportunity to figure out how to handle tough emotions themselves. They learn to increase their own ability to be flexible.

Rather than immediately leaping to scolding and threatening to punish… be present. Be kind. Give your a child a supportive environment to struggle within themselves and figure things out. Don't fuss and act out yourself. Your gentle understanding allows your child room to realize other possibilities… and develop their own resilience.

As Dr. Delahooke observes:

> "If you're never flexing
> you'll never learn to be flexible."

Thru her caring research it has become clear… "You need the ability to flex through change and the unexpected… which could be anything from finding out you have to leave the park… to discovering that you didn't get your favorite teacher in school… to getting the wrong color cup. Every moment of the day is an opportunity to be flexible."

Exercising this ability to be flexible extends to both child and parent. It is not a requirement that you react to your child's raw emotional behavior the same way your parents reacted to yours. Rather than flying off the handle at your child "acting out"… develop your own flexibility. Be in that moment with… "What's going on for you, Little Buddy?"

Yes, in the thick of it all… it takes A Lot. Requires A Lot.

Yes, it can all be way exhausting. Relentless comes to mind.

Ongoing concern about what-ifs. Keeping track of gear, snacks, and schedules. Keeping track of the kids themselves and the multitudinous aspects of their lives. Dropping kids off. Picking them up. Picking stuff up. Putting stuff away. Picking stuff up and putting it away again. Yes… there can be a grueling grind to it. Or a golden opportunity. Here again… what you see is what you get. How you call it… is what this Life is for you.

How you call it… is what parenting is for you.

There are moments of cuteness and fun. Goofiness and giggles. Discovery and cuddles. The wonderment of seeing the world anew thru a child's eyes. Snuggling together in a cozy chair reading. Angel babies as they sleep. In nearly every moment spent with kids… there are major trade-offs. Mind-bending, heart-expanding trade-offs.

Let your heart fly open.

As I said . . .

> The greatest gift your child will ever give you
> is this vast and wide opening of your heart.

The greatest gift you will ever give your child
is this vast and wide opening of your heart.

Many times parents are so involved with their important, adult stuff and things... they "just don't have time" to engage. They don't take time... they don't make time... to engage. They don't settle into the moment long enough to be awed by their kids.

I see the word "engaged" comes up a lot here. Engaged: actively participating. Involved. Positive interaction. Helpful. Kind. Each and all... instruments of good parenting.

At age 67, Steve Martin... actor, comedian, Renaissance man... became a first-time father as he and his wife welcomed their daughter. When asked... how is it being a parent at this time in your Life? He replied, "My daughter makes my Life rich." He went on to say... "If I'd had a child earlier, I would have been a lousy father because I would have misplaced my attention on my career."

"Misplaced my attention." That's a perceptive way to put it. "Oh, where has my attention wandered off to? Have I misplaced it again?" When it comes to being with children... adults definitely demonstrate a tendency to direct their attention somewhere else. Anywhere else.

Distraction shows up in many forms...crucial, subtle and otherwise. Adults are distracted by:

1) supporting home and family
2) work and chores
3) things needing to be or look a certain way.
4) our children needing to look or be a certain way (lest they reflect poorly upon us, you know.)
5) our addictions... drugs... booze... shopping... fretting... working too much.
6) our electronic devices... phones... television... YouTube... video games.

What keeps parents from wanting to be being present and engaged with their young kids? Yes... most definitely there are the chores and upkeep. Lots of chores. Lots of upkeep. Always *something* to do. And many concerns... about money, time, and maintenance.

We also have to consider how easily we adults are victimized by our own distractions, addictions, and attitudes. Take a moment to recollect... in your childhood... were your parents more inclined to be giving their attention to something else... choose from this long list... when they were hanging out with you? Or were they present and engaged... interacting with you a lot of the time?

As this chapter began, you read:

"I hope my children look back on today
And remember a parent who had time to play.

There will be years for cleaning and cooking
But children grow up when we're not looking."

These words are from a little framed sign I found at a yard sale when my kids were very young. Writing these words here makes me kind of misty. The tenderness... the truth of this unassuming, friendly reminder. This little sign hung in our kitchen for years. I've looked for the author. I'd like to thank them. "Unknown" is all I've ever found. This little pearl of wisdom now hangs in Lyla's kitchen... still a gentle, friendly reminder as she raises her 2 remarkable bunnies.

Being a parent calls you to your highest and best. Again and again. Perspective is gained... priorities assembled as we each recognize...

You and your choices...

Your actions and responses...
Your caring and accessibility...

Are growing the future of humankind.

55

CHAPTER TWO

Advanced Upgrade
Enhancement Seminar

"The gift that keeps on giving."

Welcome back to The Interpretorium.

It's a beautiful day in the neighborhood… and wonderful to see so many of you here again. This is quite a sight… all of you sitting here looking right snazzy… decked out in your simulant B.E. Suit. Hands, feet… ears, eyes… nostrils, elbows… such a remarkable vehicle is this Earthtone Human Suit. With its 3-body apparatus and 5-gear sensory mechanism… such an effective ensemble to interact with Planet Earth's mental, emotional, and physical environments.

Plus... I know quite a few of you find this human simulator a fun costume to wear at certain social functions here in our Light-Filled Beyond Etheric Realms.

As your Interpretorium Activities Director... it is my pleasure to welcome you back. And offer a hearty, "Good on you!" for choosing to participate in our Advanced Upgrade Enhancements. As you know... these Enhancement Seminars here at Team Interpretorium offer you A Deepening—a "prime your pump" opportunity. That's a human colloquial expression meaning "encouraging the success or growth of something." We're here to develop your instrument's capabilities... expand your understanding... explore specific areas of interest... and further prepare you for your upcoming Incarnation: Human On Planet Earth.

These Seminars are indeed designed to "encourage your success and growth." As you are riding the range in your incarnant instrument... with its assorted nuances and irrationalities... we want you to be having a good time, a full realization experience... in your impending Earthtone Life.

Yes, you're right. Thanks for asking. To make your time here as realistic as possible... we will definitely be engaging our extended service interface with good ol' Realizmotron... to create action scenarios and authentic human Life dioramas.

Drawing us together today… are your interests expressed in our earlier Orientation Moment. We are here to advance and broaden your perspective and perceptions in these following areas of human endeavor:

Incarnating as an engaged, loving parent… guiding younglings. Providing them with Life skills to become effective adult humans who then lovingly raise their children = The Gift That Keeps On Giving.

Grokking the intricacies of human relationship… communicating. Aptitudes to create smooth interface. These karmic/dharmic personal interactions are the ultimate reason beings Incarnate: Human On Planet Earth.

Ageing in place and caring for ailing elders. Respecting the parameters of human ageing on 2 fronts: 1) ageing well yourself… and 2) caring for others in their advanced human years.

I'm sure you know, but I want to state clearly… your intentions and efforts to equip yourself with these competencies of kindness and compassion are much appreciated by The Ongoing Unfolding of All Things.

Within the vast latitudes of incarnating human on Planet Earth… relationship is totally "where it's at"… to use a popular Earthtone expression. Regarded with particular consideration are the relationships… the caring human interactions... at both ends of the incarnant journey. Between parents and children... as parents guide and nurture their younglings. And between adult children and their parents... as ailing elders... coming to the end of their Earthtone journey... are cared for.

Misinformed by their incarnant associates... some beings spend their precious human Life involved in the meaningless endeavors of vengeance, blame, and retribution. Others... their vision askew in a different manner... believe the purpose of Life is to amass perceived power or a great fortune. Ahh, but alas... without including and sustaining caring human interaction... a Life is squandered. As a human leaves incarnation... this acquiring of wealth and prominence... which people think is so "important"... so "successful"... proves to be only dustbin details.

At the end of your incarnation... crossing your Terminus Threshold back into Light... the emphasis of your Incarnant Exit Interview is not "What did you *do*?" "Did you wield power over others?" "Did you acquire more money than you could ever possibly spend?" "Did you attain accolades?" "Did you win?" Rather, your Life In Review is based upon... "How did you *be*?" "Did you help others?" "Were you contributing and kind?" "What did you learn from your experiences?" "Did you gain insight and awareness?" "Did you help others see their own brilliance?"

I know you are aware that... your gleaned perceptions... your realizations and Life comprehension... are the significant elements collected from your human forays. The dynamics of these aspects... accumulated and distilled... are placed in Etheric Safe Deposit to build your future dharmic lessons and karmic opportunities.

As you begin assembling your kit for your next human incarnation... Safe Deposit delivers the etheric web you have been compiling for many incarnations. Your web comes charged with system structures built from your previous incarnate attitudes and awareness. Included are your various Life-purpose dharmas... as well as your accumulated talents, strengths, and phobias.

This harvest gleaned from past Life perceptions will shape and influence your inner beliefs... your human interpretive capabilities... and your outer expression. Upon this etheric web, your evolving human instrument will be assembled.

This procedure begins with processing previous incarnate experience and acquired insight. It is this "acquired insight" that beings go into human incarnation for. A distillation of each Life's accumulated realizations sculpts future incarnant prospects... and, hopefully, upgrades. These fibres of attained awareness... along with activated karmic factors... weave into Your Etheric Sconce... the energy sheath stitched from the fabric of past incarnate traumas and realizations.

Note to self: Nowhere will these traumas and realizations be more vivid than in the latitudes of your far-ranging, human emotional nature.

This etheric web is the substrata... the underlying foundation... of your upcoming Earthtone incarnation. As you get born... your human suit arrives enveloped in Your Etheric Sconce. There will be nuances, difficulties, and deep knowings woven into your karmic package which you have no way of anticipating. Unpredictable and impulsive facets of your self... and your Life... will just spontaneously erupt. Especially after your splash of free will is swirled in.

Riding the Rodeo of Life. When The Show is on... The Show is On. You suit up. You ride. Best you can.

As you've heard... this series of Enhancement Seminars is known as "The Patience Olympics." The reasons for this moniker will become abundantly clear. If human relationship requires anything... it certainly requires patience. Tolerance. Fortitude. Resilience. Understanding. And, yep... *lots* of patience.

Here, again... as we engage with human Life... we find ourselves in the midst of poles and spectra. I'm sure this comes as no surprise. Poles and their resulting spectra are a popular experience format on Planet Earth. Near universal in its application. Deeply ingrained. You find them *every*where.

Not only are there numerous poles and spectra in the physical world of Planet Earth: the spectrum of light… of sound… of magnetism. North Pole/South Pole… and the climate spectrum in between. Solstice/Equinox… and the spectrum of the seasons. Full moon/New moon… with its resulting tidal activity.

Also within the emotional environment of Earthtone reality… there are numerous poles and spectra of relationship. From neglect to overbearing. From hatred, disregard, and animosity to warm respect, admiration, and loving good will. From grasping… "I want mine!" To serving others… "How can I help?"

As you prepare for your upcoming incarnation… there is a fascinating appeal in exploring the polarity and spectra of human relationship. Boy-yo! Boy-yo! Such a dizzying spectrum rockin' between these 2 poles! Every feeling, sensitivity, and emotional out-picturing you could ever imagine! The emotional body run amok… or most sublime… depending on the players.

In every moment… the qualities and attributes of any emotional exchange… any emotional environment… are determined by and dependent upon the particular human units involved.

Some humans truly do bring out the best in others. Kindness and encouragement rule.

In more formidable cases... not so much. There are folks who seem to think they're on Planet Earth to be grouchy and mean. Unpleasant. Self-obsessed. Wasting a good incarnation.

Keeping in mind these emotional poles and spectra... we cannot overstate the significance of guidance and, hopefully, the sense of well-being... a youngling human incarnant receives from their parental hosts. By far... parenting is the most meaningful evolutionary factor affecting human Life on Planet Earth.

So much developmental time and potential is lost as human adults battle their way out of the straight jacket of being poorly parented.

Such a drag. Literally. Dragging down potential. Inhibiting becoming. Blossoming ssquashed. So sad.

So counter-evolutionary.

I'm sure you recall from your earlier Orientation Moment... on Planet Earth, Humankind is the pivotal 4th Kingdom, the bridge between the 3 lower Kingdoms of matter and the 3 higher Kingdoms of Spirit. Humankind is *the* interactive element in this whole Earthtone realm.

Spirit, Matter, and Consciousness...the trinity of human Life. Planetary Life... evolving.

Interestingly... the evolutionary set-up on Planet Earth has the 4th Kingdom finding its way to awakened, participating consciousness thru the human emotional nature. Oy!

Woo hoo hoo... that is one crazed and complicated human emotional body!

Awash within their unruly, barely manageable emotions... Earthtone humans are transfixed by their anxiety, doubt, and fear. And their rage. Not only do they believe their agony is real... they believe their fear, pain, and upsets are *reality*. The myriad other possible emotional options... hardly noticed. Rarely even entertained.

Variations on human components are active in other Planetary Realms. We frequently use the planets Kanohaloa and Euripdiacez as examples. Humans thrive on those planets... conscious of the part they play in the Planetary design and objectives.

Living within this degree of awareness is possible because... thru tender, aware parental guidance from birth ... their emotional body is nourished to express its true nature... as a Clear, Light-Reflective Surface for the Light of the Soul.

These humans do not batter themselves with the falsehood of harsh self-judgment.

The harmonious evolution of Earth's Planetary Life will not advance until Humankind finds its footing... its healing... to finally awaken. This healing... this awakening... occurs within the emotional nature.

You undoubtedly recall from your earlier Orientation Moment... "healing" does not mean there is anything "wrong" with you... that you need to be "fixed." Healing is your journey from dull, doubting and apathetic... to awake, aware and alive.

The bottom line: Human Life on Planet Earth... inner and outer... will transform as children are raised by conscious, affectionate, and respectful parents. Parents who are also kind and respectful to themselves.

Children are not mere rug rats to be tossed scraps... of caring attention, guidance and direction.

Each child born is a miraculous Light being. To be embraced, supported, and nurtured... as they endeavor to figure out:

1) What they are doing on Planet Earth
2) What's showing up on their incarnate agenda.

Treating a child with dignity and simple humanity builds an action figure well-equipt to advance onward in The Game of Life. Much human potential is displaced... destined to dormancy... as the sparkle of many wondrous younglings is dimmed by the painful effects of being poorly parented. Their parents showing up as their anger... rather than their affection.

I know you remember the Recent Returnee who visited us a couple times during Orientation… sharing her many incarnant pointers and thoughtful insight into humanosity. You may have already realized… her area of specialty is healthy human parenting. Growing glowing younglings. She will join us again to contribute her realizations to this seminar.

As human Life develops within this period of Extreme Consciousness Sport on Planet Earth… engaged, attentive parenting is the single most significant factor cultivating this current evolution of human awareness. Cultivating is an excellent way to express this. Similar to cultivating young plants in healthy soil. Encouraging. Fostering. Nurturing.

Healthy parenting is the foundation… the key… to establishing vigorous personal well-being. The early home atmosphere lays the groundwork of each incarnant Life. A healthy childhood home encourages younglings to remember… Who I am as Spirit living a human experience.

Each young human is ripe for Life. A nurturing homelife allows each being to develop. To improve. Upgrade. "I am blessed to become All I am here to be."

Extreme Physical Sport calls for agility and strength… boldness and bravado… athletic skills and derring-do. Extreme Consciousness Sport calls upon your competence… your agility … in the realms of compassion … kindness … understanding. Patience. Paying attention. Waking up.

When focused on evolving, uplifting awareness… keep in mind… this is Planet Earth we're talking about here. Stupid is going to happen. You won't always get what you want. It won't always happen on time. (Whatever "it" may be.) Messes will be made. Any strands that can knot or tangle… will.

A healthy dose of patience develops the human capacity to tolerate delay, trouble… disappointment, even sorrow … without undue anger or upset. Without getting fritzed. Tweaked. Knocked out of commission.

Patience fosters serene fortitude. Remaining centered. Mindful. Present in the moment.

Another worthwhile note to self:

> Getting tweaked and steamed
> *never* improves the situation.
> Being perpetually fritzed
> only makes the hard parts of Life harder.

Extreme Consciousness Sport calls an incarnate human to become proficient within a whole *other* set of competencies. Calling forth other notable areas of skill. An evolved capacity of Life-artistry.

Relationships with others… friends, lovers, coworkers, sundry cohorts… is an arena of elegant endeavor. How well you get along with "others" in your Life… how well you get along with yourself... makes or breaks the luminous well-being of your upcoming human incarnation.

As an incarnate human...
much of your success relating to others
is based upon the way you relate to yourself.

You may recall a suggestion I shared during your Orientation Moment... put yourself in the "Install Your Patience Here" line 3 times before going into incarnation. Embracing this triple treat will equip you with the stamina required to deal with the trials and frustrations awaiting you on that blue-green Planet of Paradox.

Sitting here in The Interpretorium... even in your wildest imaginings... you cannot grasp the many jagged, rough edges showing up on Planet Earth. Mental, emotional, and physical. *So* many irritants. Mosquitos, setbacks... mean people. Pesky, pesky irritants. And as we've established... a whole lot of stupid.

Being fortified with an innate capacity to accept and tolerate delay or trouble... without fritzing into anger and upset... avoiding a royal tizzy... comes in really handy in humanland. There are many annoyances, difficulties, and complaints... petty and *grande*. Interruptions. Slow pokes. Miscommunication. Traffic tail-gaiters. The majority of humans simply succumb to botheration. Getting all fussed.

Agitation is not the ally it pretends to be.

Standing in the steam and hassle... without getting chafed and vexed... is quality wiring you truly want to have.

As you are human... being able to sustain your calm composure and tolerant nature... in the face of aggravation = cool beans. Try my suggestion. Stand in that "Install Patience" line 3 times before you bounce into incarnation. Give it a whirl. You'll be glad you did.

Being well-equipt with a tendency toward patience... will serve you well.

An emotional nature fortified with patience is the buffer... the cushion... the shock absorber... you'll need to maintain your equilibrium... your general good attitude... as you navigate interactions with your fellow humans. Specifically... your good attitude is the inner nuance required to not tear your hair out (again, a quaint human phrase)... as you negotiate the vast and vigorous realms of all things relationship. Especially child rearing. Especially when caring for ailing elders. Especially as you interact with yourself.

Be amused. Avoid the impulse to whine. Resist the urge to make the hard parts of Life even harder. Let go of grumpy. Refuse to be a jerk.

Making sure everyone knows how seriously inconvenienced you are about "things" is not a requirement.

Why bother with grudgement? What's the attraction? The fascination? What's the use?

I believe you should know this, my friends: Pathetically… many aspects of human Life on Earth are currently mired in a muddy quagmire of grievance. Gripe. Complaint. Laser-focused on what's wrong and who to hate. *I've* been wronged. Somebody else is getting mine. "It's *their* fault!" Leaping to insult. "Everybody who does not believe the way I believe is wrong!" Diagnosis: Absolutely tedious.

Many of those in positions of governance… known on Earth as "politicians"… seem to have forgotten… their function is to govern. To help. To serve their constituents. Instead, many politicians focus entirely on getting reelected. They will also tell you who to hate. Who to be afraid of. Who to blame. Ranting. Raving. Obscuring possibility. Objecting for the sake of objection.

What happened to serving the people?

I know I've mentioned at least 100 times… what you see is what you get. Why do I keep saying this? Because it's true!

When your interactive filters are attuned to grievance… aggrieved you shall be. You're getting what you're looking for. Things to be angry and upset about… you betcha! You get what you see. When you are sure you're being slighted… insult shows up in your world. Because you're looking for it. As you are firmly entrenched in complaint... everybody and everything is wrong.

This indicates a very limited bag of interactive tools. Engaging only tried and true annoyances limits your collaboration with your Life. Your ability to team... to partner... to relate.

An insight noted in the human 20th century:

> If the only tool you have is a hammer,
> everything looks like a nail.

As you are human... there are a zillion other ways of being. Ways of collaborating. Aspects of Life to give your inner attention to. All the ways you've been wronged do not always have to be at the top of your list.

Your gripes are magnified because that's where you choose to place your attention. Where you are "paying" attention. You search thru Life's occurrences for evidence proving your allegations of being treated poorly.

If you were looking for joy... fulfillment... balance... guess what would show up?

When you're searching to justify... gathering evidence to prove your Life is unfair... full of strife and poo... it is.

As you are busy being human... this tendency to look for and focus on what's wrong is brought to you by... tun da da… *toxic habit thought.* You just keep thinking about it. Picking at it. Making everything worse than it is. It's a habit. A mindless, Life-sucking habit. Spinning your wheels in the mud flats of Life.

Humans, continuing to fixate on their wound… their grievance… their "I'm so pissed"… grind a psycho logical groove into their brain. Continuing to focus on the wronged and hurtful… carves a trench in your inner Life processes… into which all other thoughts, feelings and interpretations fall. And accumulate.

You're in a rut.

This rut of grievance is not serving you well. Focusing on emotional potholes does not make for a smooth ride.

There are so *many* other things going on. Other Life possibilities. Other things to think about. So many options you could choose to focus on.

Options and possibilities
which are *also* available in your Life.

Like slices of a pie. Your Life is a pie… 1 slice is your well-being… 1 slice is your finances… 1 slice is your anxiety, frustration, and concern. 1 slice is your interests… your talents, hobbies and capabilities. 1 slice is your interactive competence… your people skills. 1 slice is your weak areas.

It is a human tendency to focus on one slice... usually money problems... limitations... frustrations... and call that slice the whole pie.

Taking a moment to even look at your whole pie... with all of its different slices... has a transforming effect on your entire Life perspective.

There is much more to you than your woes and gripes. So much more than your anxiety, doubts, and fears.

You're missing out... as your thoughts and perceptions tumble into that open trench of complaint. You become a gripe magnet. Hypersensitive to grievance. Why let yourself become calcified searching for upset?

Consider this... walking down the street, you need to know what time it is. You look for and find all the clocks... on buildings... inside shops... the wristwatch of a passerby. If you weren't looking for the time... you wouldn't even notice the clocks. When you're walking down the street... moving thru your Life... looking for how you've been wronged. How you are losing out. Guess what you find?

As children grow up in a house full of grievance... "I been done wrong!"... the soil of their childhood environment is noxious rather than nurturing. They take on these toxic patterns of gripe and grumble. They enter adulthood *set up*... looking for... finding... fixating on... all the things in their Life that are wrong.

When you stop looking for gripes… Life is not so gripe-full.

As we discussed during Orientation… it's *all* here. All the time. Whatever "it" may be.

A child who grows in an atmosphere of optimism and encouragement develops a very different mindset. Their youngling environment offers an enhanced impression of what Life is. What's available to be and to do. For the whole rest of their Life.

An adult who grew up in harsh toxicity lives their Life in a distinctly different world.

As you are well-aware… here in these realms of which The Interpretorium is a facet… our focus is on each individual's personal transformation. What did they glean from their experience as a human of Earth? Relevant to our interest is the range of their Earthtone excursion… from who they believed themselves to be… to who they became. Who did they blossom into? Did they grow into their whole, glowing, vibrant self as their human Life unfolded? How did they interact within their karmic relationships? And with their Life's other humans? What did they do with those few precious decades they were in human form?

It really does fly by in a blink.

Again, I will state this one thing very clearly:

The majority of human anguish... confusion... torment...
will be *transformed*...
as Earth's children are treated
with more active engagement and loving regard.
Nothing else compares
to the importance of younglings being treated well.
Being embraced and guided
with care and happy, loving attention.

Here, I will pop in a good word for repetition. Practice. Rehearsal. Repetition is a human learning strategy. Becoming fluent in another language takes practice and repetition. A person learning to play the piano... practices... over and over. A play, a concert, a dance recital = lots of rehearsals.

Repetition builds acuity. Insight. Perception. Skills. Understanding.

In this Enhancement Seminar... you will hear points and insights repeated and revisited. This is the human instrument's way to anchor and develop comprehension.

At times, there can be a hasty, knee-jerk closing your ears... an automatic "I've heard this before." I will point out... that was then. This is now. Be open to concepts you may have heard before. You are not *now* who you were when you heard them *then*. Allow yourself to hear these matters fresh.

As you are open to new possibilities… insight may enter your awareness in a different way. Make yourself available to receive new nuggets of realization. Just sayin'…

Onward.

Observing current human Life on Planet Earth, it is glaringly obvious… the effects of poor parenting are as notoriously tenacious and stubborn as prickly, entrenched blackberry vines. With nary a thought... 9.5 times out of 10, adult humans turn around and parent exactly the way they were parented. For good and for ill.

Even if they didn't like what their parents did to them... humans tend to mindlessly muddle thru their own parenting opportunity. Carelessly applying the same mistreatment to their children as they received. Generation after generation. Earth's younglings are treated poorly because it simply does not occur to human adults to wake up. Pay attention. Learn to parent differently. To parent better. To stretch beyond the familiar. Training themselves to be more loving, effective parents.

A short-sighted state of affairs is being passed along. Most of the agony transpiring on Planet Earth right now... is, in fact, humans playing catch-up. Catching up with finding and building a vibrant Life… out of the gloom of disregard, neglect and ignorance inflicted upon them in their younger years. This neglect and disregard stunts Earth's younglings as they grow.

This stunting happens on a physical level as well as mental and emotional levels. Studies by human psychologists reveal... the brain's neural pathways thrive and flourish in a baby who is showered with loving attention. This affectionate stimulation causes these all-important pathways to multiply and intersect... looping thru-out remote regions of the brain. As you can see in this explanatory graphic... these neural pathways charge thru the brain like a national highway system under construction. Establishing side roads... pathways to personal creativity.

The same studies show... in the brain of a neglected baby... lying alone and unattended... whose smiles go unanswered, not responded to... fewer neural connections are built. Early in their incarnation... this all-important neurological potential goes undeveloped. These significant neural doors are closing. The baby falls silent. This lack of early warmth and affection influences this person their whole Life thru.

In these growing children... this early homelife of careless disregard... shapes their deepest beliefs about who they are... what they can accomplish... and what this Life is all about. Influencing how to be. How to act. In turn, shaping and influencing the entirety of the Planetary Life.

Consider this bit of cosmic arithmetic: Each child treated with kindness + raised with loving, attentive awareness = the entire Life environment on Planet Earth evolutionized.

One generation is all it takes. One generation choosing… insisting upon becoming more engaged, loving parents… changes this dynamic of inflicted limitation. For all of time.

This transformation by "one generation" parenting more effectively… highlights our Recent Returnee's central area of concern. She joins us now to share her insight into the relevance of this Life-altering choice available to humans of Earth as they raise their future.

Aloha compadres. I'm happy to be back with you. It's good to see so many of you here for your Enhancement Upgrades. So clever of you… equipping yourself with all the attentive awareness available before you inhabit your upcoming carbon-based Earth-suit. It's always a good idea to be well-equipped for the multi-dimensional human escapades coming your way. I'm sure you recall… there's good reason Earth is known as the Planet of Paradox.

During your original Orientation Moment… I spoke of several different human-centric topics. Healthy, loving parenting. Forgiveness: The Human Super Power. Sexosity. The Tantric Way… the Yogic Way… and light-filled sensual pleasure. As these different areas of Life-relevance intertwine in a healthy, happy way… a truly luminous human Life unfolds before you.

Your Activities Director is correct… parenting *is* my area of greatest interest. I find The True Work lies in helping you foster skills and aptitudes… your own personal flair… as an engaged, loving, encouraging parent.

There is no way to emphasize enough how important mindful, aware parenting is… in graceful service to the evolution of humankind. Especially in this epoch of Extreme Consciousness Sport.

And yes… the consequences of "one generation is all it takes" to evolve parenting ways… are definitely at the center of my focus on parenting children. Children who become thriving adults. Many times… in the frenzied activity of caring for little kids… it's hard to keep in mind you are guiding and growing the future.

In the day-to-day kid crazies… a lot of your focus is on just making it thru.

Here's the A#1 reason I focus on one generation changing parental interaction: Those choices. That change. It continues to unfold its gentle, guiding influence thru generations to come. A person raised with loving awareness will very likely raise their own children with loving awareness… who will then raise their children with loving awareness. And on it goes. Uplifting the betterment of human interaction.

Truly… the gift that keeps on giving.

Yes, occasionally, there are some humans who revert… due to their own innate karmic predisposition. They do not follow this evolved, loving guidance. Relapsing to the struggles of neurotic limitation. Limiting themselves. Limiting their children. Fortunately, this does not happen very often.

You, yourself, may incarnate into a family with a generations-long history of child abuse and parental mismanagement. It will be yours to change things. To make things right. For your children. For their children. For the future. For yourself.

Mindless neglect and abuse of children is a repetitive gambit. A miserable tactic. "I harm the way I was harmed. Why would I even think about doing it differently?"

Each human incarnant is charged with breaking the cycle of family violence. Of family neglect and abuse.

All it takes is one generation standing up… saying, "This is not right." Doing what it takes to break the cycle.

> The living of Life… transformed
> for the generations to come.

Evolving human awareness on Earth is hindered by the "snail's pace clause"… developing, moving forward slowly. Oh so slowly.

I do have to say… this is now apparent… healthy, loving parenting *is* having its evolutionary effect.

Shift happens.
Awareness develops.
Evolution rocks!

As you are in incarnation… let the people you love know you love them. Show them you love them. Tell them you love them. Don't get lost in withholding or being shy. Love 'em up good.

Let the people you love know how much you *value* them. How important they are to you and your well-being. Especially the younglings in your Life… let them know they touch your heart. Let the young ones know you see them. You see the magnificent, creative, bright beings they are. Let kids know they are important to you. That they are important to this world.

As your children grow older, let them know you approve of the way they are living their lives. Don't quibble. Let your adult children know you respect their choices. Even when you question their decisions. Even when you know you are "right."

No need to spread around your dissatisfaction. Really… how helpful is that?

Disapproval is not the ally it pretends to be.

You will be astounded as you travel your Earthtone journey by how many people crave hearing approval from their parents. It can be as simple as a tender "I love you." Perhaps a small, acknowledging kindness. Older kids and younger kids all deserve to know they are valued by their folks. By their kin and relations. By their teachers and coaches.

The lack of kind encouragement in the human world is so pervasive... and yet it's almost invisible. Mentally, you'll hardly even notice it's missing. It's "just the way things are." As you navigate your human instrument, you need to understand... your *feelings* notice that lack. You're seldom able to identify the culprit. "Why do I feel so down?" So sad. Depressed. Worthless.

When you do notice this absence of kind emotional generosity... you will be struck by what a large issue this is for humans. Generally, they do not know why they feel loss... lack... ill-regard. "Why are my feelings hurting?"

It very well could be... while incarnate you, too, will experience this absence of being affirmed and valued.

Note to self: Do the best you can to not become a perpetrator yourself.

How about a "Good job!" from bosses or colleagues? Observing this absence of positive acknowledgment, one can't help but wonder... does it not occur to folks to mention the favorable and encouraging? Are humans afraid of affirming others?

Does expressing positive acknowledgment to another make a person feel diminished somehow?

It seems like recognizing a job well done would deliver just the opposite... a feel-good moment.

While incarnate, as I observe other humans, I've noticed... there seems to be no limit to finding fault. Some folks will even tell you... it's just more "natural" to judge and criticize. Taking a moment to express positive acknowledgment calls for more of a stretch.

I hear you wondering... Why *is* that? Believe me... I ask myself that question, too.

Who knows? Maybe it's the human tendency to be victimized by their own habit thought. It's just a habit... to think in a judgmental, disapproving manner. And then spew. It's one thing... keeping negative, unkind thoughts to yourself. Spraying the grouse around... poisoning the emotional environment... is quite another.

Most humans seem blind to the truth... energy follows thought. People don't seem to realize focusing on the sour... fixating on the negative and nit-picky... has a toxic effect within themselves.

As humans stew in this self-generated toxicity... their emotions absorb the noxious fumes. Feeling bad. They seem to think the criticism and disapproval they spray only affects the "other person." In fact... their hurtful habit thought creates... perpetuates... their own dismal inner atmosphere. Theirs becomes a numb and weary inner Life. Which proceeds to a favorite human maneuver... looking outside themselves for "who's to blame" for their misery and discontent.

Flipping the coin on this mindless toxic spew and its reckless effects... what do we find? Oh look! The other side of the coin... being kind and encouraging... has a powerful ripple effect on your world and the humans in it.

As a human of Earth... teach yourself... train your interacting abilities... to be acknowledging and encouraging of others. Really... it's not that hard. After a little practice... "Good job, you!"... comes pretty easy. Offering its own reward.

While you're at it... train yourself to be encouraging to your own fine self.

As you know... I've been around the block a time or 12... or 250, or more... as a human of Earth. Those incarnate experiences have made crystal clear what I now share with you. While you are being human... speaking kindly... acting with gracious consideration... is the route to take.

Some humans are born with a kind nature... knowing innately "do no harm." Having incarnated on Planet Earth numerous times before... these beings have learned:

1) Over time… the emotional cul-de-sac of being steamed and grumpy loses its allure.

2) It wears other people out. How to lose friends and contaminate relationships.

3) Upon examination… grudgement, hatred, and vengeance truly help nothing and nobody.

4) Such a limited reactive nature only reveals inadequate creative response mentality.

5) The tendency to blame others… rather than taking personal responsibility… exposes a flaw in us, not in the world.

6) Grumpiness is a waste of a precious human incarnation.

7) Harming others guarantees karmic backwash. Future difficulty and discouragement is set in motion for incarnations to come.

I suggest paying attention to… and learning from… such karmic indicators as they fly by while you're being human.

You may find… kindness is a capacity available to develop thru your younger years. Not because it's beaten into you. Rather… this flair for kindness is modeled for you in the behaviors of those around you. Particularly, in the way you are treated by your parental hosts… and others significant in your early Life. Magnified… as you observe the way they treat themselves.

This brings us to consider a broad human dilemma… is human behavior the impact of genetics and biology… or environmental influences?

Is it nature or is it nurture? Do you come into incarnation being "nice" or "mean"… "pleasant" or "grumpy?" Or does a person learn their behaviors as a result of those around them and their general Life experience?

Humans have been preoccupied with this question since the time of the Greek philosophers… more than 2,500 years ago. That's a long time past… as the world turns. In Earthspeak, this is 100s of years before the beginning of what is now labeled "CE"… the "Common Era." The renowned Greek philosopher, Plato, and his student, Aristotle, each discoursed about this "nature or nurture" dilemma. You'll find this interesting… the deep and wise philosophic understandings these 2 long-ago humans revealed are still respected and studied more than 2,000 years after they were incarnate on Earth.

Are a person's accomplishments and the living of Life a result of their nature? Do they attract mentors, opportunities, and experiences due to their temperament… the ways and attitudes with which they come into incarnation?

Or is their Life journey more influenced by what they learn from their environment? How they are taught to be. What they learn to value as a result of the way they are treated. What they're exposed to as Life unfolds… their nurture.

It turns out Plato and Aristotle disagreed on this issue. Plato believed it was nature. Aristotle was sure it was all about nurture.

Due to the human fascination with tussle… this big question has always been framed as "Is it nature?" *versus* "Is it nurture?" For their own puzzling reasons… humans who noodled this query over the centuries… seemed to believe it couldn't be both. Had to be one *or* the other. This does not leave much room for the actual creative reality… the interaction of inborn temperament and external influences.

Nature… human pre-wiring… dynamic karmic factors generating genetic emotional inheritance and other biological features. Assigning inborn viewpoint and temperament.

Nurture… Life exposure. Learning. Experiences. The influence of external factors.

In the middle of the 19th century… which, as humans quantify time, can also be called the mid-1800s… the actual term "nature versus nurture" became part of the cultural lexicon. This context of "opposition" dominated human considerations around this inquiry thru-out the 20th century. (Also known as the 1900s.)

Then, what do you know... as the 21ˢᵗ century dawned... what should enter mainstream thought? "Nature VIA nurture." Yes! Finally. That's what I'm talking about! Of course it's both! Building an incarnation... a creative, contributing Life... by means of the exceedingly fine nature/nurture interweave.

It takes 2 to tango! These 2 elements of being human are as entwined as any dual components can be. Nature + nurture = human expression interwoven in real time. Far beyond any "either/or" considerations.

You could say... each new incarnate being is its own lump of clay... made of its own minerals and substances... its own personal qualities and nuances. Human clay... to be sculpted by their own Life. Their particular cast of characters and interactions. Relationships. Situations. Training. Oh, yeah... training. You *will* be schooled on Planet Earth. Shaped. Molded.

As a human... good thing you have choice. Choice as to how you respond to Life's impacts and influences. How you are sculpted by the bumps in the road. Dancing with your unfolding path. Pirouetting, perhaps. Or jazz hands... energy shooting out your fingertips. Or maybe you're on the sidelines... sitting this one out. A wallflower.

Your nature determines how you embrace or reject
the art of living human in Earthtone reality.

It's the Planet of Paradox. Stuff happens. I'm gonna go not too far out on a limb here and say… you'll be stunned how often stupid stuff happens. How you respond to what's happening generates your particular way of being. Your take on your Life unfolding. Your own secret sauce. Your version of the whole enchilada. With or without red onions and salsa.

Taking a realistic look at these concepts… "how you are sculpted by the bumps in the road" + "how you respond to what's happening" = your particular way of being. How you serve your own unique enchilada.

It is a Life-defining moment in a human's awareness as they begin to realize… the true test is not the pain I suffer, the trials and difficulties I endure. The true test is… what I *do* with what's happening to me. "How do I choose to respond to the pain, the trials, the adversity?" "Now that this difficulty has landed in my path… what do I do with it?" "How is this trial shaping me?" "How is my thinking… my beliefs and realizations… affecting this situation?" "How am I changed by this?"

This brings us to… Resilience.

Sweet resilience.

Resilience is the process of adapting well.

Resilience is the yoga of adjusting expectations and actuality… in the face of difficulties, adversity or trauma…

Life might toss your way. Highlighting a person's ability to recover from or adjust easily to change or misfortune. A potent characteristic of resilience = understanding Life is full of challenges. And change. Dilemma and upset will not be avoided.

Developing the graceful ability to remain open and flexible. Rather than resisting... contracting... shutting down. Recognizing the futility of fighting against challenge and change. Where does tightening up... resisting... ever really get you?

To use the human physical body as metaphor... it's the difference between stretching and gaining flexibility thru yoga practices... "going with the flow." Or... tensing up... resisting... straining. Spraining. Pulling a muscle. In this case... spraining an emotional muscle.

Looking at the characteristics and disposition of resilience... we observe psychological differences between people who are insecure within themselves... who fight against challenges and unexpected trials... believing Life is out to get them. And humans who are centered and secure... at ease within their internal framework... seeing even the uncertainties of Life as offering opportunities and growth.

With these prospects in mind... to elucidate different human traits and innate behaviors... we are now going to dive into a realistic Realizmotron diorama. From

Orientation... I'm sure you remember the wonders of Realizmotron's authentic scenarios.

An aside... have you checked out the Realizmo action in The Interpretorium Locales Library? I know you know about Realizmotron's dioramas giving you experiences in different living environments and Earth venues. But have you checked out the action sequences Realizmo provides... where you move back and forth thru time in an area you choose? It is super fun! And totally informative. Mind-blowing, as they say.

Here today, to augment your current upgrade training... I will adjust Realizmotron's whiz knobs. You will not only observe an authentic human Life scenario... you'll also *feel* what our 2 main participants are feeling.

Realizmotron will generate 2 men... Rob and Tony... their boss, Mr. Howard... and his assistant, Ida. Ah... there they are. Their exchange in this out-picturing occurs in a work environment. You will easily recognize Rob as the one who has not discovered his resilience capabilities. He is insecure... short on self-assurance... and sweating. While our man, Tony, is just pretty fascinated with what's going on. A study in resilience and fortitude.

As you know by now... this type of scenario is my favorite. One situation... 2 people... each with a totally different take on the ol' what's what.

Whiz knobs calibrated. Away we go.

"Hey, Rob. Here… I brought you 1 of those double-shot lattes you like."

"Boy, can I use this! Thanks, man. I'm a wreck. This upcoming meeting with the boss really has me on hot coals. My career hangs on whether they choose our presentation for the new campaign."

"Whoa, guy. Don't be so whacked on yourself. Being this stressed out is no way to mentally prepare yourself for our meeting. This *isn't* Life or death. They're either going to choose our graphics and ideas for the new ad campaign… or they're not. No need to wig out about it."

"Geez, Tony. I don't know how you do it. You're always mister calm, cool, and collected. My stomach is in knots. I need to find an antacid. This sure feels like Life or death to me."

The phone rings. Did you feel Rob startle? He's freaking out.

"Oh man. They're calling us to the meeting."

Answering the phone… Tony says, "Thanks, Ida. Tell Mr. Howard we'll be right up."

"Rob, we've done our best. They've gone thru our portfolio. They're just going to let us know what they've decided. Come on… let's head to the 5th floor."

"My palms get clammy every time I'm on the 5th floor. I am so stressed. This is a lot of pressure, man."

"Wow, Rob. You're making this a lot harder on yourself than it needs to be."

"Oh shut up, mister cucumber cool. Ugh. Let's get this over with."

Rob and Tony take the elevator to the 5th floor. As they walk to the conference room…. Tony says hi to Ida, who is sitting at her desk outside Mr. Howard's office. Rob is sweating. He looks like he may throw up.

"Oh, man… we're the only 2 here. That's not a good sign. If our presentation had been chosen… more people would be here. I knew they wouldn't choose ours. We're so screwed."

They sit down to wait. Let's take a moment to really experience their 2 very different psychological states. If you didn't know… it wouldn't cross your mind they are each waiting for the same meeting.

Rob looks like he feels sick. His insides are in a triggered state of over-reaction… like he's about to face a firing squad. Then there's Tony. Other than feeling bad for Rob wallowing in his bonkers emotions… Tony's interested to see what's going to happen.

Tony leaves the conference room to ask Ida if she has anything to help Rob's upset stomach. She pulls a box of Chooz antacid chewing gum out of her desk drawer… "Here you go."

"Thanks, Ida." Tony returns to the conference room… offering the Chooz to Rob.

"Thanks, man." Rob belches. "But no way am I going to be chewing gum when Mr. Howard shows up."

They wait a little longer. Looking miserable… Rob has beads of sweat on his forehead and upper lip. Tony's strolling around the conference room, checking out the large, framed, black-and-white photographs on the wall.

"Oh man! Look at this one from the 1930s… those construction workers all sitting on steel skyscraper beams… eating lunch. *Way* above New York City! I've seen this shot before. It always blows my mind!"

Rob moans.

Mr. Howard walks into the room. Tony strides right over to shake his hand. Rob struggles to stand. He doesn't put his hand out because his palms are so sticky.

"Go ahead… sit down, fellas. I've only got a couple minutes. We really like the pieces you came up with for the new ad campaign. Your graphics are spot-on. But we're going with the designs Betty and her team created. Her concept is more in line with the customer's vision. We like what you've done. We're thinking we'll use your ideas in a few months… as the campaign evolves."

Leaving the conference room… Mr. Howard calls back over his shoulder… "You 2 keep up the good work." And he's gone.

"Oh, man. Rejection. I knew it."

"Rob, he said 'Keep up the good work.' And that our graphics are 'spot-on.' They may use our work in a few months."

"Tony... 'in a few months' isn't now! Who knows when 'a few months' is going to be? I needed a win now. I'm going to lose my job."

"You do great work, Rob. You're not going to get fired."

"How do you know that?"

"Ah, chill man."

Ignoring Tony's suggestion... Rob lurches on... "How could I think I'd make it as a graphic artist? Totally ridiculous! I'm in way over my head. 'Fake it till you make it.' Suuuure. Easy enough to say. I'm an idiot to think my puny artistic skills could succeed in this career. Man, I feel sick."

"Rob, your skills are fine. You've got real talent. Look... our presentation wasn't chosen to roll out the campaign. That doesn't mean we're going to get fired. They're not going to throw our work in the toilet. You know what they say... 'This or something better.' When one door closes... another one opens."

"Are you kidding me? That's a bunch of horse shit! Our careers are doomed. Let's go to Alph's and get drunk."

"Rob, that's not gonna help anything."

"It'll help *me*."

"I'm not ready to leave yet. It's not even 3:00. I've got another project to work on. I'm heading back to the ol' drawing board."

"Suit yourself, man. We are so fucked. What a mess. I'm going to tie one on. I may not make it in tomorrow."

"Take care of yourself, buddy. If you don't come in tomorrow, I'll cover for you. Really, Rob… things aren't as bad as you think they are."

"Says you," Rob sneers.

Tony glances heavenward… "Geez, man." He's on his way back to his desk.

Rob grabs his coat and heads out the door… muttering, "A stiff drink… that's what I need."

Realizmotron winds down.

Humans would say… "clear as day"… observing the completely different take-aways these 2 men generated from the same interaction.

Ya gotta love good ol' Realizmotron! Allowing you to *feel*… as well as watch and listen to… these realistic scenarios. Did you feel how Rob couldn't stop awfulizing? In his mind, everything was bad and getting worse. He was terrified inside. Totally beating himself up. Already convinced he'd failed.

Tony… being his upbeat, resilient self… sailed along. Ho hum. La dee dah. Just another day in the Life. Not only did he hear Mr. Howard's positive, encouraging comments…

he believed them. "They'll choose our designs and concepts another time. Good by me." He keeps on keeping on… steering his creative energies toward his next project.

Rob's going to get drunk. All he heard was a horrible outcome. Failure. It's gotta be a bummer living inside Rob. Exhausting.

This scenario offers an excellent example of the ways a human's inborn disposition and childhood training play out in adult Life. Based on all we've been talking about today… you can't help but wonder… was Rob born with a fretful temperament? Or did his early childhood environment teach him to be anxious and self-abusive? Fraught with disaster? "Watch out!"

Was Tony born easy going? Or did his homelife teach him to go easy? As we know… most likely it's a combination of both. "This… or something better."

A human youngling is constantly deciphering early child-hood "ways and means." Methods and resources. "What's *this* all about?" "How do I fit in here?" "Am I in trouble?" This internal effort to decode and make sense of those perplexing early-Life experiences… grows up to become adult behavior patterns and self-belief. Healthy or harmful.

Diving into humanosity… you'll be doing yourself A Huge Favor as you cultivate a willingness to adapt. Modify. Be flexible.

Yes, responding to Life's quirks and fancies with patience, curiosity and resilience does play a significant role.

Fine tune your ability to stretch and bend. Emotional yoga. Seek solutions.

I'm sure you recall this suggestion from the closing of your Orientation Moment:

> Dare to take the step...
> with the eye lifted... away from the chasm...
> fastened upon the Light.

Do that. Lift your inner eye. Fasten on the Light.

Your inner gaze perpetually fastens *somewhere*. Might as well fasten on uplift and clear vision.

Life is going to happen... groovy or grinding. It's always a good idea to learn to dance with it. Sway to the music. Enjoy the twirl. Embrace the tango. Become a dance instructor. Moving with the sway and twirl makes for a Life way mo' betta' than hunkering down inside... tensing your emotional muscles. Hardening your heart. Struggling. Making Life harder than it needs to be.

For many humans, struggle is just "the way Life is." Struggle is a human construct. A determination to make the hard things harder. As if Life can't happen any other way.

But the day does come... realization dawns... "This fritz and freak out... I'm doing it to myself." Whoa. "There's got to be a better way. What did I do with that resilience guidebook?"

Resilience truly comes in handy as you are raising children. Handy dandy. In the day-to-day on Universe Kids... whatever you thought was going on... can change in a flash. Best to be psychologically equipt to roll with those instantaneous adaptations. Modeling resilience is an exquisite gift you give your kids. Children learn to be resilient... or not... as they observe the way adults in their world respond to Life's dilemmas and upsets.

Remember... children are observing... absorbing... taking it in. All. The. Time.

Further gifts parents give their children... the gift of your attention... your time. The gift of your interest in them and what they're doing. What's fun for them. What they like. What troubles them. Who they are.

I'll be right up front with you... in many of my Earthtone childhoods... this gift of parental interest and attention was sorely, sadly lacking. Many of the other Recent Returnees I've spoken with tell me they also found their parents' disinterest to be a significant part of their experience as a youngling of Earth.

In my most recent human incarnation... I was an only child... raised in an environment of benign neglect. I wasn't hit or berated... just mostly ignored. Neither of my parents had any idea what it might mean to be an engaged, involved parent. It would not have occurred to either of them there could be a different way to do what they were doing.

Such indifference and disregard is a quiet, yet profound, form of mistreatment. As a child in that Life... I often felt like a piece of furniture my parents needed to move from Point A to Point B. I was a "complication" in the midst of their busy, distracted lives.

My kid-self used to wonder... *Where's the juicy stuff?*

As is the Earthtone way... childhood neglect resides within its own spectrum. Neglect... benign and otherwise. Sadly, there is a cruel "otherwise" on the neglect spectrum. From mindless disregard and indifference... to contempt and harsh mistreatment... to deserting and abandonment.

Neglect... being left alone... might not seem "that bad." It's certainly not "as bad" as being beaten or abused. Yet, I will tell you from experience... neglect leaves its own deep-seated, stealthy scar.

Within... a neglected child carries deep perceptions of unworthiness... subtle and profound. Becoming an adult who is easily overwhelmed or discouraged. Children of neglect grow up in emotional poverty. They learn early to disregard, discount, and deny their own needs and talents. They grow into adults who believe (unconsciously), "Who I was and what I had to say sure wasn't important to my parents... Why should what I have to offer now be important to anybody?" The living of their adult Life is constrained... stunted by this constricting false belief. A stealthy mark, indeed.

An aspect of youngling Life... "childhood," as it is called on Earth... which many Recent Returnees spoke of was how apparent it was that their parents had many "more important things" to do. Busyness seemed much preferred over engaging with the kids.

Especially, it seems, in "developed" countries... as parents are with their children... they frequently have their nose in their personal electronic devices... a book or newspaper... the television or a video game. Occupied in their own appetites and addictions. Many times... when "interrupted"... the parent is impatient and snappish. "Don't bother me, kid." As if children are a nuisance... an inconvenience. Adults give off the vibe... or show by their actions... "I have something 'more important'... 'better'... to do than spend time with you."

Do these adults give a moment's thought to how this feels to their child? To what this says to their children? What example are these parents setting about the value of human interaction? How will these younglings respond later in Life... when their parent wants or needs their attentive interaction?

Parents will boast about their kids to friends and colleagues... telling them their children are the most important thing in their lives. This does not mean their kids ever hear any of that. Evidently, my most recent human father would brag about me and my accomplishments to colleagues and neighbors. Or so I heard from them... after he died. Thru our years of Life together... he didn't have much acknowledging to say to me.

Based on the way they are actually treated... criticized... neglected... ignored... kids often have little evidence to realize they are valued by their parents.

Blinded by their plight... harried and harassed... many parents don't give "the kids" enough time and quality attention to truly comprehend their amazingness. A great disservice is done. To their kids. And to themselves. Many parents act like taking care of the kids... or hanging out with them... is drudgery. "Let's just slog thru this so we can get on to better... more engaging... more adult things."

Believe me, I do know... a human adult always has A Lot To Do. Especially as a parent. You will be up to your eyebrows in "to do." Get dinner on the table. Do laundry. Plan daily Life. Work to earn money... to pay the rent or mortgage... to keep the lights on and food in the fridge. Buying and maintaining a car. Saving for a family vacation. Total overwhelm. I know. I've been there. I am not for one moment downplaying the human adult's ongoing deluge of required Life activity.

Yet... even in their down time, many parents are absorbed with their other, "more important" things.

In conversations with other Recent Returnees... and from my own human experiences... I just want to say to you... as you plan to have kids in this incarnation... be attentive... be engaged. Avail yourself of the opportunity to "love 'em up good."

In the mid-20th century... a well-respected children's doctor observed... "Unless a person has gone thru a significant change in their own consciousness, they will parent exactly the way they were parented." Sometimes this is a good thing. Many times... not so good.

As mentioned in Orientation... many children on Planet Earth grow up in difficult... dysfunctional... even horrible... childhood circumstances. As these children grow to adulthood... contemplating the possibility of becoming parents themselves... the fear and pain of their childhood leads them to 3 different Life prospects:

- "I'm sure never going to have children."
- "I had a miserable childhood and I'll be damned if I'm giving my kid anything better or kinder than what I had to put up with."

- "I am determined to give my children... the love... the caring heart... the fun... the happy childhood... I didn't have."

Plan 1 is an understandable choice. Plan 3 has a vast beneficial variety of plans, goals and diversities.

Let's talk about Plan 2. As it is your intention to have children... even tho yours was a miserable childhood... refuse to perpetuate that on your kids. Don't do it. Make this active choice. You detested the neglect and abuse you experienced. Don't allow it to continue. Do not mindlessly repeat the pattern.

As a parent... do everything you can to *not* perpetuate the pain you endured. Take parenting classes. Read books. Observe parents you admire... watch the way they interact with their younglings. Learn to parent differently. Stretch beyond the way you were parented. Resist becoming the same ol' same ol' you hated. Do better.

If not you... who?

Train yourself to become a good parent. It is more than worth the effort to be present and engaged in crafting a pleasant, happy home life. Make *those* choices. Healthy for your children. Healthy for your self.

Please keep this in mind...
in the human realm...

joy and fulfillment have as much to teach you
as pain and limitation do.

Likely more.

CHAPTER THREE

Your Ability to Cope

"Oh, Dana, I'm the lucky one."

"People will forget what you said,
People will forget what you did,
But people will never forget how you made them feel."
~ Maya Angelou

How true is that? Pretty doggone true. Perhaps you are speaking with a friend… recounting one of your Life-episodes… "I don't remember exactly what she said… but I sure remember the way I felt."

The "feels" are anchored at a whole other latitude in our authentic human reality. That's why emotions are able to "pop up" the way they do. Sometimes in a happy, cheerful way. Sometimes in a dank and dismal way.

I know you know… feelings are definitely not thoughts. Inside you… feelings are generated and stored in a totally different place than thoughts and ideas. Emotions resemble more of a random-access file. Arbitrary emotional elements… oft times showing up willy-nilly. Sometimes at just the right moment. Other times throwing you completely off-kilter… "Uh, what was I just saying?"

Appraising these "other latitudes" speaks to the value of personal experience… the reliability of your inner realizations. Grasping your own blossoming insights… resonating deep within… holds a different clarity … a more profound certainty … than anything someone tells you from "the outside."

This multifaceted well of emotion begins developing in our earliest days… retaining moments… interactions… feelings. Watching. Learning. Absorbing. Altho most people do not remember Life elements that happened before their change of baby teeth… around 6 years old… all of those early memories are the rudimentary components of your deepest self.

My 2 children retain within them some measure of my awe and delight with each of them when they were little. Our mutual enjoyment and appreciation of each other as they grew into the caring adults they are... are a beacon of certainty and inspiration for each of us.

I stand in admiration of Isaiah and Lyla. This was certainly true when they were little. Moreso now as they are adults. I've always felt we have such a great time together because of them. As a mom, I lucked out. I received excellent kid material to work with... twice. So, as I mentioned... when folks would say "You should write a book about raising kids"... I'd think, "What in the world would I say?" It took me a while... a few decades... but I figured it out.

It is clear to me now. How *not* to do it.

Scott and I moved to Hawaii in early February, 2009. Soon after our arrival, we met a lovely young woman and her brother. He was in his late teens. She, in her early 20s. Their parents had divorced years before. Their mother was also our friend. At that time, their father was out of the picture.

Life... cleverly arranging itself, as it does... handed me the opportunity to help this young woman and her boyfriend put together their submission packets applying to the culinary arts program at a local college. Working together thru this process... I had the pleasure of getting to know the 2 of them.

Our wide-ranging conversations and hearing a few stories about her dad... helped me develop a glimpse into the kind of person he was. And the kind of parent he had been. His friends would chuckle about his drugging, drinking, and womanizing. Before even meeting him... I had the impression he was actually a teenager... walking around in an adult body. Yes, that has a ring of the familiar. Thru the years, I've met more than a few adults who live their lives as tho they are teenagers still.

When this young woman was in high school... she tried to talk with her dad about going to college. His response... "You're not smart enough. Don't even think about college. Just hook up with some guy and make babies." Way to instill confidence in your daughter. (Not even a little bit.)

After knowing this family for a few years... the dad came to visit. He was pleasant enough... for a few minutes. He's kind of surly. Definitely full of himself. It didn't take long to recognize... he lives in the world of "all about me."

Watching him interact with the few small children who were around... Holy Cow. What a jerk. He'd throw his weight around. Blustering. Shouting at the little kids... "Shut up!" "Get out of here!" Making them wrong. He was a big bully. Literally. A. Big. Bully. Ranting and raving. A self-absorbed tyrant.

He could host a seminar... How To Be A Lousy Parent.

In my younger years, I would fall for that bullying crap. Feeling intimidated. Nervous. Scared. I'd react to their coercion. Moving thru the years... interacting with my fair share of humans… I am less inclined to be tricked… stymied by their acting out. Their irksome harassment. I've come to understand… blustering bullies are revealing only themselves. Their own fear and insecurities. Their own lack of skill in human interaction.

When kids are bullies… 9.7 times out of 10, they are displaying behavior they are exposed to… terrified by… at home. Seriously mistreated by a parent or older sibling(s). Bullied themselves. Scared. Scarred. These kids learn their interacting style as they follow the family example. Sharing their emotional legacy. Looking for somebody they can terrorize.

Adult bullies act all tough and domineering… hiding the insecurity they feel. Covering up the gaping chasm of their own sense of inferiority. They're afraid. They suck all of the oxygen out of the room… dominating others so they can feel in control. "In control"… so they can feel safe. To not feel so afraid.

There is no good excuse for their domineering rudeness.

Which circles back around to nature and nurture. Some folks are born fussing and howling. Cranky. Contrary. Mean little humans. In some cases, their "nurture" makes them only more that way. They learn to interact with their world thru a coarse cloak of intimidation. Picking on others. They are, in fact, emotional terrorists.

Gentle-natured souls born into a harsh emotional environment simply shut down. Feeling attacked. Scared witless. They curl into themselves... for protection. Rather than becoming a bully themselves... they are emotionally cauterized. Seared victims of the cruel, callous atmosphere of their early home Life. They remain withdrawn. In hiding. Sometimes never to emerge.

Here in Hawaii... I'm watching this dad interact with his family... with his world and the people in it... large and small. All of a sudden... the clouds part. All becomes very clear to me. Now I see what I can write in a book about parenting.

Don't be a jerk.

A bright light shines on the great human dilemma: selfless or selfish. Apparent in so many aspects of human Life. Facing your children as a good parent or a crummy parent lies in that beleaguered interactive realm... between generosity of spirit and "Hey! It's all about me." Heart open or heart hard. Amiable and accommodating or entirely self-absorbed. Here to help. Or here to hurt.

Self-absorbed parents make being a kid hard.

That's what finally clicked for me... the chasm between being a selfless, loving, joyful parent... and being a self-absorbed, "It's all about me," "Sit down, shut up" parent.

Once recognized... it seemed so obvious. Yet, I'd never seen it exactly that way before. So clearly. So blatantly.

When you live in the realm of "all about me"… there's no room… no feelings… no concerns… no empathy… for anybody but *Me*.

Tho, I do notice… there seems to be plenty of room in their selfish world to criticize and belittle.

There we have it… this divergence alive in the vast human spectrum between being open and responsive to others… and being closed off. Totally self-absorbed.

The self-absorbed often utter that plaintive cry… "What about me?" "Pay attention to me!" Well… what about you? Your frustration. Your rudeness. Your domineering ways. Here's a clue… other folks don't find your self-fixation nearly as fascinating as you do.

Being so self-centered is an interwoven aspect of both nature and nurture. Intermingling with our fellow humans… it is totally clear… we each show up in our own unique, individual packaging. Each with our own strengths and talents… phobias and limitations… attitudes and aptitudes. Our tender inner tendencies are either nourished or derailed by the way we are treated as children. By the mental-emotional environment we grow up in.

Sure, it's true… in the territory of just plain being human… we each are some degree of self-centered. That's how we roll. Each human focused on themselves. We each feel vulnerable and doubting. Vulnerable about our own capabilities... about "winning" and "losing." Doubting our own worth. Anxious to fit in. Trying to hide our fear and uncertainty.

This sense of self is not a bad thing.

This very sense of self and "how things need to be" motivates us thru Life. It is the foundation of our individual personality. Our attitude and approach... our Life expression... is built upon our sense of self. What makes your Life... your interactions with your experiences... enhancing or debilitating is constructed upon how secure or insecure you feel within yourself. How resilient you are.

A person who feels secure within themselves is assured, settled, solid. They live within a sense of certainty. Their inner emotional stability is not easily rattled by Life's varied and various disturbances. Even recognizing their own shortcomings... they maintain a healthy degree of self-confidence. An emotionally secure person does not find it necessary to fritz... dragging themselves over hot coals... when something goes awry. They are able to cope with and handle unexpected changes.

An insecure person lives within a vast and wide uneasiness... feeling nervous... awkward and anxious. Easily agitated. Minor Life setbacks can trigger bouts of depression. Perceiving themselves to be inferior or vulnerable... they frequently need to showcase their accomplishments.

Bragging about their Life and skills. Boasting to others… as they try to convince themselves they really do have worth.

The inner self-talk of a secure person sounds like… "Can do." "So far, so good." "We're doing okay." "Is that a silver lining I see?" While the inner conversation of an insecure person would be more along the lines of… "I can't do this." "I'm not good at anything." "What a mess!" "Everybody better not blame me."

Abraham Maslow said an insecure person… "perceives the world as a threatening jungle and most human beings as dangerous and selfish."

Abraham Maslow (1908-1970) was a psychology pioneer and a highly creative thinker. In 1943, at the age of 35, he published his 5-tier Pyramid of Needs… recognizing the interconnectedness of a person's basic needs, psychological needs, and self-fulfillment needs. His Pyramid with its clear elucidation of human development is a mainstay of psychological analysis. As a psychologist… Maslow stressed the importance of focusing on the positive qualities in people… as opposed to treating them as "a bag of symptoms."

Fascinated by the relationship between mental health and human potential… Maslow is famous for his ground-breaking psychological studies of self-actualizing people. Humans who fulfill their Life's potential. This led him to develop and practice Humanistic Psychology… which is grounded in the belief that people are innately good.

Maslow is noted for his observation… "If all you have is a hammer, everything looks like a nail." This insightful comment says basically… you may not clearly interpret what's going on in your world if you only rely on 1 particular tool or mindset. The world looks like a different place when you develop various helpful tools and useful techniques to fortify your psychological toolbox. Always a good idea.

Feeling secure or insecure is not an objective evaluation of a person's abilities. It is purely subjective. Self-doubt is a personal emotional creation constructed from fear and uncertainty.

While others… in their inner world… live within an architecture of calm confidence.

These innermost constructs are not a conscious choice. For the first however many years… 17… 32… 48… your inner reality is the sea you're swimming in. Just "the way things are." Where you live inside yourself. What you see as you look out at your world thru the window in your personal "front door." There are no questions about secure or insecure… calm or anxious… optimistic or pessimistic. "This is just reality, man."

A moment comes in each person's Life when all of a sudden, things… Life… relationships… possibilities… are seen differently. Sometimes this comes as a result of study or meditation. Personal inquiry. Sometimes it arrives in an unexpected burst of insight. This is not hocus-pocus. This is you remembering who you are.

All of us experience emotional vulnerability and have the capacity to be hurt. Pain and uncertainty are not only the domain of insecure people. Emotional insecurity is a difference in self-perception. Two people with the same capabilities… or in the same prickly situation… can see themselves and the situation very differently… experiencing entirely different levels of security or insecurity within.

Insecurity… like bitterness or being defensive… is often rooted in childhood. These personality aspects develop in a multi-layered fashion… nature via nurture. A person may be born with anxious, uneasy personality characteristics (their nature). Tense, angst-ridden dynamics in their childhood environment (their nurture) can cause these personality traits to develop into an immobilizing force. Establishing a tendency to self-doubt and self-limitation thru-out a person's Life.

Intention, meditation… therapy, study… self-reflection… are tools a person can explore to lift themselves out of the self-constriction of an innately anxious temperament.

Here we have one of those tools… right on cue. Let's talk about the wonders of emotional resilience. A dazzling human super power!

Resilience speaks of your overall ability to cope as you navigate human Life. Your capacity to remain open and flexible. Willing to adapt to change. Drawing a deep breath. Recalibrating to center. Moving on.

Resilience profoundly affects how your world works. Your physical world as well as your psychological world. Your world of interacting with your children. And with everybody else.

Cultivate Your Belief in Your Ability to Cope.

Resilience is your capacity to bounce back… rather than fritz out. Your ability to adapt when things don't go as planned. You… interacting with your Life events. Stretched… like elastic. Extended beyond… then springing back. To your original shape. To your sense of well-being.

Yes… this takes intention and in many cases effort to achieve. Developing resilience = you… avoiding creating your own emotional mishaps as your environment changes. Caught in the swirl as situations evolve… yet not drowning in a whirlpool of negative self-talk.

Resilient people don't wallow in self-reproach… nor dwell on the fumes of failure. They acknowledge the situation… learn from their mistakes… and move forward.

Key item here…
They learn from their mistakes.

Rather than beating themselves up for "not doing it right." Rather than pointing a finger, blaming someone else. A resilient person not only learns from their mistakes... they *look for* the lesson to learn here.

Some people may read this and roll their eyes. "Oh sure, like when everything's totally messed up, I'm going to 'look for' the lesson. Yeah, right." Well, yeah. Right.

> In the middle of the fuss and fume
> is exactly the best time
> to make yourself available to "the lesson."

The emotionally resilient do not let themselves be defeated by criticism or setbacks. Rather than getting all defensive and losing their temper... acting out... they process loss and frustration in a healthy way. They are not inclined to avoid the dilemma... blame someone else for their difficulties... nor allow themselves to be consumed by it.

This makes me think of American inventor, Thomas Edison. He tried a zillion different ways to perfect the construction of the electric light bulb. He is quoted as saying... "I have not failed. I've just found 10,000 ways that won't work." In the very middle of the fuss and fume... in the midst of those "10,000 ways"... he persevered. (We humans of Earth are glad he did!) Even tho things looked bleak... he *knew* he would find a way. Now, that's resilience!

Vocabulary plays a significant role. Here, Edison basically says, "Hey, I don't see this work as failure. This is experimenting... learning... and moving on." As so well-stated in the revered *I Ching*... "Perseverance furthers." It's especially challenging to persevere when you're beating yourself up. While you perceive yourself to be a failure.

Every mistake... every misunderstanding... every situation... every failed experiment... has within it the power to teach you something worthwhile. Look for the lesson. Look for the possibilities. Don't be tricked... overcome by setbacks and momentary obstructions. Allow yourself to develop clear vision.

Unencumbered by self-reproach... you see what is there for you beyond the frustration mumbo-jumbo.

A twinkle of admiration here for the resilience of Captain Jack Sparrow ... maneuvering amidst his challenges as a pirate of the Caribbean: "Problems arose... ensued... and were overcome." Go, Jack.

How you talk to yourself about your challenges and frustrations... how you talk about them with friends and colleagues... makes those situations what they are for you. The words you use matter.

The words you use cement your reality. As you talk about the experience in your inner dialogue. As you describe to friends how it all went down. Words you use soon after the event... and in the years to come. The way you choose to describe it. What parts you emphasize. This is how you construct your truth. Your thoughts and words build the scaffolding... then the architecture... of what your experiences are and how they influence your ongoing perceptions of your self and your Life.

Give attention to what you say... how you describe... your incidents and encounters ... your realizations. Your Life. Energy does follow thought. Your words do matter... in your inner world... and to those you encounter and interact with.

A hallmark of resilience: Resilient folks don't let setbacks and difficulties spill over into unrelated areas of their Life. They don't misplace their frustration and take it out on others.

Considering a particular dilemma... you would hear a resilient person say, "I'm not really good at this"... rather than making the hot leap to, "I'm not good at anything."

These folks see the future in a positive light... maintaining an optimistic outlook. Envisioning brighter days ahead. They also step outside of their own small world... reaching out to help others. As they develop and practice their own resilience... they consider ways to help others recognize *their* own resilience.

Resilience is based on inner encouragement. Choices we make inside. Realizations we choose to practice.

I am reminded of a poignant example of resilience in action I wrote about in chapter 13 of *Holy Wow!*... now the last chapter of Volume III. I shared the Dalai Lama's approach to challenging situations. When considering what has happened in Tibet... the Dalai Lama's cherished homeland... Archbishop Desmond Tutu asked him... "How can you not be morose?" The Dalai Lama responds with a practice he uses:

> "If something can be done about the situation,
> what need is there for dejection?
> And if nothing can be done about it,
> what use is there for being dejected?"

The Dalai Lama went on to paraphrase... "When you experience some tragic situation, think about it. If there's no way to overcome the tragedy, then there is no use worrying too much." This blew the Archbishop's mind! This approach was almost too incredible. A person could stop worrying just because it was pointless to worry? Whaaat? Archbishop Tutu responded... "I think people know this with their head. You know that it doesn't help worrying. But they still worry. We have no control over our feelings. Emotions are spontaneous things that arise."

This conversation occurs in *The Book of Joy*, published by Avery-Penguin-Random House. Douglas Abrams,

Archbishop Tutu's longtime collaborator, moderated this exchange of ideas between these 2 remarkable men. Mr. Abrams commented, "This was a point that the Archbishop and the Dalai Lama would disagree on during the week: How much control do we have over our emotions? The Archbishop would say we have very little. The Dalai Lama would say we have more than we think."

More than we think.

The Dalai Lama could have also added… "If I'm always thinking about how dejected I am… I wouldn't have any mental or emotional capacity to think about or do anything else."

Debilitated by dejection. Victimized by a self-inflicted emotional double whammy.

I am inspired to reiterate 1 of my favorite bits of worry-be-gone wisdom:

> Worry is interest paid in advance
> on a debt you may never owe.

Give yourself a break already.

Use your great mental-emotional capabilities to reframe the dark and dismal to something hopeful and manageable. Cognitive reframing is you consciously choosing to modify your mindset… shifting the way you look at a situation or relationship. Looking for… finding… and establishing a different perspective... can transform how you are processing Life inside yourself.

Resilience. Recalibration. Moving on.

How well do most humans know themselves emotionally? Emotional self-understanding makes a tremendous difference in how you live your Life... how you feel inside your own skin. Especially... how you are able to interact with your world and the people in it.

Emotional resilience is an outstanding "survive and thrive" technique here on Planet Earth.

Yes, it *is* an inside job. Yes, some of us are born with a more emotionally optimistic and resilient nature. This could be based on emotional heredity... biochemicals... DNA. Most certainly our childhood environment and interactions... our nurture... plays a significant role as we develop our relationship with living Life. And... there are ways to teach yourself... to train your responses to be resilient.

Relax. Practice releasing conflict and concern. "Wait a minute! I am your most grievous conflict... your deepest, over-arching anxiety. You can't possibly *release* me! You can't just *let me go!*" Well... drawing a deep, centering breath... it turns out you can.

Relax your anxiety and apprehension. Taking care of yourself... your body... your mind... your heart = a huge step toward being able to develop a more resilient relationship with your Life.

As I researched "building emotional resilience," I had to smile. After you relax… you are encouraged to "practice thought awareness." Hmmm… Do I hear a familiar ring? You may recall in earlier volumes of Holy Wow! I share my "3 Steps to Greater Awareness." The First Step = "Listen to your thoughts." How do you talk to yourself? What are you telling yourself, day in and day out? Is your inner dialogue optimistic? Pessimistic? Secure? Insecure? Fearful? Rehashing the past. Anxious about the future. Or is your self-talk resilient … flexible… confident? Moving forward with a positive outlook.

It is possible to edit your outlook. Because you have choice… you can develop and practice "cognitive restructuring." You can choose how you respond to your Life. You *can* change the way you think about troubling situations or difficult events. You can see them as "Life tutorials." Look for the possibilities… the lessons to learn. They *are* there.

Do yourself a big favor… don't fall for feeling, "I'm being screwed with!" Don't look for slights or evidence you've been mistreated. As I've mentioned… it's *all* here. All the time. Your Life takes figure and form from what you give your attention to and what you focus on.

Your Life assembles and builds according to what you think… believe… say… is happening.

You hear people say… "Don't take it personally." Or the even more ridiculous… "It's only business." Yeah… easy for you to say. That's corporate-speak for… "Sure I'm messing with you. But, hey… *I'm* not taking any responsibility for this."

I have a clear memory from elementary school of someone saying "don't take it personally." I remember thinking… what does that even mean? How does a person not "take it personally?" To clarify for myself… I just looked it up. "Don't take it personally" means don't be upset or offended by what someone says or does. The example given… "He says unkind things to everyone." In this case… how come "he" gets a pass? Have you ever wondered why "he" gets off the hook for talking trash? As you are supposed to just suck it up and roll with it.

Let's explore another way to look at "don't take it personally." Rather than reacting… getting vexed, peeved, twisted… by something rude a person says… you get to choose. There are no rules saying that anyone's remarks or actions have the power to pollute your inner Life. You have the choice… to not get in a snit. To not let this stupid person ick your wow. You get to choose who you are… and how you're going to be. It's yours to decide. You get to be who *you* are. In this moment now.

And in this moment, too.

You have undoubtedly noticed… in the living of human Life… everything is not always perfect. Things go wrong. You make mistakes. Sometimes you will not be chosen. There will be misunderstandings… miscommunications… missteps. Your lesson is not the fact that "obscure things happen." Because they do. Your lesson… your realization… your growth… is found in what you *do* with these things that happen. How you respond. What you tell yourself. How you proceed.

Don't get stuck looking back. That's not the way we're going.

Basketball legend, Kobe Bryant, put it like this… "Everything negative… pressures, challenges… is all an opportunity for me to rise." Amen.

As this Life of yours unfolds and "stuff happens"… the following becomes clearer than clear:

Happiness and resilience…
disappointment and frustration…
your mental health… your general well-being…
your happy heart…
all are tightly bound to your early emotional environment.
To the inner connections you made…
beliefs, attitudes, perceptions…
as a child.

Why do the majority of humans walk around feeling angry… guilty… wounded? Because we were not "recognized" when we were children. Not only were we not joyfully welcomed and embraced… recognized as the tremendous beings of light we each are… most of us were treated as if something was wrong with us.

Especially tweens and teens hear a variation on… "I'm sure you've done something wrong." Or you're going to. Teenagers are treated as persons of suspect. Often with harsh outcome.

Most of us are taught… Life is a crisis. Not to be trusted. With more emphasis placed on what is wrong than what is right. Fear and self-loathing are the result of childhood misguidance. Abuse. Neglect. Intended or unintended.

In a Parade magazine interview, actor Sylvester Stallone revealed: "My father was an extraordinarily exacting man. If what you did wasn't a photocopy of the way he did it, then you had no abilities and had to be chastised and corrected. And quite often the correction was, you know, shocking. He made me feel extraordinarily inept. 'Why can't you be smarter? Why can't you be stronger?' I didn't have one virtue. He never said he was proud of me."

Sons are destined to disappoint their fathers. Fathers are destined to disappoint their sons.

Of course, this also applies to daughters and mothers.

Family relationship can be done better.
If not by you… then who?
If not now… when?

People will tell you their children are the most important things in their Life. Do their kids know that?

They should.

As a parent… it is yours to create a home environment that fosters a sense of security and well-being in your child. As a human… it is yours to let the people you interact with know that you see them… that they are valued.

Here's a question: How much do you let your insecurities… your tender awareness of your own limitations and vulnerability… guide you? Impose upon you? These doubts about yourself seep out into your Life. This self-uncertainty affects what you do with your Life. How you create your living expression. Who you are.

It's all about where you place your attention. How you see and experience who you are. What you believe this Life of yours is all about. You get to call it.

I was in my early 50s when Scott and I attended a Full Moon Meditation Event in the early 2000s. The speaker shared a point that really leapt out for me. "You grow up to give what you did not get in your childhood."

Whoa! I grokked that immediately. Whether you are conscious of it or not… as an adult, you offer to others what was missing for you when you were a kid. A remarkable revelation. Right away… I knew what was missing from my childhood. And what I was giving to others: Feeling valued. It is important to me in my adult Life to let others know I value them… especially my children.

I definitely did not feel valued as a child. I've already mentioned… it seemed to me… I was a piece of furniture my parents needed to move from Point A to Point B. "Oh, right. Don't forget to put Dana somewhere."

I'm going to again visit perceptions I gleaned from *Children: The Challenge.* Yes… applying and practicing its insights and suggestions made for An Extraordinary Parenting Experience… guiding me to actively express to Isaiah and Lyla how much I value them.

As well as guiding me to be a better parent… these suggestions and realizations brought an added bonus. The perceptions I gleaned from *Children: The Challenge* also improved my relationships and interactions with my fellow humans in general. The clerk at the grocery store. The bank teller. The gas station attendant (yes, once upon a time there were people who pumped your gas, checking your tires and oil each time you pulled in). Sending notes to friends letting them know… "I'm thinking of you. I am so glad our lives touch."

I grew up seeing my dad send greeting cards to his aunts and cousins... post cards to friends and relations thru-out the land. It was just what he did. I love sending notes and post cards. I didn't realize till later in my adult Life... oh look... I get this particular inclination from Daddy. Applying pen to paper... many times colored pens... with hearts and star stickers to visually liven things up. Enthusiasm for the remarkable people who touch my Life. Snail mail. A little unexpected treat. Showing up in your mail box in real time. Lyla carries on this family tradition.

When my kids were in their early teens... I started a new Women's Circle in Portland. As per usual, some women I was meeting for the first time... others had been in my Circles for years. I was late arriving to our 4th Circle gathering. By way of explanation... I said, "Sorry I'm late. I'm very popular at home." Engaged in family Life was, indeed, the reason I was late arriving. One of the Circle women I was just getting to know said, "If you are popular at home... I definitely want to know what you know." She made it clear her home Life was not so great. If I was "popular at home"... she wanted to know what I was doing to pull that off.

Such a difference a generation makes. Parenting in the 21st century definitely presents challenges that were not a part of the scheme of things as I was raising my kids in the '80s and

'90s. So many of the current Life-features ... Internet, video games and social media to name a significant few... weren't even a blip on the screen back then. Today's parents are in a whole new world. Greatly unknown. We have no way of perceiving the consequences this technology may be having on our children's hearts and minds. Behaviors and attitudes.

One unfortunate side-effect is pretty doggone clear... hiding behind the anonymity of online interactions and social media allows humans to become keyboard gangsters... spewing their worst.

Social media is a fascinating microcosm... revealing both humanity's worst instincts and our better angels.

Yet, what do we do but keep moving forward? Doing what we believe is best for our children.

As a child, I always felt something was "missing" in my Life with my parents. I didn't know what "it" was. I just knew it wasn't there. Little girl me would have conversations with myself... about being a different kind of parent than my parents were. Of course, I didn't know exactly what that meant or *how* I was going to be different. I just knew I was going to be having a good time... and letting my kids know it. I would let my kids know I enjoyed being with them.

Recently I was musing about how Lyla's younger daughter likes to pretend she's a baby. We all play along with her. "Oh, such a cute baby." "We'll take good care of this sweetie pie baby." When Lyla was little, she liked to pretend she was a baby, too. Scott and I both played along. "Such a cute baby." As I was smiling, thinking about this… all of a sudden, in my head, a scene appeared from my childhood. I'm 7 years old. My mother is talking on the phone and I am rolling around on the floor at her feet cooing, gurgling… making sounds like a young baby. As an only child, I always wanted a sister or brother. In my kid mind… I was pretending to be a baby so the person on the other end of the phone would think we had a new baby at our house. My mother completely ignored me. She didn't even look at me. I was making a bit of a baby-spectacle of myself. She didn't comment or engage in any way. That would not have occurred to her. Seeing this scenario… remembering that moment… led me to realize… my parents did not interact with me in an engaged way. Never any, "What's going on with you, Dana?" "You funny little thing… what are you doing?" "Let's have fun together."

As adults, Lyla and Isaiah both make it clear… I'm a good mom. They thank me for that. Many times I've tried to figure out… what did I do to be "a good mom?" What did I do to actually enjoy being a mom? Recalling this "baby" scenario suddenly brought a clear realization.

I enjoyed my kids. I still do. To me… they were marvelous, fascinating bunnies. Funny. Bright. Fun to be with. I *wanted* to engage in their world. "What's going on for *you*, Sweetie Pie?" "What do *you* like?" "Yes, of course… I'd love to play, too!"

This level of engaging would not have occurred to my folks. I don't remember even one time either of them involved themselves with little Dana in Dana's World. In the moment of my recent realization… I saw this as a *big* difference in the way I chose to be with my kids.

Now, I get to see the sweet, encouraging way my daughter and son engage with their kids. Bonus!

I wasn't particularly fussed at my parents. I wasn't a particularly fussed little human. I just went along with the program. I knew something was missing.

In the vast and multi-faceted realm of parent/child interactions… compared to what other kids have had to deal with at the hands of their parents… mine could be seen as "first world problems." My parents did not hit me. They did not berate me. Yes… I am *very* grateful for that. My parents also did not engage me… did not interact with me in Kid Land. They did not nurture me. Not because they were withholding. They, literally, did not know how. I was pretty much on my own. Adrift. Occasionally, I wondered why they didn't like me. Especially my dad.

Even in the context of a gentle home environment… this "something's missing" was significant for me. I am aware… and at times unaware… of the ways this affects my inner being. My adult self. My interactions with my world.

It is Absolutely Mind Blowing how much… how multi-dimensionally… our childhood environment… and all we come to believe about ourselves… colors and animates our adult Life.

My folks had family friends named Lydia and Brownie. They had 5 kids. As my little-kid self became aware of their family… the 5 kids were all in their 20s, starting families of their own. As I grew older, I learned more of their family's story. Lydia was married with 5 young children. Brownie was her husband's friend and coworker. Lydia's husband was killed in an accident… a very unexpected death. Brownie offered to marry Lydia and help her raise her 5 children. Wow. Good story. Their family had an easygoing way with each other. They all got along just fine.

My folks kind of lost track of Lydia and Brownie when I was in my teens. Years later… I was 30 and very pregnant with Lyla… my mom and I, with 3-year-old Isaiah, were shopping in a large Sav-On drug store in the weeks before Christmas. I saw a woman who looked like Lydia. Lydia was a very distinctive-looking woman… jet-black hair, strong facial features accented by a prominent mole. I walked over to my mom… "Mama, doesn't that woman look like Lydia?" My mother gave her a glance… "That *is* Lydia!"

We went over to them and had quite a warm reunion… right there in the busy Christmas aisles of Sav-On. We all marveled… running into each other "after all these years." Lydia and Brownie were delighted to meet Isaiah and congratulated me on my very apparent pregnancy. Lydia and my mom walked around together as Brownie, Isaiah, and I looked at greeting cards. I said to him, "Brownie, I want to tell you… I've always thought it was so great that you married Lydia and helped her take care of all her kids." Looking me straight in the eye, Brownie said in his sweet Southern drawl, "Oh, Dana, *I'm* the lucky one."

I was so touched. Kinda blown away. Tears came. He saw *himself* as "the lucky one." Not the put-upon one. Not the yeah, it-was-really-hard-but-someone-had-to-do-it one. He is the *lucky* one. Wow.

Just as I'm writing this, I realize… Life set it up so I, too, am with a man who sees himself as "the lucky one." Lyla had just turned 2 and Isaiah was 5 when Scott and I met. As time went on… Scott became the guy who shared Life and love with the 3 of us. He "helped out" a woman with small children. Just as Brownie did. (I have literally never seen this life similarity until right now!)

The years unfolding the way they have… our rather amazing Life… living within the love that is our family…

now with 3 glorious GrandBunnies... Scott would readily tell you, "I am the lucky one." So cool.

During our first year together... Scott mentioned that as a boy, he would daydream about being with a woman who had 2 small children. Hmmmm. As my Daddy would say, "Well how about that!"

Here's another reason I'm telling you about Lydia and Brownie. When I was a kid, Lydia and Brownie would come to visit. I'd say hi to them when they arrived. As the adults chatted in the living room... I would go down the hall to my room. Every time they came over... Brownie would eventually come down the hall to see what I was doing. To visit with *me*. Interested in what I was up to. Attentive as I told him little stories about my dolls and their goings-on. Or he'd listen to me play a tune on my Melody Bells or my violin. I fondly remember... Brownie came to visit *me*. He was interested in what was going on with me. No other friend of my parents ever did anything close to that. I felt like Brownie saw me as a viable human being. I was his friend, too. Obviously... this was memorable.

Living as we do in a time when motives are suspect... when a man expresses interest in a young girl. I want to be completely clear... this was not the case with Brownie. These were not uneasy, leering encounters. These were moments when a sweet, caring man came to see what his friends' little girl was up to.

I know the difference. When I was 11, my dad started buying eggs from a man who kept chickens and sold fresh eggs. The first few times, my dad and I drove to the guy's farm to buy eggs. Then he started delivering eggs to our house. I was a mature young girl... "developed" for my age. I distinctly remember the few times I was home alone when the egg man came by. Those moments he was in the house with just me definitely felt creepy. Fortunately, nothing came of these times. I do remember the feeling, tho. I certainly know the difference between the leering energy coming from the egg man... and the kind, twinkly energy coming from my friend, Brownie. God love him.

A day or 2 after my above-mentioned realization about how my parents didn't engage with me in my little kid world... out of the blue, a woman friend of mine commented, "I wish I had taken more time to enjoy and play with my kids while they were growing up." Wow. Pretty remarkable... her random musing fit right into my developing realization.

Her comment got me to thinking... you don't ever hear an adult say, "Sure wish I hadn't played so much with my kids when they were young." I haven't ever heard anyone say that. I doubt I ever will.

Because I always felt I was going to be "a mom"… as I was growing up, before I ever had children… my inner filter was attuned to collecting pieces of information… points of possibility… about being a parent. Just as I would do with my "pieces of the puzzle," I would store these wise tidbits away. Compiling them. Mulling them over. Having them ready to pull out and apply when I became a parent.

Growing up… "feeling ahead" into my future… it always seemed to me I would be a teacher. The possibility of being a meditation teacher never once occurred to me. It couldn't have. There was zero framework in my early Life for an awareness of meditation to grow on. In my youth… meditation was light-years beyond my known realm. Believing I would be a teacher… I had an interest in the field of education. In my early 20s, I developed a fascination with Summerhill… a boarding school in Suffolk, England, founded in 1921 by A.S. Neill. Summerhill is recognized as the original alternative "free" school.

Here, I will not delve into the philosophy of Summerhill and what was considered by some its radical approach to education. Nor will I write about the controversy surrounding this new way of educating young humans. Considering said controversy brings to mind one of my favorite astute observations from Albert Einstein:

"Great spirits have always encountered violent opposition from mediocre minds."

What I do want to share with you here is a story I read in A.S. Neill's 1960 book, *Summerhill: A Radical Approach to Child Rearing*. A.S. Neill was known to his friends and associates as Neill.

As Neill tells the story… at one point, a troubled, defiant teenage boy was brought to live at Summerhill. He flaunted his rebellious nature. With disdain, this boy made it quite clear… he wanted nothing to do with authority. Teachers and Neill, himself, began to wonder if they would be able to actually get thru his defiant resistance to make a connexion with this boy.

One day Neill was painting an exterior door white. The young guy stood behind him, silently watching him work. When Neill finished painting the door and stood back to look at his work, the boy picked up a handful of dirt and threw it on the door's wet, white paint. Looking at what the boy had done, Neill picked up a handful of dirt and thru it on the newly painted door. Whaaaat? In this moment of startle… the boy began to cry. Jolted by Neill's unexpected reaction… the boy's rebellious bubble burst. A break-thru moment.

Neill did not respond like "an adult" to the boy throwing dirt on his freshly painted door. He didn't yell. He didn't get upset. Quite the opposite. Neill joined the boy where *he* was in that moment. The pristine perfection of Neill's painting project was not more important than the well-being of this young man. Humanness won. Kindness won. Neill's unexpected response collided with the boy's inner world. His defiant façade was crumbled by kindness. The boy changed. He no longer needed to seethe and defy. He no longer needed to exclude himself from the world around him.

He had been seen.

This story of Neill's response really struck me. And, obviously stuck with me… here I am writing about it decades later. My takeaway: Stuff isn't more important than humans. Projects don't have priority over relationships. Don't be blinded by busyness. Don't ignore the possibility to really connect. Be awake and aware… alive and present in the current moment. Allow connexion and compassion to win.

The awareness I gleaned from Neill's gentle wisdom in that transforming moment… brings me to share with you a mindfulness jewel from the insightful works of Alice Bailey. A little sign I made with these words hung above my writing desk for many years. It said:

"Wisdom connotes skill in action…
as the result of developed love

141

and the light of understanding:
it is awareness of requirements
and the ability to bring together into a fused relationship
the need and that which will meet it."

In his compassionate response to the actions of that troubled boy… A.S. Neill gave a clear example of "skill in action" as he brought together "the need and that which will meet it."

Another attentive tidbit I appreciate came my way when I was at a party in my early 20s. A hippie potluck… lots of folks… lots of music… lots of kids. I happened upon a scenario which gifted me with another useful piece to the parenting puzzle. From across the room… I watched a young guy sitting on the floor playing blocks with a little girl. They each had their own pile of colored blocks. She reached to take a block from his pile. Instead of saying a sharp "No!" (the response I anticipated) he said, "Sure." He then took another of his blocks, asking, "Would you like this red one? How about this blue block?" Instead of being all "no, no, no!" he was all "yes, yes, yes!" Rather than keeping his blocks for himself or making her feel she'd done something wrong… he was encouraging and kind as they built a block tower together. "Would you like this one?" Cool.

That moment… that exchange… really opened my eyes. It opened my heart. Awareness dawned. When interacting with kids, an adult doesn't always have to say "No!" Being all punitive. Chastising. Controlling all outcomes.

Present in the moment… an adult, a parent can say, "Yes." "You're right." "Would you like this one, too?" Elevating possibility for the child. Connecting in the here and now.

I am always grateful for insight delivered in Life's subtle moments. Awareness shows up… when you're not even looking for it.

In my early 20s, I was on staff at California Institute of The Arts when it opened in Valencia, California. Among its *many* artistic endeavors… Cal Arts is home to a gamelan ensemble. Gamelan (GAM uh lawn) is the traditional orchestra of the islands of Indonesia… with bronze xylophones, gongs, drums, and bamboo flutes. In a conversation, one of the gamelan musicians told me… when young children display an interest in the gamelan instruments… they are encouraged to play with the bells… the drums… the xylophones. If a child shows no interest in the instruments… rather than being forced to learn gamelan… they are encouraged to explore other things. Note to self: When you become a parent, Dana… utilize this approach.

My own inner voices gave me another useful piece of parenting wisdom. When I was a kid… every now and then a voice in my head would say, "Remember what this feels like." This voice showed up randomly... not at colossal, significant moments. Just here and there. I knew it was saying: "Remember how it feels to be a kid." Perhaps in service to clarity... as I became a teenager, the message altered: "Remember what this feels like, because you *will* be on the other side of it." I took note and, ultimately, made good use of this helpful statement. I raised my kids remembering what it felt like to be a kid. Especially, to be a teenager.

In this conversation about the significance of healthy parenting... the most important element we can discuss is stopping... transforming... the ongoing family violence that travels, mindlessly, from generation to generation to generation.

If yours is a family of unhealthy, abusive parenting... you know who you are. You know how it feels living in such an onslaught of toxic dysfunction. You also know this cannot go on. We cannot continue poisoning the emotional well-being... the emotional reality... of the future.

It is up to us... each one of us...
to break the cycle of family violence.
Of family neglect and abuse.
All it takes is one generation standing up...

willing to say, "This is not right."

Doing what it takes to break the cycle.

For the generations to come.

This I know from my own family history.

My father was on the younger end of 9 children... 3 girls and 6 boys. He was number 7. His mother was an incredibly loving woman. In her living room was a small alcove with 3 shelves. Here she had framed 8x10 headshots of each of her 6 sons. I remember, at age 9... looking across the room at this array of her photos and thinking, "Her sons love her so much."

In my heart and mind... she has long been Angel Heart Woman of The World. My grandmother was remarkable. An exceptional presence of love.

My granddaddy, on the other hand, was cut from a completely different piece of cloth.

From various family stories I've heard... I'm convinced Granddaddy had mental health issues. He had a meanness about him... and an achingly limited view of the possibilities of Life and this world we live in. He would sometimes say to my grandmother... "I get mighty fussed at you, Mary." Yet he was never physically abusive toward her.

This same tolerance did not extend to his sons. With them he was both physically and psychologically abusive.

To add an extra scheming twist... he made sure his cruelty happened outside of my grandmother's view. He berated and beat his boys. They scornfully called him "Chunk." My dad was so wounded by his father's mean, controlling ways... he moved from Florida to Southern California in his early 20s... rarely to return to the family home.

Now, decades down the line... here's what I know. Even tho my uncles were seriously abused... not one of them ever hit their own children. My cousins and I did not have good fathers... but we were not beaten. Being raised by a terrible father... my uncles and my dad had no role model showing them how to be a healthy, loving father. Being men of their generation, it did not occur to them to learn to be engaged fathers. But they did not abuse their children the way their father abused them.

In my 30s, it occurred to me... my father should have been on antidepressants since the 1950s. Outside of our house, he would be amiable and fun... with strangers, coworkers, occasional visiting family. When he came home... he went in his den and closed the door. Folks regarded him as a charming, Southern gentleman. In our home, he was sullen and silent. Consumed by his wound.

As you know... Scott and I cared for my parents in their final years. One day, as I drove Daddy to a doctor's appointment... he said to me, "I should have been more involved with you when you were younger." Altho I agreed with him 100%… I didn't say anything. A minute or 2 later, he said… "I just thought you wanted me to leave you alone." As he had wanted his father to leave him alone. This last part was unspoken… but his implication was clear.

I was never hit as a child… not even spanked. Daddy had his "mad face." I was a compliant child. I wasn't inclined to act out. When he was displeased… his mad face was all it took to straighten me out.

I've often thought… a karmic agreement existed between my grandmother and her sons… to defuse Granddaddy's mean, nasty ways. To neutralize his toxic approach to Life. She and her sons were, in fact, successful. Chunk's cruelty was not passed on to his grandchildren. I am grateful to my grandmother and my uncles… and to my dad… for their consistent choices not to pass along the violence they grew up in. Together they defused my grandfather's harming, hurtful manner of parenting.

Abuse grows from fear. Needing to be in control grows from fear. Instead of engaging Life creatively… finding positive solutions… many people can only think of wielding a big stick to get their way. Their way should not be confused with the best way. It's just the way that feeds their particular neurosis.

As you are a parent… as you are a functional, contributing human being… show your affection. Not your affliction. We have all been wounded in some way(s) by painful childhood experiences. As we grow, evolve, mature… it is ours to move beyond interacting with others from a place ruled by our wounds. The last thing you want to do is mindlessly inflict your pain on your children.

Find and show your affection.

This is good for your kids… as you interact with them in a warm and friendly way. Good for other people in your Life… as you treat them with kind regard. Finding and showing your affection is especially good for your own fine self.

A note to your ever-evolving inner self… you know you're on the path to personal healing when you are able to look at your parents… and see them as people who were dealing with their own unresolved Life trauma.

∽ ∽ ∽

Now let's take a look at the power of parent/child possibility from an entirely different perspective. Here, I share with you a tool you can use as an adult to release your wounded psyche from childhood trauma or mistreatment. I have used this technique many times in my own Life. I've guided a lot of people as they embrace this process to find their own balance, healing and self-worth. You will find this to be a helpful tool.

Living your adult Life... many times as you experience a painful emotion... you'll find it can be traced to experiencing the same emotional distress when you were young. When you were a child... and powerless to do anything about the situation you were in.

Find yourself a quiet place where you can focus your attention for a few minutes. As the adult you are now... allow yourself to feel your current painful emotion. Drawing a deep, centering breath... allow your mind to recall a situation where... as a child... you felt similarly upset, frightened, or wronged. You may be surprised how readily these painful childhood memories show up.

Looking at this childhood moment in time... allow as many details as possible to fill in the setting. Take the time to recollect specifics and features of that moment. Where were you? Were you in a room? Outdoors? Is it sunny? Rainy? Nighttime? Do you see what you were wearing? What is going on? Who is there with you? Are you alone? Feel what your child self is feeling. Are you frightened? Mad? Sad? Be aware of the circumstances, and the person who is mistreating you. See whoever or whatever else is present contributing to your fright or upset.

When you have the details of the scene and your child-self feelings before you... in your imagination, step into the scenario as the compassionate, caring adult you are now. Confront the situation or person who mistreated you.

Rescue your child self.

In your mind and heart... show up as the person your child-self hoped would come. Save the day! Defend your child self. Advocate for the well-being of your child-self. Be your own champion.

Confront the mistreating person... the adult or older child... and let them know their time is up. They are outta here! Don't hold back. Give them a piece of your mind. Send them on their way.

As your adult self... resolve the situation so your child-self no longer feels scared, angry, powerless. Acknowledge your child-self... so they (you) feel valued. Seen. Be a buddy to your younger self. Scoop your little self up in a warm, reassuring hug.

Congratulate your kid-self for being brave and courageous. Reassure them they were not bad or wrong. Let your child-self know the adult mistreating them was out of line. They were not right. Just bigger.

Having resolved the situation... take your child self out for a really good treat... an ice cream cone comes to mind. Or a toy. Or an adventure.

Let yourself feel your child-self's relief.
The wonderment of being rescued.
Of being supported.
Of being saved.

Feel your child-self's delight at getting a treat. Let your adult self and your child-self *feel* your loving connexion. Don't rush it.

Savor this marvelous moment.

Here is another possibility... a powerful and empowering variation on this healing blessing. In your mind:

Go to yourself at the moment of your birth.
Just as you crossed the threshold into this new Life.

In your mind's eye... receive your newly-incarnate self with welcoming joy. Gently hold your newborn self in a warm, loving embrace. Acknowledge your new self... your brilliant presence... for coming here to Planet Earth. Acknowledge how the planet welcomes you. Needs you. How thrilled the waterfalls... the evergreens... the oceans and deserts... the beasts and the butterflies... are that *you* are here.

Be with your newborn self. Provide this openhearted foundation. Welcomed... fortified with love... as you arrived in this Life. Again... as your adult self... as your just-born self... savor this moment.

Applying either version of this healing rescue mission as an adult, you'll be amazed at the peace... the deep sense of well-being... it can bring. Generously give yourself this process of transformation... this healing gift... time and again. Relish the experience. You are remixing the basic ingredients of your Life. Healing. Transforming your inner foundation.

If you were a lonely or misunderstood child... go to your child self as a kind, encouraging presence. You will feel the deep, peace-full effect.

Any adult will tell you... what happens in your childhood rides with you... rides on you... for the rest of your incarnation. Be willing and ready to defend and save your child self. You were not able to rescue yourself then. But you can now.

You are the liberating Super Hero
of your inner psyche.

This excursion into your child self... this revisiting and release of past emotional trauma... allows you to be in your adult Life in a more congruous, compatible, harmonious way.

Be willing to stretch.

Be willing to heal yourself
from childhood neglect and abuse.

Do everything you can
to not pass along that mistreatment.

Be with your kids.

Love 'em up good.

CHAPTER FOUR

You Contain Multitudes

"From bliss to blisters."

I know you are each jazzed about your upcoming incarnation as a human of Earth. Who wouldn't be? Such a spectacular venue! Evergreens, oceans and polar bears… oh my! So many possibilities! Highs and lows. Steaming hot to freezing cold… and everything in between… physically, emotionally, and mentally.

Ride that ol' Rodeo of Life!

Look how brilliant you are… here to equip yourself with the insights, techniques, and specializations offered in these Enhancement Upgrades. You've heard us say here at The Interpretorium… as you launch into your human Life:

Show Up... Be Kind... Contribute.

You are refining your instrument's ability to cope and thrive... as you prepare to play your part... "strut your stuff" as humans say... on that blue-green Planet of Paradox. Actually... does "paradox" even begin to elucidate the enigmas of Earth? Mysteries within riddles... wrapped in conundrums. Hints and clues... some hidden... others right out in the open. "In your face" as the locals would say.

As is true in every human-based planetary system... if there's one thing you are guaranteed to encounter on Planet Earth... it's the reality of relationship. Relationship is the plot, the theme, the character development... the display and the exposition... of Life on Earth. The human story writ large. Clear and obvious. A reality in which you will sometimes find rhyme... occasionally, even reason.

Just as poles and spectra dominate the landscape of Earthtone Life... so do relationships. One relationship motif applies to connexions between humans... lovers, children, teachers, colleagues, frenemies. Also to be considered is your relationship with your home... your condo, your apartment... your yard, your house. And how you "keep" it. You will have relationships with your interests and your hobbies. Your creativity. Your skills and abilities. Your doubts and anxieties.

Humans develop relationships with their work, their play... most certainly, with their creative expression. A wise acknowledgment you will hear from humans of Earth:

When you love your job,
you never work a day in your Life.

Some degree of employment is destined to utilize your time and pay the bills... you might as well like what you spend many hours of each day doing. Truly. If you hate your job, each day is drudgery. If you are "working for the weekend"... or only to make it to retirement... the grind definitely grinds.

You'll have a relationship with yourself. Your personality. Your free will. Your resistance. Your ways and means. Your physical body... its aches and pains... your stamina and prowess. And for sure, you'll be deeply relating to the roller coaster of your emotional nature. Ups and downs... valleys, chasms, peaks... like you cannot even imagine as you sit here in The Interpretorium.

You will have a close affiliation with your thoughts, your perceptions, your ideas. Your beliefs and attitudes. Your education. Will you be a scholar? A dropout? A strong student? A creative thinker? Whatever quality or quantity of education your Life presents... and you embrace... will strongly affect your ongoing relationship with your human Life.

You may even have a relationship with not having relationships.

As you can see… relationship is not only about liaisons with the humans you will interact with and get to know. Altho, in the vernacular of Earth… the term "relationship" does most frequently refer to the tingle as you mingle. With the people you care about… as well as the ones who infuriate you.

Humans are wired to be social creatures. Interaction with others is key to humanosity. When you are being human… relationship will indeed rock your world. And roll it. Occasionally… even roil it.

Our commitment here at Team Interpretorium: Equip you with skills and awareness… so you can live a fulfilling, bodacious Life while you are a human of Earth. As a carbon-based Life-unit, you will encounter So Many Activating Components rolling… and roiling… in the mental, emotional, and physical environments humans are alive in. Relationship underscores that complexity. It's the undercurrent. The substrata. The very foundation of the living of Life.

You will not hear me say the dance of human relationship is easy. It's not.

Well, you know… sometimes humans *do* luck out. They connect with an outstanding match. Two people find each other… click… and move harmoniously thru Life together. The supreme good pleasure of discovering another human who enjoys the same things… walks on the beach… a hike in the mountains… a rollicking game of backgammon. Whipped cream on their café mocha. Coffee, black. Chai tea. Country music. Reggae. Classical. A loving family Life.

Amicable, cordial connexions like these are golden. And more rare than you might think. 'Tis a beautiful thing when it happens. A blessing to be a part of. A marvelous fabric to wrap around yourself and exist within.

Compatible. Rather than combatable.

Many times… based on the conflict, the hostility in their early homelife setting the stage… wounding their nature… some humans live in a world of combat and lashing out. As an adult, finding themselves in a volatile, hurting relationship… there is a sense of the familiar. Deep, down inside… "this feels like home." Not necessarily a healthy, happy home. But at least, I know what to expect. How to suffer. How to lash back.

A totally different universe than the friendly, congenial harmony some people create and thrive within.

How does this loving, supportive connecting come about? Is their connexion a longstanding cosmic agreement? Or just plain karmic good luck? Kismet, perhaps.

Is their supreme good fortune based in their nature? Or their personal nurture? Divine providence? Pre-destined happenstance? Is it a gift? Sure feels like a gift. Or is it completely inexplicable?

Each human involved in such a gift of good fortune will agree... this grace-filled, affable relationship is a Life blessing. A Life saver. A Life evolver. Not to take for granted. "I know how lucky I am. I nourish our relationship every chance I get." Good strategy. Thumbs up.

"Thumbs up"... fold your fingers into the palm of your hand. Extend your award-winning opposable thumb vertically. This is a positive human gesture representing... "A-OK!" "You betcha!" "Well-played!"

Speaking of good strategy... allow me to suggest... while incarnate on Planet Earth, it helps to listen. Many times, humans just want to talk. Getting their point across. Clarifying. Mansplaining. Showing others... "I know important stuff!" "You are not listening correctly!" "My idea is the winner here!"

Some folks just want to be the one talking. Explaining. Expounding. Telling the story "the right way." Impatient as others are speaking. "Yeah, yeah, yeah... shut up already so I can talk!"

Listening opens doorways to communication.

Stand in the "Listening Capabilities Installed Here" line before heading into incarnation. Equip yourself. I base this worthwhile suggestion on personal experience. You will find listening to be a Life skill many humans have not developed. Rein in always having to be the one talking. The one getting *your* point across. Even tho you know you're "right." Other folks want to express their points, too.

Listening speaks volumes.

Frolicking in the human realm, yes, there's listening… and there's looks. Demeanor. Comportment. Appearance. Looking *good*. You'll be amazed… in the realm of humanosity, physical appearance is a huge factor. A mind-boggling component of human interaction. Yet, the vast realities and reckonings of relationship skate so far beyond looking foxy… being attractive. Yes, to humans, a striking comportment is seen as a boon. "Hubba hubba!" some say as they express their approval and enthusiasm for another person's appearance. For many humans… male and female… it feels good to get "dolled up." Stuff, strutting.

A human looks "attractive" to "catch" another person's attention. But once you've "caught" that attention… now what? What you gonna do with it?

There are a lot of "sprout relationships." People who are good at starting relationships… "sprouting" interaction… then moving on to sprout another. Sprouting is not sustaining. Yes, sprouting capability is an essential… it is the first few pages of a book… the previews to a movie… the first few bars of a tune.

But then what? What happens next? Where does the whole book come from? The entire movie? The rest of the song?

Starting a relationship is one thing. Nurturing and sustaining a relationship... building something that works well for all concerned... is quite another.

This relates to any kind of relationship. With other humans. With work. With creativity. Playing a musical instrument. Learning a new language. Continuing your education.

Hmmmm... well, lookie here... we have more fertile ground for growing patience. Tolerance. Fortitude. Resilience. Exercising *those* muscles.

Naturally... humans learn a lot about nurturing or harming relationship in the context of their youngling home Life. Children... those little sponges... eagerly soak up all that's going on around them. Watching. Listening. Absorbing. Learning. All. The. Time.

So deeply immersed in their ongoing blossoming... children are not even conscious of their "taking it all in" process. Steeped within watching and learning... young children rarely think, "watch and learn." They just *are*. Watching. Learning. Absorbing the details and nuances going on around them. Drawing in all the actions and the inactions... dithering, procrastination, lethargy. Simmering in the stew of their family's feelings... psychological cues and miscues. The interactions in their environment. Multidimensional psychological osmosis.

Ensconced within your Karmic Package... your human suit comes equipt with built-in connexions to a variety of people... your parents, siblings, teachers, school chums, coworkers. Some of these relationships are charming and delightful... encouraging you to discover and express your very best. Others can be bullying and demanding... causing you to question your self-worth.

Discovering these connexions continues thru-out your incarnation. Even in your older years... new friends, cohorts, and adversaries show up. Remember... Planet Earth is an intergalactic melting pot. You're going to find every kind of human there. Some people you will be immediately drawn to... others, not so much. At times, a new person will seem immediately familiar to you... as if you have known them before. Most likely, you have.

Incarnant in this current Earthtone time frame, you will come across something new and different in the world of communication and human relationship: The Internet. And its kindred posse... social media. This vast electronic universe will provide you with *many* interactions. Some you will find engaging and informative. At the same time... there are other aspects that will annoy the stuffin' out of you.

You'll be learning new ways to communicate while human. Including new descriptive words and phrases. Trolls. Memes. Hacking and hacktivists. Blogs and vlogs and bloggerati. Cyberspace. Cyberbullies. Chats and spats. Cookies which are neither sweet nor tasty. Dot-coms… not to be confused with rom-coms.

The Internet and social media generate an electronic intergalactic escapade you will have little or no actual control over. Items and exploits go "viral"… viewed by millions. Who knows why? Some things just click, connect and escalate. A screen shot. Video… sometimes sweet… sometimes shocking. Or commentary. "Trending." Widely viewed and discussed online. Wildly popular. Then gone. Poof! A momentary diversion. Yet forever to be found… somewhere in the electronic universe.

Social media = a captivating facet of 21st century Life. Multi-faceted in its captivation. So. Many. Facets.

Like the Internet, social media offers much to appreciate and much to scorn. Amidst its myriad aspects of human inter-action… social media offers a startling degree of anonymity. Realizing "I am anonymous"… "no one will ever know it's me"… people use their online comments to target others… fellow students… complete strangers… anyone who thinks differently than I do… with criticism, ridicule, and hostility. Thus the term "cyberbully." This degree of feeling "concealed" incites folks to come out nasty. Mean. Vindictive.

Twitter warriors… ready to judge… to chastise and rebuke. While sitting on the couch… sipping a latte… tossing back a beer... guzzling an energy drink. Making the time to be sure others know... "you're fat"... "you're stupid"... "you're wrong." Passing judgment. Frequently accentuated with hostility.

You may recall... during Orientation you learned about "sedentary agitation"... and its sidekick, the "nebulous gnaws."

Sedentary agitation occurs as a person gets all worked up by their particular grudgement *du jour*. Trigger(s) activated... politics... immigration... gun-control... feminism. "I don't like how they talk... what he's doing... the way she looks." Not only are there so many different triggers... there is such willingness to *be* triggered. This internal activation comes with little or no inclination to get up off the couch and engage in any sort of meaningful Life participation.

Frothing and fuming. Stewing in their righteous indignation. Getting all worked up. Tendencies to fester... festering away. "I'm really upset... at them... those people... the ones who don't see Life exactly the way I do. What's wrong with them? I'll write something harsh and hurtful. I'll show them!"

Ok, so you're going to love this. A learning moment. Be advised. Humans have formulated a mathematical set of rules called *algorithms*. These "rules" specify how a group of data behaves. In social media, algorithms assist in ranking search results... synching web applications...

directing pages and content to display in a certain order. A certain manner.

Here comes the "be advised" part. Fascinatingly… social media's algorithms are set to amplify drama. These "mathematical rules" promote hateful speech and prioritize negativity. You gotta wonder… who thought *that* was a good idea?

A precept in human Life acknowledges most humans are naturally drawn to conflict, negativity and mayhem. "Bad news sells"… newspapers… TV broadcasts… advertising… online and otherwise. Humans of Earth are drawn to stories of disaster, corruption and incompetence. They want to hear or read news accounts tinged with a negative tone… fraud, sleaze, hypocrisy. Another person's difficulties, setbacks, and poor choices are common fodder and frequently a popular read.

Makes me think… hmmm… maybe it seems like problematic relationships are more common among humans than congenial, loving ones… because the difficult relationships get more press. More air time. Like… who wants to hear about people sweetly getting along? Maybe the ouchy stuff and the yuck are more prevalent because then, a person can feel better about the hurtful, limiting shenanigans in their own Life. "At least I'm not *that* bad."

Researchers in human psychology point out… people say they prefer good news and feel the media is too focused on negative stories. Yet, in fact, humans interested in "the news"... current affairs, celebrity sightings, politics... are more likely to choose the bad news. These researchers' experiments reveal solid evidence of the human "negativity bias."

In the world of Earthtone humans... "bias" is a tendency... an inclination of temperament... toward the narrow-minded. Prejudiced. Unreasoned judgment. Favoritism.

"Negativity bias" is a term psychologists use to describe humankind's collective hunger to hear and remember bad news.

This draws out another popular human phrase... "So, what's up with that?"

Well, as it turns out... here we have human cognizance showing off its mental/emotional ancestry. Tossed right back into their limbic systems. Their reptile brains. Welcome to the frightful arena of the *amygdala,* folks: 2 almond-shaped clusters of nuclei located deep within the human brain. The amygdala (uh MIG duh luh) is the neural system's core for processing fearful and threatening stimuli. This brain component evolved very early... along the lines of... "Do I eat it, or does it eat me?"

The human brain is comprised of many different areas... each with its own functions, whys, and wherefores. The amygdala's gig is fear and frightful emotions. Flooded with the stress hormones, cortisol and adrenalin... the amygdala flies into overdrive. Working overtime.

This leads to… now here's a fascinating term… the *amygdala hijack*. An immediate, overwhelming emotional response… triggered by the perception of threat. Not necessarily actual threat… the *perception* of threat. "Hijack" refers to the way-out-of-proportion amygdala freak-outs a human experiences… as compared to the actual stimuli. Thru vigilant hyper reaction to… news, people, events… always searching for the threat… how I've been wronged… "They're out to get me!" Some folks are inclined to chronically over-stimulate their amygdala. Leading to a Life lived in perpetual frantic freak-out.

Sounds exhausting.

Why self-install freak-out lenses thru which to view your world? There are so many other ways to observe and interact with Life and humanosity.

Continuing along this agitated vein… nearly 90 percent of all media news is negative. Bad news sells because the amygdala is always looking for something to fear. Humans evolved to react quickly to potential threats. This bad news signal is wired to interpret input… "Yeow!" "Look out!" "Avoid danger!" "Fix that! Now!"

Those zany humans are at it again. Racing around in their own self-created fritz. Freaking out. Paying more attention to the hostile and adverse.

A direct line can be drawn... showing the human physical instrument's evolvement from its animal ancestry. In early human history, the key to survival was: "Watch out!" Be attentive to negative threats in your world. "It's a matter of life and death!"

To keep things in captivating perspective... to this day... when stimulated, the amygdala can lead a human... or a group of humans... to react irrationally and destructively. To go ballistic in the here and now.

Negative information grabs human thought... and hangs onto it. Automatically. Like a magnet. A lure. This reflex controls human attention. Once grabbed... human awareness finds it challenging to focus on anything else. Like... oh, I don't know... Life's uplifting positives perhaps.

In addition to the conduct of the amygdala and the limbic system's reactive behaviors... there are many significant ties between human instrument biology and its animal ancestry. Noteworthy is the human instrument's high-level response to visual cues. This brings us to another aspect of humanosity's current electronic age... the proliferation of video games... constructive, violent, educational and otherwise.

Altho these games are considered "entertainment" and "play"... as an incarnating human, it is important for you to know what you are getting into here. All is not recreation and amusement. A vast number of these video games encourage hunting, stalking and killing... shooting... with an absence of any actual consequences.

The country currently known as the U.S. of A. is dealing with an onslaught of mass shootings and general public mayhem. Altho much is spoken about "gun control"... which certainly has the ring of deep sanity... evidently many U.S. humans consider being able to have a gun, or multiple guns... way more important than the safety of their children and general well-being in the public arena.

Interestingly... as these shootings happen again and again... you will hear nothing about the influence and impact the easy violence in video games has on the human ability to cope within the stresses of daily Life.

Young human males are especially susceptible to the visual cues and self-management options offered as they shoot, maim and kill with abandon in the violent video games they "play." In this case... self-*mis*management is the more accurate term. To an undeveloped male mind... with rational thought, empathy and self-control not yet fully on board ... the shoot-em-up solutions offered in video game violence, with no direct consequences... readily transfers to "how to do" human Life.

"Oh, *that's* how you do it!" A viable response to anger, upset and feeling offended is to just shoot them. As this plays out in the reality of human Life... it comes with a complete lack of awareness of the magnitude of outcome in the shooter's Life. A complete lack of awareness of the painful, disruptive aftermath in the lives of the many people affected by their casual shooting, maiming and harm.

In addition to regulating access to guns and bullets... awareness must turn to the mental, visual, real Life effects of being awash in casual, no-consequence violence.

Granted, millions play these games. It is a small percentage of these people who actually become killers. Is it in their psychological DNA to consider this violence a solution in the realm of their daily living coping options?

In their evolution... or devolution... the Internet, social media and video games have normalized callous conduct, harmful actions and bigoted comments. Racist or homophobic posts. Easy violence. Harsh, irrational criticism. Spewing harmful, hateful words.

Interestingly, at the same time you will also find online remarks and observations demanding moral purity. Expressing distraught upset... dismay and consternation... over others' hurtful comments. Oh, those scolds of social media. Showing up in full regalia. The scold flies fast in both directions... from admonishing to antagonistic. Sometimes plain obnoxious. Generating a particularly unforgiving online environment.

Complimentary and approving remarks *are* there, too... just utilized far less. Perhaps a lot of humans find it "more fun" to snipe. And be cruel.

Let me assure you... there is good, too. You will find many positive uses of online resources. Definitely beneficial for all kinds of research. Lots of DIY (Do It Yourself) tutorials... about zillions of things. Make-up. Cooking. Rebuilding a carburetor. Knitting and crocheting. Growing anthurium, ginger, or pomegranates. Painting with water colors. Plumbing. A vast accessible encyclopedia of "how to."

Reading or writing reviews = definitely popular. These reviews offer personal opinions and evaluations for a wide assortment of goods and human services. Occasionally this, too, is misused... when disgruntled folks feel they need to take aim at certain targets... sharing their dissatisfaction... political... imagined... or otherwise. They just gotta concoct somebody to shoot their disgruntle at. "I'm tweaked. (Choose from this long list of tweaked and twisted.) Everybody's gotta know how put out I am!" Sure. Feel better? I didn't think so.

For the most part... online reviews can be helpful in making decisions about work you may need done. Choosing a restaurant to go to. The chiropractor... hypnotherapist... mechanic... hair stylist... you're looking for.

It is safe to say the many aspects of social media offer some of the highest highs and the lowest lows of the Internet. Multi-faceted riding the range. A wide and wild gamut from chaos and conflict to caring compassion. Grab your hat… your online avatar… a classy moniker… and hang on for the ride!

The Internet presents another interesting reveal… disclosing an additional fixation in human nature. In some humans' natures. I'm sure you recall our conversation during Orientation about… sexness and sensuality… the Tantric Way and the Yogic Way. The "Human Sexness Rocks" seminar. Vast and various conduits for humans experiencing their sexosity.

It turns out… a large percentage of Internet bandwidth is completely taken up with pornography. Known to its friends and detractors as "porn." Pornography is visual material explicitly describing or displaying human sexual organs and activity. Engrossed in the erotic. The aesthetic… not so much. Of all the multitudinous data transferred across the Internet… at least 30 percent of it is porn. Considering the vast and wide realm of interaction that is the Internet… 30 percent is a lot of bandwidth engrossed with a single subject. Reflective of… a particular preoccupation. Get it while you can. How you can. Just get it. Oh, those titillated humans.

Skating around the roller rink of social media... you may find yourself bruised by rude online contusions. Do yourself a favor... remember:

When a critical person is telling you "what's wrong"
with you or your body...
your beliefs or your choices...

Hiding behind their keyboards...
they reveal more about themselves
and their short-sighted view of the world,
their constricted belief systems,
and they're need to criticize and attack...
than they reveal about you.

This is a variation on the way some folks find a photo, a post, or an article hilarious... while others find the exact same item disgusting. Each human... wired... wound... wounded. Reacting. Responding. Criticizing.

Wired in their one-of-a-kind karmic packaging. Wound like a coil... ready to spring. Festering in their own distinct sensibilities, beliefs, and Life happenstance. Wounded as they internalize... in their own way... their interpretations of "slights." Blame. Disapproval. Condemnation. Interactive discontent... from their own experience of Life.

Before you become full-on human... engage your Recall + Retain Button to remind yourself... every human incarnate is living their own distinct Life. Residing on a planet uniquely their own. Each in their own Youniverse. No other human thinks... believes... reacts... the same way you will. No matter how "close" you may be.

You're in your package. They're in theirs. You do you. They are doing their own self.

Each human incarnant contains multitudes. Multitudes of emotion. From bliss to blisters. Compassion to hatred. Centered self-kindness to harsh self-abuse. Multitudes of thoughts, ideas, perceptions. Multitudes of cells, biological chemicals, and assorted genetic functions coursing thru-out their bodies. All of that is just *inside* the human. As you can easily imagine... the multitudes of activity going on *outside* the human are vast and complex. Multitudinous activity... work, play, interaction, creative expression. Complexity. Grace. Pain. Building. Destroying. It's all in motion. The ball's in play. All the time.

Critical humans stand before you disclosing *their* "issues"... their nit-pickyness. Yes, they may be calling it *you*... but they're not disclosing anything insightful about you. They reveal themselves. Fussing in their own fussedness. As if their "fuss"... their take on things... is, as they say, gospel. And their way is "the way things are." When in actuality... what they promote so emphatically... is "the way things are" *for them*.

Life... a fascinating gambit on Planet Earth.

As a young human trying to make sense of things... trying to figure out this paradoxical Life... you will create beliefs, defenses, and attitudes that make sense to your child self. Within your inner Life... which is ON and firing from the get-go... these beliefs and attitudes calcify... becoming structures of Life response. These childhood beliefs cruise on... often creating formations of self-constriction and false information intake.

Not always do these calcified, self-constructed attitudes and defenses serve you well as you build the architecture of your adult Life.

In the midst of the twirl and swirl of adult human Life... as you are Up To Here within all the goings-on... you bump up against these self-constructed constrictions. Hmmm... something definitely does not feel right here. "Could I be creating my own difficulties?" Hmmm...

This is a transformative moment in human self-awareness. "I've got to stop playing the victim... believing 'it's *their* fault' or 'They're doing this to me.'" The moment arrives... "I see now... it's mine to take responsibility for my interactions. For my own pain and doubt."

As you get over blaming everybody else for your difficulties and resentments... your problems and glitches... you arrive at the point you want to... you need to... make some internal adjustments. "I can't keep creating these difficulties and obstacles. I can't keep tripping myself up."

"They're not doing this to me.
I'm doing this to me."

It takes a while for you to begin to see... your habit thought creates your own obstacles. For the first many years of your incarnation... or for many incarnations... your knee-jerk reaction will be to blame somebody else for emotional mishaps in your Life. It takes a long time for most humans to realize... their self-awfulizing creates their agony and conflict.

Oh, this is funny. Not ha-ha funny. More like "Well, look at this!" funny. Here we have another set of human awareness poles... humans self-awfulizing at one end. Humans self-actualizing at the other. And the vast spectrum of all the healing... evolving... becoming... in between.

Ok, so maybe not *that* funny. It would be funny, perhaps, if not so revelatory. Examples of the 2 poles: Awfulizing all over yourself... "I don't know what I'm doing. I'm such an idiot!" "I will never get this project done." "I'm such a fool to think these people would like me." Ouch. Serious tying together of shoe laces at the beginning of the race.

Versus the other end of the human awareness spectrum... becoming more and more the person you are capable of being. "I see how I've been limiting myself. I know I can change these self-restricting patterns." "I can figure this project out and do a good job." "This conference is a perfect opportunity to make new friends and connexions." Onward.

Examining these 2 particular poles and the human awareness spectrum dancing between them... we find resilience and a positive attitude boils down to... "So far, so good."

So far, way good.

I ran off on a little self-awfulizing/self-actualizing tangent there. Ha ha. You will find tangents show up as a very human conversation trait.

Now, back to making some internal changes... so you can "stop tripping myself up." Absolutely key in this human endeavor is finding the time... making the time... to figure out what's what. "How am I holding myself back?" "Why do I keep having painful relationships?" "How is it I keep falling into the same dark hole?"

Here is where the ol' Emotional Boogie Man leaps up with his most convincing ruse: "What if, as I look inside, I don't like what I see? What if I find out something awful about myself?" Steady big fella. Let's call this what it is... subterfuge. A trick. A big emotional smokescreen. Unfortunately... tender human nature falls for this again and again. Halting any personal awareness progress. Sigh. (The "snail's pace clause" rides again!)

Until the day *does* come. The day when an exasperated human says... "Oh, let's get on with it."

Then... the next self-imposed obstacle pops up. Even as you are weary of your general Life mayhem... you may continue to limit your movement forward with the familiar whine... "Who has the time?" Or, more accurately... the motivation... to dig around inside. To self-explore. To develop any sort of inner understanding. To open the door to self-clarity.

Who *does* have the time? Where *is* that motivation?

Excavating internal archaeology takes time and intention. Focus. Attentive mindfulness. Self-kindness. Self-care. Finding and developing effective tools and resources. A human doesn't "just know" how to find healing and awareness while stuck in the muck of the great ongoing.

Mindless psychological sludge perpetuates recurring Life drama.

You can count on this emotional muck and mire doing little or nothing for the health and well-being of your self... or your relationships. There is a certain numb comfort in its familiarity, tho.

I'm sure our earlier Seminar Session made the following pretty clear. As an adult human... whether you are consciously aware of this, or not... the way your parental hosts treated you... how they treated each other... how they treated themselves... assembles your initial roadmap for developing relationships in your Life. Childhood-created emotional structures affect both an adult human's way *to* relationship... and their way *in* relationship. Many times... as your adult Life evolves... these early emotional configurations cramp your style.

Or, they just plain give you cramps.

When unhealthy relationship patterns are a part of daily Life... children draw them in. Believing "this must be how you do relationship." If children see their parents hit each other... oh, that's the way you handle conflict... you strike out. You shove or hit. You break their things. You hurt them.

Hurt them for hurting you. Or, even, hurting them *before* they hurt you.

A deeply insecure person fixates on controlling their partner. Telling them what they can and cannot do. What they can and cannot wear. Who they can and cannot be friends with. This level of control speaks of mental instability. "I can't control myself... I don't even like myself. But I sure am going to control you."

"I love you... therefore, you will do everything I want you to do, because I love you." Believe me, *that* is not love. Nowhere near it.

One partner dominating in a relationship is not love. Terrorizing… violence, or threatening violence… is not love. Threatening to do something drastic is not love. "I'm going to leave you if you don't do what I want." "I'm going to break your blown glass collection if you don't act the way I want you to." "If you leave me, I'll kill myself." Red flags flying.

Jealousy is not love.

Jealousy may seem "cute" at first. "Oh, he's so jealous. That means he really loves me." Note to self: Rethink that one immediately! Suspicion and jealousy are hostility in action.

Believing you have to change your behavior and act a certain way to avoid upsetting your partner… is not love. That is "walking on eggshells"… as humans so perceptively put it.

One partner pressuring or forcing the other to have sex against their will… without their consent… is not love. It's sexual violence.

Once upon a time… humans devised what they refer to as The Golden Rule: "Do unto others as you would have others do unto you." You will find that bit of human relationship wisdom is not followed by all.

How would a sexual predator or violent partner feel if the tables were turned? If *they* were the ones being tormented? Abused? Victimized?

Blinded by their own appetites and perceived needs... the perpetrator doesn't give their victim's well-being a moment's thought. But if they were in a relationship where they are the mistreated... they would squeal the loudest. Interesting... that ol' turning of the tables.

Depending on your Earthtone upbringing... you may need to educate yourself as to what being in a healthy, supportive relationship can be. You may need to learn what love is. What love feels like. What love can be.

As a parent of human teenagers (age 12-21)... you do them a great and loving service as you guide them to understand the value of mutual respect... and what a healthy, intimate relationship looks like. Especially... what a healthy relationship *feels* like. In the reality of your own human emotional Life... you may or may not be able to coach them or model for them healthy relating.

Especially your human daughters... help them be aware of healthy relating... so they are not victimized by belligerent, over-bearing, immature boys.

So many times... a young person just *wants* to have a boyfriend or girlfriend. Like it's some sort of badge showing "I'm okay." "I'm grown up." "Somebody likes me." Young and unexperienced, they are naïve... uninformed as to how they should be treated. Not realizing... you do not have to put up with being treated poorly.

If you feel you are being mistreated… you *are* being mistreated.

Good communication and mutual respect are the 2 pillars supporting the structure of healthy, loving relationship. This is not just true of a romantic relationship. Every relationship… school chums, coworkers, cousins and relatives, social media friends… deserves respect and good communication.

Patience with yourself. Patience with others.

You've heard me suggest… you may need to take parenting classes as you are an adult human to overcome deficits from your childhood environment. You may also need to find classes and opportunities to help you develop communication skills… empathy… good listening capabilities. Such valuable self-development training is available. Choose to make good use of it.

Facets we share with you here… pre-incarnation… settle deeply into your inner human psyche. Hopefully, these components will alert your incarnant self to know when "something is not right."

You know what? Right here… right now… engage your Retain and Recall Button. Plant this counsel both deep and ready. So when you are actually being human… you'll *remember* the value of seeking out psychological tools… partaking of training courses. To help your human self succeed… in living a worthwhile Life. And having meaningful human interaction.

A huge factor in every human relationship is each person's own self-confidence. An insecure person can be grasping, clingy, overbearing, suspicious and not know how to express themselves effectively. Many times, they have their radar tuned to finding slights and "offense." Not knowing how to listen and empathize with their friend or partner. There is very little "I understand how you feel"… because the insecure person doesn't understand how they, themselves, feel. Rather than be concerned or sensitive to their partner's feelings… an insecure person is absorbed in "how *you* should be making *me* feel."

In a healthy, loving relationship… each partner:

Values the other person…
and who they are. How they are.
Is supportive and encouraging of their
partner's work, goals, and ideas.
Is tolerant and kind… open-minded about differences.
Is willing to get a grip
on their own anger and learn to fight fair.
Is willing to compromise and problem solve.
Listens to their partner's opinions and suggestions
without forcing "my way is the only way things are."

When you are being human... there is always room for growth and change. Always more to learn and become. Don't waste your precious time on Earth beating yourself up and believing you've been wronged. Look for things in your Life... for ways and connexions... that help you feel gratified. Nourished. Fulfilled. Be grateful for what *is* working.

Give yourself the benefit of the doubt.
Give your Life the benefit of the doubt.
Have faith in yourself.
Let yourself off the hook.

What you were is not who you are now.

Let's round out today's session with a trip down Realizmotron lane... for a couple of interrelated scenarios. The beginning of each scenario is the same. How things work out is based on the temperament and characteristics of each participant. We begin:

Melanie is just starting to make dinner... anticipating her man, Tad's, arrival home. The phone rings. It's an urgent call from her neighbor, Julie... who is very upset. "Melanie, please come over. I don't know what to do. I need someone to talk me down. You are always the best at times like this. Please." Hanging up the phone... Melanie puts down what she's doing... wipes her hands, and heads over to Julie's.

This means Melanie is unexpectedly not there when Tad gets home. Dinner has not been started. More than an hour goes by before Melanie walks back in the door.

And there's Tad. Can you feel how he's gotten himself all worked up? He is fuming. Jumping up from the chair he's been slumped in… Tad grabs Melanie's upper arm hard. Furious, yelling, "Where have you been? I've been sitting here in the dark for more than an hour! You said you'd be here! Where's dinner? You were out with Joe, weren't you?"

Melanie is caught completely off-guard. Shocked, she stammers… "Joe? Why would I be with Joe? Stop, Tad, you're hurting my arm. Let go!"

"Don't you think I know your old boyfriend is in town? You couldn't wait to hook up with him!"

"You are so full of it!" She yanks her arm away.

"Don't sass me, bitch. Where were you?"

"Julie called. She was real upset. She begged me to come over. I thought I'd only be gone a few minutes. But things with her were worse than I thought. I…"

Interrupting… "You think I believe you were at Julie's? Where did you hook up with Joe?"

"Tad, stop being an idiot! I was just…"

Interrupting again… "Don't call me an idiot!" Raising his hand… "I'm gonna smack you, you cheating, lying whore!"

"Tad! Shut up! Don't call me that! I knew you'd be a jerk about this. You won't even let me tell you what happened!"

"I don't give a damn what happened! You liar! You were out sneaking around." Again, he raises his hand... yelling, "Don't tell *me* to shut up! You make me so mad! It's your fault I'm gonna hit you!"

Instead of hitting her, Tad shoves Melanie toward the kitchen. "Get in there and make dinner. Make me a drink. You're lucky I don't smack you hard! Bitch!"

Her jaw clenched tight, Melanie stumbles into the kitchen... tears streaming down her face. "Asshole!"

Realizmotron winds down.

Well, that was a ride! Did you feel how insecure Tad is? How immature? Out of control. Totally accusing. Terrifying. Only thinking of himself. Immediately making up a story where he is the victim. He's made himself a cuckold. Convinced Melanie is cheating on him. Enraged... he's not interested in anything going on with her.

Tad neither listens nor communicates. He can only terrorize, shout, and blame. He has no tools to help himself. Or to be receptive to Melanie's explanation. He's not able to actually be present in the situation. Obviously, Tad has done nothing to deal with his searing emotional baggage.

Now here's a question... does he accuse Melanie of being "out with Joe" because if Tad were not at home, he'd be out with some other woman? Is he accusing her of doing something he would do? This has been known to happen.

What kind of evening do you think they're going to have together? What sort of Life?

Oh, and... don't *ever* fall for, "You make me so mad! It's your fault I'm gonna hit you!" It is never "your fault." You are not the one "making" that other person do anything. The person doing the hitting is responsible for their own actions. You are not responsible for their out-of-control behavior. If you find yourself in such a situation... my advice to you... get yourself out of there.

Now we'll fire Realizmotron up again. As I mentioned... the beginning of this scenario will be the same.

Carly is just starting to make dinner... anticipating her man, Jack's, arrival home. The phone rings. It's an urgent call from her neighbor, Julie, who is very upset. "Carly, please come over. I don't know what to do. I need someone to talk me down. You are always the best at times like this. Please." Hanging up the phone... Carly puts down what she's doing... wipes her hands, and heads over to Julie's.

This means Carly is unexpectedly not there when Jack gets home. Dinner has not been started. More than an hour goes by before Carly walks back in the door. She finds Jack in the kitchen.

He's glad to see her. "Oh, hi… there you are, Honey. I thought you said you'd be here when I got home. When you weren't around, I started making dinner. It's almost ready."

"Thanks, Jack. I was getting started on dinner when Julie called. She was really upset. She begged me to come over. I had no idea I'd be gone so long."

"Oh, wow. Is Julie okay? You're such a good friend to drop everything and go help her. I really admire you… how caring you are. This worked out fine. Gave me a chance to get creative in the culinary department. You're gonna like what I cooked up."

"Thanks, Sweetheart. It smells great! I'm starving. I had no idea I'd be at Julie's for more than an hour. She can really get herself in a tizzy. I appreciate you being so understanding. Sitting there with her… I knew you'd be okay with how things were turning out. I really appreciate you, Sweet Stuff."

"Thanks, Honey. I appreciate you, too. Sit your fine self down. I'll bring you a glass of wine before I serve dinner. I'm glad you're home. I'm looking forward to our evening together."

Realizmotron winds down.

Well, then. As humans are inclined to say… "That was as different as night and day."

Jack is secure within himself… so he's not thrown off by Carly's unexpected absence. He doesn't make up a hurtful story. Unlike Tad, who was immediately rageful... Jack's inner resilience allows him to respond to the situation with... "Something must've come up." When left to his own devices... Jack goes about making dinner. Taking care of the needful. I'm sure the possibility of helping out by starting dinner never entered Tad's mind. Evidently, he could only fume and make up a hurtful story to explain Melanie's absence. Getting himself all worked up... he just waits... fuming... for Melanie to show up so he can berate her.

When Tad isn't fuming and erupting... he's probably an okay guy. Even insecure people who cannot control their emotions have a few fine qualities. Let's hope. Otherwise, what would keep Melanie with a rageful guy like Tad? You know... she could have her own insecurities... so she'll take what she can get just to be with a man. Depending on her childhood emotional environment... Tad's hostility may feel "like home." It could be... Melanie believes she does not deserve to be treated any better than she's treated by seething, insecure Tad.

Here, we return to commentary from the beginning of today's session. In the most basic sense... caring friends and loving partners... show up. They're kind. They contribute.

Let's take a look at these attributes:

Show up: Be present. Don't stay snagged in the white noise of squalls and upset. Dust storms spinning in your head. Be engaged in the ever-evolving world of this relationship you're in. Do not neglect or take for granted your caring connexion. Figure out ways to nourish… and flourish… your special bond.

Be kind: It could be said, "This speaks for itself." However, "Be kind" is worthy of elaboration. There are so many ways to be kind. Just as there are so many ways to be sour, disrespectful, and mean. Consciously choose to be friendly. Considerate. Supportive. Encouraging. Live your Life with A Generosity of Spirit.

Contribute: Participate in what's going on… the fun stuff and the not-so-fun stuff. Be willing to cooperate… and collaborate. Don't show up apathetic and half-hearted. Show up whole-hearted and involved. Be a positive influence. Bring all of yourself to situations and interactions. Be fun.

You are not incarnating in human form to be misery. You are not on Planet Earth to agonize and be melancholy. You incarnate in human form to lift the gloom. To wage hope. To heal misery. To be a restorative instrument of good.

An instrument of caring.

A catalyst of becoming.

Being human is a captivating enterprise. Being human in relationship is an immense endeavor … vast and wide. Calling humans to their highest and best.

191

Calling human patience to its highest and best.

Beings incarnate on Earth to give and be their best. "How can I help?"

Centuries ago... in Earth time... Shantideva, a wise sage in the tradition of the Buddha... spoke this ode to the vastness of relationship and all things human.

This is The Bodhisattva Vow

For as long as space endures
For as long as living beings remain
Until then, may I, too, abide
To dispel the misery of the world.

Ah ho.

CHAPTER FIVE

It's All Between You and You

"From meltdown to mastery."

"Experience is the hardest kind of teacher.
It gives you the test first and the lesson afterward."
~ Oscar Wilde

I laughed out loud the first time I read those words. Holy Cows! Does that totally sum things up, or what?!

Life is a tapestry of experiences... interweaving... one experience after another. At times, several of Life's occurrences pop up all on top of each other. Twists... loops... knots. Situations. Interactions. Setbacks. Accomplishments. So many threads and filaments... diverse textures, multiple colors... entwining. Weaving the tapestry of experience, context and nuance that is your Life.

Tests. Trials. Lessons. There is so much Life in experience. There is so much experience in Life. Whether we are inclined to learn from "Life's lessons," or not.

Some experiences we have control over. Many of them, we do not. There are experience-generating Life choices we consciously make. Others are made for us... by circumstances... our parents... financial reality... our own self-beliefs.

The amusement park of Life. At times you're cresting the peak of the roller coaster. Yeeooww! Plunging! Descending at top speed. Thrills! Chills! Hopefully, not too many spills.

Other times you're riding your favorite horse on the merry-go-round.

Or, there you are... swaying gently at the top of the Ferris wheel. Taking in the view.

Anyone care for a chocolate-dipped banana on a stick? Cotton candy? Churros? Tossing a ring. Winning a prize. Sometimes... blasted by too much sun. "Let's sit this one out in the shade." Sipping a cool one.

These various rides... situations... relationships... keep us amused and entertained. Certainly fascinated. Laughing on the inside. Frustrated and grouchy. Upbeat. Repulsed and resistant. Head spinning. Annoyed... yet captivated.

Frolicking amongst the amusements.

The bumper cars of Life.

Jugglers and acrobats.

Clowns aplenty.

Occasionally… fireworks.

I know you know what I'm talking about. The whole wild-eyed shootin' match. The is what is. And then some.

The true test of living human on Planet Earth is how we respond to Life's amusement park features. The pain. The doubt. The joy. What we *do* with our experiences is what makes Life Life. As duly noted… from meltdown to mastery.

Confucius in 500 BCE… had something to say about this:

"Our greatest glory is not in never falling,
    but in rising every time we fall."

Basically… take it all in and make sure you get back up. Or as some would say… "Keep on keepin' on."

I mentioned earlier in *Holy Wow!…* Life can show up with some pretty serious whacks. And wouldn't you know it… our reaction to a good, stiff whack *can be* to open to aspects of ourselves we haven't previously explored . "That whack sure did turn me around and sit me right down. Maybe there's a different way to look at things. Who do I get to be now?" Where to from here?

As I shared... that is exactly what happened in my world when my first husband told me he was in love with another woman. Whack! Ow! My Life *changed*... inside and out. Years... experiences... realizations... went by. What do you know? That whack became... "the scar that turned into a beauty mark." Blistering hard as it was at the time... I wouldn't change a thing.

Returning to the quote from Oscar Wilde... do we actually grok... seek... find... "the lesson" after "the test?"

As we navigate our internal merry-go-round... the spin is about who or what we let "win." Win our attention. Win what we believe. Win how we show up in Life.

Do we let frustration win? Do anger and rudeness win? How about resistance?

Do we let calm consideration win? Does generosity of spirit win? Love? Kindness?

What happens in a relationship when annoyance wins? "Do you want to know how annoyed I am with you?" Plenty.

Where to from here? Annoyance breeds annoyance. Generating disapproval. Displeasure. Provoking discontent. Is this the slippery slope we really want to be scrambling on right now?

If there was a Master Class in Being Human, you would learn... right up until the moment you realize you have choices... you don't. "What do you mean I have choice?

I *have* to react this way! This *has* to be this way. I don't have a choice!" You're right. When you are blind to other possibilities… they're not there for you.

Rarely are we taught… at home, at school… we can choose how to react or respond in a situation. With no awareness or consideration of options available… we forge blindly ahead. Options? A possible different decision? Alternatives beyond my botheration? Hmmmm… I hadn't thought of that.

As things are currently unfolding… we do not enter adult Life with a whole lot of emotional intelligence. Because we are not taught differently about experiencing our emotions… they seem to reside in a dark, foggy hinterland. Devoid of light. Of awareness. Devoid of choices.

Yet, in truth… like a power generator… our emotions fuel and fire our particular amusement park ride thru Life.

Oblivious within our emotions… we certainly can't trust them! Many people are just plain afraid of their emotions. Believing their feelings are to be squelched. Suppressed. Ignored.

We don't know our way around… within our emotions… because we've never been taught about our emotional nature. We've never been encouraged to explore. To poke around and see who we may be inside. We haven't been coached to not be scared of what we'll find.

We humans *are* able to find our way within the complexities of our emotional universe. Our emotions *can* be "managed." Handled. Dealt with. Believed. Explored. Transformed.

In 1990, the term *emotional intelligence* began showing up in the Western World's cultural lexicon. I remember thinking… "Oh, that's good." "Good" not only because "emotional intelligence" is a worthwhile concept… but also because it's helpful to have an identifying word phrase to be able to talk about it.

It's good to be able to talk about and amble around within your emotional self. Good to have a word phrase to facilitate that exploration.

This is similar to "Maylaigh: The Love That Heals"… introduced in earlier volumes of *Holy Wow!* This word… *maylaigh* (may LAY ikh)… shines a light specifically on *that* love… The Love That Heals. Having this word gives us a term, a handle, to speak of that love easily and accurately.

Now, as we exercise accurate ease to speak of emotional intelligence… the basis of our conversation would be:

How do you *do* your emotions?
Who are you in your emotional Life?
How is your relationship with your emotional self?

Are you afraid of your emotions? Do you self-terrorize? Are you numb? Apathetic? Do you lash out at others? Are your obstacles… doubts… grudgements… always somebody else's fault?

Are you pretty okay with yourself? Acknowledging there are ups and downs? Good days. Not-so-good days.

Life has its moments. Are you generally not inclined to get your panties in a twist? Do you tend to see the good in other people?

Are you willing to let other folks off the hook? Do you remember to let yourself off the hook?

Emotional intelligence is about your relationship with yourself. The very relationship creating the playing field for the way you relate to others.

Here on Planet Earth… in all its many facets… relationship is the name of the game.

At some point in your Life you realize… you are the one creating your ups and downs. Slathering your various breads with your many and varied butters and jams.

For a long time… years, decades, incarnations… you want to be blaming others. "It's *his* fault I'm in a bad mood." "*She* made me make this mess." "It's *their* fault I didn't win." The day eventually dawns… sometimes in a blinding flash… other times, the darkness lifting slowly … you begin to realize… "I am creating my own adventure." My own pain and limitations. My own setbacks and obstacles. My own Life experience.

This can be a sobering realization. Don't be too hard on yourself. Don't freak yourself out. Best idea? Draw a deep, centering breath. Then another. Proceed.

You begin… or continue… this process of investigating and exploring your inner Life… developing your emotional intelligence… by taking 3 big steps in the right direction:

1) **You develop your self-awareness.** Delve into your own feelings and motivations… your character and personality. Your individuality. Take a look around inside. Let go of being afraid to get to know yourself. You begin to comprehend your own thoughts and behaviors. You become more comfortable in your own skin. As you understand yourself and other people… you move thru your Life mindfully. Purposefully. Rather than "Oh, what the hey!"… and just winging it. Stride on, Noble Human. Stride on. Advance. Develop. Improve.

2) **You grow your ability to self-regulate.** Develop a measure of personal management. Recognize you *can* guide your thoughts… your responses… the way you *are* in the world. The way you interact with others. Become your own supervisor… instead of looking to (and resenting) an external authority telling you what to do. How to be.

3) **As always... you develop these inner abilities with a healthy dose of self-kindness.** Your admirable ally. Proceeding without self-kindness... your harsh self-talk will drag you down. "You're so stupid!" "Why don't you already know this?" "I can't believe it's taking you so long to pull yourself together!" This unforgiving self-talk and surly self-analysis dominates your inner conversation. This does not serve you well. You cannot proceed while you are tearing yourself down. Be kind.

As I mentioned earlier in *Holy Wow!*... if you talked to your friends the way you talk to yourself... you wouldn't have any friends.

Learn to be a friend to yourself. Truly. Self-kindness. Self-compassion. Self-understanding. Each and all... your powerful compadres... as you travel your path to your awakening. To greater self-awareness.

Another key to emotional intelligence is motivation. What gets you out of bed in the morning?

Motivation has you firing on all cylinders. Cognitive and biological forces are involved. Emotional undercurrents and social dynamics activate your actions and behavior. Compelling your general willingness to do stuff. To keep things tidy. To meet goals. To be creative.

Truthfully... I am not, by nature or nurture... a very motivated person. Didn't ever give it much thought. Until I gave birth to my daughter, Lyla. Holy Moley! Seriously... I did not *know* a person could *be* so self-motivated! She is a wonder to behold. This sweet, fantastic girl of mine Gets Things Done! Wowza! When she was a kid... Scott would say, "We just stand back and take notes." Lyla is an impressive force for good in this world.

In its own fascinating fashion... motivation is not always the paradigm of reliability. Not always traveling in a straight line... motivation can come and go. For some people... like Lyla... motivation is a consistent Life companion. An active impetus coursing thru her days and choices. For some people... like me... not so much. There can be days... maybe even weeks... when I am "up and at 'em!" Getting things done! Then there are times... days... maybe even months... when motivation seems to have packed its bags and headed for sunnier climes. You just can't seem to get that ol' engine firing.

The last time Lyla visited... she and I were organizing my office... piles of papers and miscellaneous stuff. This is a common pastime for the 2 of us. At one point, turning to me, she said, "Mom, you live in a diffuse universe." In the midst of the random clutter of my scattered reality... I laughed out loud. "You are so right, Honey."

At an earlier point in my Life... I might have gotten defensive at her acknowledging my "diffuse" ways. These days... I am at peace with the way "organization" plays out in my world. Hers is a spot-on observation. No need to get my panties twisted when it's true.

As I mentioned earlier... why just crastinate... when you can go pro?

In the 1981 movie... *The First Monday in October*... Walter Matthau describes the jumbled mountain of papers on his desk as... "The wilderness of free association." Another laugh out loud moment for me. I made a banner... The Wilderness of Free Association... and hung it in my living room.

"A diffuse universe." Indeed.

In addition to exploring your inner Life and what motivates you... there are 2 additional components in the sphere of emotional intelligence. These both involve your interactions with the other humans in your world. Empathy and social skills.

Empathy is a human super power.

Clearly, we live in a world of relationship. Being caring toward others... respecting their individuality... understanding the way they feel... is your secret sauce. Human interaction lubricated.

Develop your capacity to experience what another person is feeling within *their* frame of reference... within the context of *their* Life. Willingly growing your awareness in this way bridges the gap. Decreasing the differences between self and other.

Our perceived difference between "myself" and "others" is a psychological construct. A carry-over from animal instinct... which focused on fearing and fighting the "different" just in case they are going to make a meal of me.

In the reality of human awareness... "me/us" and "them" are each and all water molecules swimming in the same ocean of Life.

Opportunities arise to exercise your compassion muscles.

"Walking a mile in *their* shoes." Understanding not everyone thinks or feels the same ways you do. That doesn't make them "wrong." That just makes them themselves.

Within each person a *multitude* of diverse factors shape their interior landscape. Their thought processes... emotional responses... decision-making.

Folks are wired the way they're wired. Differently. Each making their own distinctive choices and decisions. Finding their own solutions to Life's complications. "That's not the way I would do it." Which is, of course, the point. It's not your way. It's *their* way. Sure, their decisions or solutions may seem illogical to you. They are making their own choices. Weaving their own Life tapestry. Being "me" their way.

Our temperaments, attitudes and past experiences influence the decisions we make each day. Every person's cognitive processes... their chemical synapses and brain connections... are influenced by myriad factors. Including childhood trauma and poor parenting.

As children, teenagers and adults... Life is made sweeter by being and having a friend. An interactive 2-way street... of support and encouragement. Life takes on a glow... a deep and certain knowing... when you have a kind, compassionate friend. We are each blessed when we get to be that friend.

Being a friend... supportive and encouraging... demonstrates your social skills. Your capability in interaction... communicating with your fellow humans. Your competence in respecting others. In respecting yourself.

Social skills = communication skills. Skills which are both verbal and non-verbal. Conveying connexion thru gestures, facial expressions... body language. Making eye contact.

A good communicator is a good listener... an active listener. Many people listen passively... blah, blah, blah... yeah, yeah, yeah... impatient for their turn to talk. An active listener is engaged in the conversation... concentrating and responding. Paraphrasing to show mutual understanding. Remembering what is being said.

As with so many aspects in the realm of relationship…
effective listening is about self-awareness. Being comfortable
in your own skin lets you relate to and communicate with
other folks. And enjoy it.

Frequently, people who are anxious, stressed, or depressed
feel socially awkward. Altho they may long for friendship
and connexion… feeling accepted… they don't grok the
value of developing their own social skills. Or even how
to go about doing that. This is a venture taking time and
intention. Reaching out. Not always waiting for the other
person to make the first move. Being comfortable as you step
outside yourself. Recognizing connection as a 2-way street.
Letting another person know you find them interesting.
That they're important to you.

Caring to connect.

Moving thru your Life equipt with solid social skills
allows you to relate to and connect with other people.
Establish meaningful friendships. Navigate your Life with
a greater degree of satisfaction and fulfillment.

Your emotional intelligence tool kit:

    Self-Awareness
    Self-Regulating
    Motivation
    Empathy
    Social Skills

Contemplating these characteristics… these qualities of emotional intelligence… I realize… a lot of what I share with you in *Holy Wow!* resides in exactly this arena:

Be more aware in your emotional self.

Be more alive inside.

Be more comfortable with yourself and your Life.

Be more at peace within.

This was not "my plan" when I began writing *Holy Wow!* in March, 2016. Can't really say I had "a plan." Yes, I had been on the verge of writing "my book" for decades. All those years I did write… fleshing out different ideas. Composing phrases… bits of chapters. I knew I had something to say. Life survival tools to share. And a few good stories. After my 5 successful hypnotherapy sessions… the first 13 chapters of *Holy Wow!* tumbled right out. (Finally!)

As I read and reread *Holy Wow!* preparing for publication… I saw, hmmm… I've written a lot about:

Becoming more at ease within your emotional self.

Not so freaked by the Emotional Boogie Man.

Not so freaked by your own fine self.

Not so much stumbling around in your emotional nature.

Less bumping into self-created inner obstacles.

Less bumping around in the dark.

More assured in your emotional environment.

More willing to take it all in.

Allowing more light within.

Contributing. Processing accordingly.

Giving back better than you get.

Participating in Life's vast panorama of potential
and promise."

Again, I hear my Daddy, in his deep Southern drawl…
"Well how about that!"

How about that? How about feeling more at ease…
at peace… within your own skin? There are choices you
can make. Actions you can take. A process which is very
similar to developing the health and well-being of your
physical body.

There are exercises… trainings… practices… psychological asanas… you can apply to the health and well-being
of your emotional self. You'll be amazed by the similarities
in the ways you approach wellness in your physical and
emotional bodies.

I write this in 2021. The psychological wellness boom
has been in full swing since the 1960s. There are so many
"ways:" tools… insights… workshops… therapies… available in the realm of developing emotional well-being.

You would not ask your trainer or coach to do your
physical exercises for you… expecting their workouts to

have a worthwhile effect on your muscles and fitness. To see any results… you have to do those exercises yourself. Lift those weights… run those miles… stretch.

Ditto in your emotional body.

You have to look for… find… and apply… stretches and exercises… practices… to develop the health and well-being of your emotional self. Emotional aerobics. Calisthenics of the heart. Exercising self-kindness. Self-awareness. Self-compassion. Developing your friendship with yourself.

If not you… who?

Repetitions are where it's at with physical exercise. You don't do one set of push-ups and think… "There. Done. I won't have to do another push-up for the rest of my Life." You keep at it. Over time, you build your muscles and stamina to develop the physique and endurance you're looking for.

This is also true as you foster the health and well-being… the resilience… of your emotional nature. Some are inclined to say… "Yeah, I meditated for a few days. Nothing happened. Meditation doesn't work for me." Just as with barbells, push-ups, and other "reps"… you keep at it. You make time to meditate daily… regularly. You repeat chants and affirmations. You develop vigilance… ejecting stinkin' thinkin'… as you consciously put more psychologically constructive thoughts in its place.

Just like building your physical muscles... you meditate... daily - regularly - frequently... for a year or 2. Or 5. Then take a moment to look around. *Then* see if you notice "results." It's taken a lifetime to construct your personal limitations and self-negativity. As you apply awakening tools... self-realization techniques... you've got to give your psychological self some time to grow and evolve.

Consistency. Patience.

Just as you would build your physical muscles... you have to empower your emotional well-being with those building inner harmony reps. It's worth the time Transforming negative self-beliefs and calcified self-limitations. You're worth the effort.

Dare I say... you're worth the devotion. Devote yourself to feeling more comfortable in your own skin. Devote yourself to being more awake and aware. Devote yourself to feeling and being better.

Sure, there's effort involved. Of course there is.

In the world of human endeavor... when is there not effort involved? No worries. The effort... the inner exertion... is so totally worth it. And so doggone fascinating. Engaging. Intriguing. Who knew something I was once so afraid of could be so fun and rewarding?

In the world of human relationship there is effort involved. There is *so much* involved. Especially as 2 people are in and building the intricacies of an intimate relationship. Especially then. So many levels of interactive capacity... inside and out.

Over the years, I've been paying attention... taking notes... while traversing the realm of close interpersonal relationships. For your perusal... here follows a few juicy and worthwhile pointers. A travel guide.

At the top of my list:

Choose To Be Amused

Yes, that *definitely* belongs at the top of the list. Choose to be amused rather than annoyed... disheartened... angry... with your fellow humans. I know sometimes it may not look like it... but we are all doing the best we can. Yes, some people's "best" may seem kinda lacking. Even a little dodgy at times.

Facing Life's ridiculousness with mild amusement can take the sting out of stupid.

An attitude of... "Silly ol' bear"... or... "That's just the way she is"... gets you a whole lot further in the realm of "let's just be getting along." Yes, it's tempting... and habitual... to express your frustration. Anger. Irritation. Your disapproval. But... ya know what? Is that what you'd want to hear from your partner?

Remember in earlier volumes of *Holy Wow!*... we talked about choosing love over fear? Here is a totally real-world opportunity... to choose love over irritation. Amusement over frustration. Understanding over anger.

It's your Life. You get to choose what's going on inside of you. And what's popping out. Are we having fun yet?

You have better things to think about than your problems. You have better things to think about than what's "not working."

The positive, the negative and the neutral = all here, all the time. Focus on the negative and it is more than happy to show up, breed, and grow. "You want to be upset? Disappointed? Dismayed? Let me readily remind you of all your disappointments. Here... I have a list of painful items all ready for you to be upset about!"

Let's pull ourselves together in the realm of There Must Be A Better Way. Let's counterbalance that tendency to scold. Here's a list for you to make:

Aspects of My Life That Are "Not Problems."

Write down what *is* working. What *does* feel good... or at least okay.

Small aspects and large. Altho "the big things" get a lot more glitz and show... it really is those "little things" weaving the fabric of your Life. As you contemplate these okey-doke aspects... be sure to write your list down. Don't just haphazardly mull it over in your head. This usually leads directly to the rut of mindless repeating.

Writing it out clears mental space. You can't keep mulling about what you already wrote down. Then... what happens in your cleared mental space?

There's room for more "good stuff"... realizations... to show up.

With your mental commentary more open, allowing and creative... freed from mindless repeating... I have another Really Good Reason for you to write your list of "okay enough/super groovy" Life-factors. You write it down to make it tangible. Concrete. Touchable. Your acknowledgement of the good in your Life now has form in the physical plane. This means you can read these good things anytime. To remind yourself.

Now having a list of "good things about my Life"... you can add to it.

Give mind and heart energy to all
you appreciate about your Life.
Recognize what you cherish.
FEEL Grateful.

Yes, this is a similar ballpark to "Don't just focus on what's wrong." Let's take that a step or 3 further. We humans are seldom encouraged to "recognize what you cherish." Which is, itself, a truly worthwhile activity. Most important, while you contemplate this activity… FEEL grateful.

Just thinking "grateful" can turn into a slapdash job. Hasty. Haphazard. Your thinkery quickly comes up with a few things. This and that. Another quick thing. "There. Done."

Sit with an uplifting aspect… a pleasing part of your Life… until you *feel* your gratitude. There is a world of difference between thinking grateful and feeling grateful. Feeling grateful brings with it a whole other level of fortifying realization. Sweet. Enriching.

Steer Clear of "You Always…" and "You Never…"

Oh golly. In the heat of disagreement… this is the easiest trap to leap into. And proves to be bogus. Fake. Untrue. "Always" and "never" are absolutes… about behaviors or situations which are rarely absolute. Consistently, in relationship… there are shades of gray. And many colors. Variations on a theme. The other person's point of view. Additional factors to consider. Most often… "I feel as if you sometimes…" is more accurate.

Treat Your Relationship Like Something You Value.

A healthy, happy, compatible relationship is a great prize. A boon. Find ways to treat your loving relationship like the gift it truly is. Actively engage in your relationship with respect and appreciation. Sure... it may not be perfect. But then... what is? There are always things to be tweaked about. Why focus there?

In ways big and small... let your partner know... "You are a treasure in my Life." Whisper sweet nothings... which are usually received as sweet somethings. Don't wait for some "big" gift-giving opportunity like an anniversary or birthday. Or to give a giant gift like a new car or a trip to Europe. Little sweetnesses speak volumes. Write a loving note... leave it where he'll find it. Does your partner feel loved when someone else (you) does the dishes? Did you think... "She'd really like that"... when you saw a cute little something? Is tonight a good night to make his favorite meal? Treats are good.

In this human Life we live... it *is* the little things.

Do Fun Things Together.
Remembering, "Oh this is why I like us!
This is why I value our relationship."

Feed your relationship. Nourish it. Don't ignore your relationship... or your partner. Come up with something(s) fun to do together. Jump out of the rut now and again... or a lot. Have experiences together that round things out. So your Life together isn't just all... work... chores... maintenance. Put a little boogie in it. Move beyond the ho-hum. Even simple things… read aloud to each other. Take a day trip to the city. Do a creative art project together. Create memories. Nurture and sustain the magic.

Falling in love is easy. Staying in love… there's the challenge. How can you keep your relationship fresh and growing amid the demands, conflicts, and just plain boredom of everyday life? It doesn't "just happen." You have to invest some of yourself. Encourage good stuff to happen. It is always worth the effort.

Communication and kindness are key.

There are partners and parents who think… "I don't have to tell her. Of course, she knows I love her." And yes, she, he, or they might know you love them. But that doesn't mean it doesn't hurt to say it sometimes. It sure feels good to hear it sometimes.

Just because your parents may not have actively demonstrated their love… that doesn't mean being undemonstrative is the best or only way to do it. It could be that is *not* the way for you to do it in your Life.

It's easy to think about your parents' "way"… "Well, they stayed together. It worked okay for them." But, did it? Did you ever have conversations with your mom about how she felt living with your dad's emotional indifference? Did your dad talk with you about your mother's distraction? Her apathy? Her boredom?

Stretch your expressing self. It might turn out to not be that much "trouble." Chances are really good… it will be well-received. Go ahead… give it a stretch.

Blurt out your appreciation.
This may turn out even better than you think.

Relationship is worth the effort. Treasuring. Nourishing. The significant relationships in your Life are definitely worth the effort.

Writing here about relationship… and about resilience, repetition, and emotional well-being… I am inspired to revisit an insightful exchange I shared in Chapter 3. This is the conversation in *The Book of Joy* between the 14th Dalai Lama and Archbishop Desmond Tutu… as they spoke of the devastating challenges in the Dalai Lama's cherished homeland. And of perpetuating the Tibetan Buddhist way of Life… which is in great peril. Archbishop Tutu asked the Dalai Lama, "Why are you not morose?"

Again, I share the Dalai Lama's response… the practice he uses from the ancient Buddhist teacher, Shantideva:

"If something can be done about the situation,
what need is there for dejection?
And if nothing can be done about it,
what use is there for being dejected?"

The Dalai Lama paraphrased… "When you experience some tragic situation, think about it. If there's no way to overcome the tragedy, then there is no use worrying too much."

"No *use* worrying too much." As in… where does worry really ever *get* you? Not far.

Worry fixes nothing. It keeps you engaged in distraction. Spinning your anxiety wheels.

You will recall… to the Archbishop this "no worries" approach seemed almost too incredible. Someone could stop worrying just because it is pointless to worry? As revealed in his response… "I think people know this with their head. You know that it doesn't help worrying. But they still worry." Archbishop Tutu went on to say… "The thing is, don't feel guilty. We have no control over our feelings. Emotions are spontaneous things that arise."

As I noted in Chapter 3… reading their exchange, I observed… and their moderator, Douglas Abrams, commented… "This was a point that the Archbishop and the Dalai Lama would disagree on during the week: How much control do we have over our emotions? The Archbishop would say we have very little. The Dalai Lama would say we have more than we think." Interesting dual perspectives.

I repeat their exchange because these "dual perspectives"… "very little" and "more than we think"… are hugely significant in the human universe of developing and living a healthy emotional Life.

Self-understanding
makes a tremendous difference in your inner resilience...
and in your healthy, authentic interactions
with your world and the people in it.

Buddhists practice focused inquiry. What are you thinking? Are you able to direct... manage... change... your thoughts? How is your heart? Are you able to lift your heart? This is inquiry into how humans operate. How we function... inside and out.

Quiet the mind.
Open the heart.
Mindful awareness.

The fruits resulting from this inquiry? Learning about your self and how you maneuver thru Life. Your M.O... that groovy ol' *modus operandi*. Your method of being you. Your internal guidance system. Why do you do what you do? Why do you think what you think? How do your thoughts affect you? Why do you feel the way you feel? What are your beliefs about your self? Your Life? Are you "winning" or "losing?"

In your Life as it is now... do the beliefs you focus on serve you well?

Are you caring and kind-hearted? Are you stubborn and belligerent? Why?

Years ago, I saw a TV interview with Carlos Santana. He said… "I am a changed man"… as he recounted a Life-altering moment. A while back, his therapist asked him, "Why are you so angry?" "Uh… uh. I don't know." He went on to say, "My Life was perfect. I had everything I could possibly want. Everything was going great. Yet she was right. I *was* so angry. I had to ask myself… why?" Upon introspection he realized… his anger was habit thought. When he was younger and struggling… Life was hard. He was angry. As he attained success beyond his wildest dreams… without realizing… he held onto his anger. It was a habit. This was a revelation moment for him. A Life-transforming awakening. Once he saw his anger was just habit… he could let it go. No good reason to hold onto the anger cat once it's out of the bag. In this interview I watched, Carlos made it clear… he was enjoying being a happy man.

Realization + Transformation = A Renewed Life.

Focused inquiry offers you an evolutionary opportunity to look at your self. Observing without judgment. "Oh look… why do I do *that* to myself?" Can't change it until you see it. Can't release yourself until you look around and realize... "I don't need this self-generated pain and limitation anymore."

Consciously or unconsciously... what inner rules are you playing by? What are your established qualities? Your operating procedures? Your habits... mental, physical, or otherwise? This practice of self-inquiry shines light on that spectrum between... "We know very little" and "We have more influence over our emotions than we may think."

Yes... here we have another spectrum in human reality. One pole... "We cannot direct our emotions." The opposite pole... "Sure we can." With *all* that transpires between.

Oh, *that* spectrum. Unfolding from... emotions as Boogie Man. Eventually comes a growing willingness to inquire within. Draw a deep, centering breath. Then another. The spectrum... the process... unfolds. Give yourself time. Make time to look within. Personal inquiry leads to awareness of self. Clarity is revealed. Choices are made. Response-ability acquired. Another mindful breath... you find yourself at the "Life is good" pole of the spectrum.

Reading *The Book of Joy*, I observed the Archbishop saying time and again... being aware of and directing our emotional energy is really more than can be expected of a human being. This belief is the result of the Christian tradition not training its flock in competent emotional ways and means. Not highlighting the tools of healthy personal inquiry and well-being. This I say without judgment... simply longtime observation.

All the while, the Dalai Lama is saying... of course we can be more aware. We should be more aware. We *must* be more aware.

Exploring the path of a practicing Buddhist:

> **Become aware** of the emotional effect you are having inside yourself. The inner emotional environment you create and live within.

> **Be aware** of the effect you are having on those around you. The outer emotional environment you create and thru which you touch your world. How you interact with your fellow humans.

> **Teach yourself** to be more inclined to figure it all out in a mindful, harmonious way.

> **Proceed accordingly.**

Meditating... looking within... developing healthy self-awareness... is not the "navel gazing" it has blithely been labeled by those who have no idea what they're talking about. Those who have no experience in this practice. Without an inkling of understanding. Blathering in the weakness of ridicule... they belittle what they do not know. Their flippant comments revealing only their own ignorance.

Making the time to "inquire within"... a person looks into their own ways of being. In the interest of becoming healthier... more authentic and well-balanced. Choosing to cultivate interaction with the world... and the people in it... in a more capable, congenial way. Letting go of Life difficulties being "someone else's fault." Developing a personal awareness which adds to the well-being of people and situations. Rather than childishly and churlishly stirring up difficulty and discord.

Ha ha... this reminds me of another wry observation from Oscar Wilde:

> "Some cause happiness wherever they go;
> others, whenever they go."

"Developing a personal awareness which adds to the well-being of people and situations." This sounds like emotional intelligence, doesn't it? Bingo! Oscar, himself, may not have called it that. Yet, here it is.

This inner evolving from "emotions as Boogie Man" / "I'm so out of control"... to "Life is good" / "I am so grateful"... is a real and true thing. I know it is. I have lived this process... unfolding thru the course of my current adult Life. I used to emotionally terrorize myself... always sure... if faced with the truth about myself... I would "go insane." Whatever that meant in my 20-something mind.

In my early 20s, I participated in a weeklong Ira Progoff workshop. An older guy there... in his mid-30s... came up to me one day and said, "Dana, I'd like to meet with you after today's session. I want to tell you something about yourself." *Oh My God!* My head exploded! Calmly, I said, "Sure." I always managed to maintain a cool façade.

When we got together, he said, "I've been watching you this week." *You have?...* I thought to myself. I was sure I'd been pretty invisible. He said, "What I want to tell you is... you are a gregarious introvert." *I... wait a minute... what?* I was gobsmacked. Knowing he was going to tell me something awful... I'd been all ready to defend... or crumble. Steeling myself to be flayed by a tough personal revelation. Instead... I felt so *seen*. So... OMG! You're right. I *am* a gregarious introvert!

I had to laugh. He had so clearly put a truth about me into words. A truth about me I had never even thought about. But when I heard the words "gregarious introvert" I had an immediate... *"Yep! That's me."*

When he said, "I want to tell you something about yourself"... within myself, I flew into full awfulize. I knew he was going to tell me something terrible about myself. He didn't. He *so* didn't. He gave me very clear and useful information about myself... after he had only "been watching" me for a few days.

As time went on, when I began to freak out about something... I would use this exchange... which turned out so different... so much *better* than I thought it would... to talk myself down. *Dana... remember at the Progoff workshop that guy said he wanted to tell you something about yourself and you got so wigged out thinking he would tell you something awful? Instead, he gave you a very useful piece of self-information? So don't go getting your panties in a twist this time... before you even know what's going to happen.*

Yes... very useful indeed.

Studying The Nature of The Soul made me aware... I have an emotional body. An emotional nature. I live in an emotional environment. This opened vast panoramas of awareness and possibility. *I have an emotional body? Really?* I live in an emotional environment. Okay. That makes sense.

I know this becoming more aware... more at peace... within your emotional self can happen because I have done exactly that. Been there. Got the T-shirt. And the gym shorts. I wear them frequently.

To be clear... not for a moment am I polishing my medals. I'm not saying I have it all together in the vast realm of human emotions, sensitivities and feelings. My application for sainthood came back stamped **HUMAN** a long time ago. There is awareness nourishing still to be done.

Here's what I *am* saying... I'm a whole lot less freaked out by my emotional self than I once was. I used to be completely enthralled... captivated. Spellbound by the whirling and twirling of that ol' Emotional Boogie Man. Completely convinced of his take on things. It would not have occurred to me to question those gyrations. Or the Boogie Man's sovereignty over my inner crazies.

I sure didn't trust my Life. Or my self. I wrote earlier in *Holy Wow!* how stunned I was when "I trust my Life" popped up in meditation one day. Say *what*? An electric jolt! Zowie! Like sticking my finger in the electrical socket of Life. The realization struck... like a deep, reverberating gong tone. The certainty of that moment... jangled me. "Trust my *Life*?" "What?" I was shocked by the concept... the possibility. The novelty. Trusting my Life. Whoa.

Again, I assure you... this is not hocus-pocus. This is you... remembering who you are.

❧ ❧ ❧

Here is a series of insightful suggestions from a plaque mounted on the wall at Mother Teresa's Home for Children in Calcutta, India:

People are often unreasonable, illogical, and self-centered.

Forgive them anyway.

If you are kind, people may accuse you of selfish motives.
Be kind anyway.
If you are successful, you will win some
false friends and some true enemies.
Succeed anyway.
If you are honest and sincere, people may deceive you.
Be honest and sincere anyway.
What you spend years building, someone
could destroy overnight.
Build anyway.
If you find serenity and happiness, they may be jealous.
Be happy anyway.
The good you do today, people will
often forget tomorrow.
Do good anyway.
Give the world the best you have
and it may never be enough.
Give them your best anyway.

In the final analysis, it is between you and God.
It was never between you and them anyway.

I like the whole idea of this… "Do good anyway." "Build anyway." "Be happy anyway." And especially the last line… "It was never between you and them anyway." Because, truthfully… it never was.

It is always between you and you.

The whatever or however you perceive God… lives inside you. Your interpretation. Your beliefs. You are the one who defines the powers you ascribe to God. You determine how significant God is in your Life. Or isn't. You decide if God is alive within you. Or not. No judgment about being a "good" or a "bad" person if you do or do not believe in God.

Considering yourself a "spiritual" person or a "religious" person is a matter living within your own inner Life. A matter of your own quest for nourishing your spirit. The majority of times… a person simply follows their parent's religious denomination into adulthood. And hopefully, that continues to serve them well. Sometimes people "marry into" a different religion than the one they were brought up in. Other folks, as they reach adulthood, find they are not fed by the tenets of faith they grew up in. They change religions or develop their own soul-nurturing moments and practices.

In many cases, religion requires God to remain the same… to be only one way. "My way." This restrictive stance does not allow God to become the presence… the enlivening essence… the magic… God is.

Most religions demand sole belief in its own objects of worship… requiring disbelief in the divinity of other ways or sacraments of worship. These adherents practice a peculiar brand of exclusivity… insisting "My God is the only God!" "Your god isn't really God." "Their holiness is not as good as my holiness."

Years ago, I watched a documentary about the Olmecs (1200-400 BC)... recognized as the first Meso-American civilization. The narrator referred to their religious practices as "mythology." I thought, "I bet they didn't think of their religion as mythology. They were as deeply embedded in their gods and beliefs as Christians are today." Realization popped... "OMG! Future archaeologists will refer to Christian beliefs and tenets as *their mythology*." Whoa. A fascinating thought.

Many people are more attuned to spirituality as they follow their inner path. They find wisdom and nourishment in rituals and customs different from the ones of their childhood religion. They may adopt Buddhist or Hindu practices. Or their inner needs are met by embracing more contemporary methods of spiritual observance such as... Yogananda's Self-Realization Fellowship... Ernest Holmes' Religious Science... Unity Church... Quaker Meetings... Unitarian Fellowship. Sometimes they create their own spiritual "ways and means."

I have always felt that the world's religions have more in common... kindness, love, service, devotion... than the theoretical differences which appear to be dividing them.

Whether practicing a particular religion or not, many people believe in God... love God... serve God. What

God *is*... their interpretation... lives within them. If you believe in a kind and loving God... your God is caring and generous. If you believe God is wrathful and harshly judges your missteps... yours is a severe and punitive God.

For years I've imagined creating a bumper sticker:

"My God Is A Loving God. Your God Is, Too."

But who am I to tell another person who or how their God is?

Many people do not believe in God. Yet, they live kind and giving lives... attuned to their own generosity of spirit. There are people who attend church regularly... and yet are judgmental of others... living less-than-compassionate lives. Believing in God does not automatically make someone a good person. Not believing in God does not automatically make someone a bad person.

Several years ago, I came across the following on Facebook, posted by Senator Cory Booker... before he became a senator from New Jersey. The clear insight of these words resonates with me:

"Before you speak to me about your religion,
first show it to me in how you treat other people.
Before you tell me how much you love your God,
show me in how much you love all His children.

"Before you preach to me of your passion for your faith,
teach me about it thru your
compassion for your neighbors.
In the end, I'm not as interested
in what you have to tell or sell
as in how you choose to live and give."

As you serve God… you are serving Love. You are serving Life. You serve your fellow humans. You serve the situations and experiences of Life as they are unfolding before you.

You can serve your fellow humans if you don't believe in God. You can be caring and giving… kind and helpful to other people… without calling it serving God. Many people do.

The key ingredient here:

Be your best self.

You are not competing with anyone else to live your best Life.

Competition is a human construct. A chunk of very convincing psycho logical architecture. People give competition a lot of air time. Like it's something real. It's only real if you have your ticket stamped for the "Competition Is Real" amusement park ride.

There are lots of "winners." They just don't always "come in first."

In "The Best Life Category," it's all between you and you.

Not so much "who you want to be"… as "how you are showing up."

In amongst the maintenance… the complications… the chaos… the laughter… the choices you make every day bring the sacred to Life.

Let Love Win.

Don't let annoyance win.

Don't let neglect win.

Don't let frustration win.

Let Love Win.

CHAPTER SIX

Patience In Action

"A diplomat of the heart."

Oh, you guys! Walking in here today… I totally feel the buzz of excitement in the air! You lucky lottery winners! You lucky Enhancement Update folks! Your enthusiasm is palpable as you anticipate your upcoming Incarnation: Human on Planet Earth! I know you sit here contemplating the zillion and one excellent enticements drawing you to incarnate on that blue-green Planet of Paradox.

Many beings are drawn to incarnate as a human of Earth to ride a Rodeo of Life like no other. Charmed by the notion of intermingling with all of those personalities, attractions, and complexities. Others look at the discord and disarray on Planet Earth and consider it the dunce pile. As they say in human-speak… "different strokes for different folks."

Humanosity *is* such a multi-faceted incarnate attraction! A cornucopia of possibilities. The joys of being in-body! Seeing and touching! Emotions and perceptions! Inhabiting a fantastic karmic package! Go Team You!

I know you know… it's one thing to be as we are here, residing within this realm of pure cognition. Spacious flourishing as we ride the vast domain of telepathic rapport and clear light awareness. It's a whole *other* thing to be incarnate in the material elements of a mental, emotional, physical instrument.

A thinking, feeling action figure!
WooHoo!

There you be… enrobed in Humankind's Classic 5 Senses Package! The very gear and tackle making your vast sensory experiences available. Relishing the potentialities. Anticipating all the interactions coming your way while in human form.

About the features of the blue and green on that Earth-tone planet: The Infrastructure Unit has certainly outdone itself! Adorning Planet Earth with tropical rain forests… vast glacial regions of ice and snow… magnificent mountain ranges. Gardenias, papayas, and redwoods. Parading penguins and stately lions. The noble dragonfly.

Earth's Planetary Life receives robust acknowledgment for demonstrating great wisdom... insisting each kingdom be centered within an extensive incubation period before the next inhabiting component showed up. Thus, the fundamentals of The Mineral Kingdom... rocks, oceans, seasons, and gravity were all well in place... grounded... to support the arrival of The Plant Kingdom with its spores, fronds, fruits, and evergreens. Along with its tenacious vines. Its resourceful and clever roots-and-shoots mechanisms. An abundance of plant Life flourishing in the vast oceans as well. After a gajillion years of vegetation thriving... covering most of the planet's surface... who should erupt on the scene? The Animal Kingdom! Amphibians, gorillas, dolphins, and llamas... making good use of the bountiful fruits of land and sea. Amazing adaptations. A planet of plenty.

Admiring and appreciating this lush abundance... humans rightly acknowledge:

"We walk the beauty way."

There *you'll* be... in your well-appointed human instrument! Let's see... you'll have fingertips to touch your world and arms to wrap around it. Toes to wiggle. Earlobes, elbows, and eyebrows. Hips for shaking booty. Legs for walking, running, and leaping. Feet for dancing. Hands for clapping, slapping, and caressing.

And vision… taking in the beauty. Seeing where you're headed. Watching all the goings-ons. As well as reading… mapping… texting… appreciating the vast array of color and all things lovely.

There will be E.A.R.S… your 2 Enhanced Audio Receptor Systems. One located on either side of your head… creating the stereophonic wonder of high-fidelity. You'll hear birdsong and jazz. Listen to conversation and love songs. Elevator music. Ballgames. Soliloquies.

Oh, and touch… from vigorous to subtle. Those remarkable sensations felt by the tiny nerve endings thru-out your body's skin wrapper. Hot and cold. Sticky, soft, silky. Hugs and gentle skin-to-skin contact with another human. Sublime.

This skin wrapper covers your entire physical instrument… maintaining your body's temperature as it also prevents leakage of vital bodily fluids. So handy. Your skin is your largest physical organ. Here's a boggling factoid… every square inch of your skin will contain more than 1,000 nerve endings! And boggling some more… every square inch of skin is also comprised of 20 feet of blood vessels, 100 oil glands, 650 sweat glands, and hundreds of hair follicles. This is not in the body's entire skin wrapper… this is in Every Square Inch!

The nerve endings in human skin sense touch, pressure, temperature, and pain. When just one of those nerve endings is stimulated... a signal is sent to the brain... causing a person to "feel" the corresponding sensation.

So, we've spoken of sight, hearing, and touch. As this is the Classic 5 Senses Package... can anyone tell me the additional 2 human senses?

Exactly! Taste and smell.

You will be fitted with extensive olfaction action. Smelleriffic! Your high-functioning olfactory equipment allows you to completely appreciate the many fine aromas and fragrances Planet Earth has to offer. You'll find The Plant Kingdom has done wonders with Earth's Ultimate Fragrance Upgrade.

And my favorite of the 5 human senses... taste. The savor of flavor. That flabby ol' lump of a tongue... resting on the floor of your mouth... awesomely functional as the receptor of that most subtle and divine of the 5 physical senses. Humans of Earth were endowed eons ago with the full spectrum of taste enhancers... sour and sweet... bitter and salty... tart and tangy.

Thru-out your incarnation... the task of taking in nourishment to sustain your physical apparatus is an ongoing endeavor. Several times daily you are required to consume fuel and fluids. This continuous intake of nourishment would verge on the tedious... become boring, even... if not for the installation of these marvelous taste sensors.

Taste... making fuel intake a much more enjoyable requirement.

So, you'll like this... as if there isn't already a ton of evidence illuminating The Profound Order of All Things... your taste function and your sense of smell work together. Completely harmonized. Seamless compliance with the necessary. Perfection. Enjoyment. Survival.

There will be times... you smell something luscious and the taste buds on your tongue will squirt little, enthusiastic bursts of saliva... joyfully anticipating flavor and ingestion. As you enjoy your taste sensors' range of zest and tang... rather than guzzling your fuel intake... you will learn to savor the flavor. Ever alert to distinguishing the dynamics... the aromas... the subtleties... of Earth's vast taste and fragrance spectrum.

As mentioned during your Orientation Moment... beyond the frills of pleasure... taste and smell co-operate in 2 highly crucial functions:

1) Alerting you to nearby food-partaking availabilities... "Are those pomegranates I smell?"

2) Warning if a fuel item has moved beyond prime to putrid. Always heed the stinky! If it smells ick... it'll make you sick. Don't eat it.

That bodacious Earthtone human body… with its myriad fascinating and user-friendly mechanisms! We always get raves about that marvelous 5 Senses Package!

And, you will easily come to find out… 5 digits on each hand is really all you need. That super deluxe opposable thumb and 4 fingers… an ideal, well-designed apparatus. As a young human and thru-out your Life… you will delight in developing your "hand-eye coordination" and "fine motor skills"… as they are called

And you already know so well… the physical body with its eyes and ears… arms and legs… its basic get up and go… isn't all there is to this human equipment. Within the framework of a human Life well-lived… there is vast dimensionality *beyond* the realm of the physical body. There be… intelligence, perceptions, witty banter. Always fascinating explorations into the parameters of good judgment and common sense. You will have viewpoints… opinions… attitudes. On your own… you will establish context… determining the significance and implications of…interactions… events… mementos.

While in human form… there are moments… opportunities… to experience the deepening light of compassion. Caring. Uplift. Sweet exchanges with other humans. Instantaneous knowing. Wisdom. Insight. Revelation. The best kind of ride! The best kind of learning about humanness.

In your enthusiasm to suit up and jump into The Game... it's easy to remember only the super groovy parts of being human. As we discussed in your earlier Orientation Moment... there are some bumps, bruises and sharp edges to watch out for in the antics and anticipations of your tri-body human suit. You especially want to prepare yourself for the pranks and capers of your deep, cavernous emotional nature. As well as the constant copious chatter of your thoughts... with their regrettable propensity for stinkin' thinkin.'

I offer you a word of caution: Humans have compelling affiliations with their appetites and addictions... drugs, booze, shopping, sex. Working too much. Anxiety. Conflict. Self-pity. Each carries its own alluring, seductive appeal. There are times these captivating seductions turn into a permanent Life component. The question then being... is this craving friend or foe?

Some humans delve into such behaviors and compulsions to... as they say... "take the edge off." Nothing wrong with smoothing the rough edges and easing the overwhelm. Other folks deeply partake of intoxicating substances... until the walls begin to move and sway. Altho the effects of ingesting inebriating substances can feel soothing and relaxing... at times, mind-altering... do proceed with care.

For humans of Earth… there is both a fine line and a vast difference between using and abusing. The siren song of mindless habits and addictive substances has its own destructive effect within a Life. These are not as friendly and helpful as they may appear. Not as friendly and helpful as they want you to believe.

Unfortunate, yet true… many well-intended incarnations are derailed by the attraction and turbulence of this broad variety of obsessive appetites.

There will be components of awareness… sensibilities… doubts… beliefs… that feel all sorts of real and realistic at a certain time in your human Life. Then a new chapter… another phase… comes along and… before you know it, as humans say… you are recalibrating and repurposing your cognizant energy.

Brain plasticity and unfolding conscious awareness transform what once was a Life certainty into new capacities. Accommodating your present tense. Current time. Serving who you are now… rather than who you were then.

Reconfiguring. Upgrade. Energies actualizing in the living of your Life as it *is*. Here. Now. Moving beyond the there-and-then.

Always ready to rise to the moment… that great human boon. The advantage… the bonus… of brain plasticity!

Plasticity refers to the human brain's ability to change... as neurons reorganize their structure... their functions and connections... in response to internal or external stimuli. Such an amazing, adaptable organism!

This is exactly how humans learn... anything. Every thing. The brain's ability to modify its connections and re-wire itself is what allows human development... from infancy thru old age.

On Planet Earth... the fundamentals of neural plasticity show up in the nervous systems of insects, mammals, amphibians, cetaceans and other aquatic beings. Humans are not the only neural, synaptic winners.

As a human of Earth you are hardwired to adapt and evolve. To learn and grow. To transform and become.

This means... no matter how calcified... how entrenched... beliefs, opinions, habits... ways of being... might be in your human instrument... you have the inborn capability to change and evolve. There is always room for renovation. Adaptation. Blossoming. Room to develop and become who you are now.

I'm sure you notice... here and there I toss in different human sayings and phrases. This is to give your ears and comprehension components an opportunity to familiarize with the local lingo. Granted, there are innumerable lingos on Planet Earth. But, here we are... engaging somewhere. Humans would say... we're starting "at square 1."

Altho this will rarely occur to you as you are a busy, involved human... transformation is, in fact, a prime requirement of each Earthtone incarnation.

If you don't get around to the joys and rigors of personal transformation in your upcoming incarnation... no worries... there's always next time. If not this one... maybe awareness awakening will occur in your next Life. Or the one after that. No reason to stress over it.

Believe me... conscious personal transformation will come and get you at some point.

Most effective approach? Be open to being open to it.

You seek The Light... and It Finds You. True story.

Fortunately, beings are able to utilize their gleaned past awarenesses, insights, and patterns... to craft a human vehicle capable of recapitulating mindful understanding in the early years of human Life. This ability to recap, reiterate, and reclaim... brings good outcomes thru the rest of their human incarnation.

I have a metaphor for this recap process... using the alphabet. For this example, we will use the English language alphabet. This process can also easily be applied to the Cyrillic alphabet... Arabic, Chinese, Bengali, Cherokee.

A person on the road to literacy learns their ABCs as their basic foundation. Having established the basics... they are then equipt to go on to the mind-expanding realm of spelling, writing, and reading.

In our example... each alphabet letter encapsulates a realization... an insight or a way of being. In one incarnation... you learn the sound-quality intricacies of the letters A thru D... then you go out of incarnation. Your next return to human form, you bring awareness of A thru D with you. Life provides you with opportunities to recollect these capabilities. They come easily... you don't need to effort as you relearn them. Moving thru D... you go on to learn or realize E thru J. Again, your incarnation comes to an end.

Another incarnation rolls around and there you are on Earth again. This process of recapitulation continues... you arrive in your new incarnation with knowings and certainties related to recapping A thru J. Now you are on to learning K thru N. This process continues thru your human incarnations until you have accumulated awareness of the whole "alphabet." Until you have accumulated awareness of a happy, healthy, contributing way of being.

A human lifetime arrives when... early in your incarnation... you recollect the complete knowledge of the 26 letters of the alphabet. In our metaphor... you have embodied many levels and degrees of perception. You have assembled your basis of knowing. And being.

Coolness ensues.

Here is where a whole new dimension opens. Remembering your basis of knowing… the "whole alphabet"… early in Life… you forge onward… learning to make and read words. "See Jane run. Run, Jane, run." "Fourscore and 7 years ago…" Ultimately these words… these Life-realizations… evolve into phrases and sentences. Novels and training manuals. Human Life makes sense to you in a whole new way. A broader cognizance dawns. Deeper knowledge. Wide realization. So, *this* is what it's all about!

Just as literacy and education transform the livingness of a person's incarnation… this metaphor offers insight into each individual's ability to kit out their instrument with Life-transforming uplift and awareness. There is more to Life than being illiterate. There is more to Life than just learning the alphabet. There is more to a human Life than wandering around in… "Who am I?" "What is this all about?" "Why am I here?" "Is this all there is?"

Each incarnation offers you opportunities to gather *realization wealth*. The prosperity of deep knowing. The affluence of wide compassion. The opulence of understanding yourself as Spirit living a human experience.

You go into incarnation as a human of Earth to become more conscious and awake while *in* human form. Rather than being overwhelmed by the turbulence and toil… you utilize Life's intricacies… its nuances… to become a more contributing human. Lifting and nourishing the well-being of your fellow humans. Lifting and nourishing the well-being of the Planetary Life.

Nourishing the well-being of the Planetary Life speaks to being functional as a person who helps. Helping other humans to live Life more effectively… to remember who *they* truly are. Being present and caring for animals. Furthering the well-being of plant Life. Conservation. Caring for the environment. The emotional and mental environments as well as the physical. Contributing to the fostering of good. Being of service as a human of Earth.

Earlier, I commended you for choosing to participate in these Advanced Enhancement Upgrades. Let me also thank you… for your dedication to living an exemplary, contributing human Life. For yourself. For those your Life touches. For all of Humankind.

So far, our Enhancement Seminar has deepened into 3 areas of human endeavor:

1) We spoke of the glories of healthy child-rearing and the intricacies of relationship. Plus, the many kinds

of relationship… with your friends, family, and frenemies. With your work, your education, and your creative expression. And how they, each and all, affect the living of your incarnation. Glorious or grumpy.

2) We've also clarified why these Upgrade Seminars are called The Patience Olympics… for myriad reasons. The obvious… and far beyond.

3) I have again encouraged you to visit the Install Your Patience Here kiosk 3 times.

I sense some of you thinking I have a fascination with patience. You're right… I do. For good reason. Many incarnations ago, I said yes to a karmic assignment: Be an emissary… an investigator… for The Dynamic of Patience in the realm of humanosity. Like a scout. A diplomat of the heart. Over the course of many human lives… this mission tasked me to observe and interact with the force of patience… or its absence… in the cauldron of daily human Life on Planet Earth.

It has been mine to experiment… kitting myself out with assorted strategies, wiring capacities and related capabilities… before going into each incarnation. Sometimes I lived a Life as patience in action. Other incarnations I rode the range in a short fused, impatient vehicle. Reconnoitering all the angles. I'll tell you… it was a profound exploration into humans and their psycho logical ways. An investigation of human perceptions. Perceptions of their own capabilities and shortcomings.

Here is what I have learned:

Patience is a capacity.
A competence any human can develop and exercise.
Patience is a choice to make.
Much like compassion and empathy.
These are emotional muscles a human
can choose to exercise.

In the human realm… much attention is given to physical prowess and stamina. Developing patience offers a different quality of stamina. Cultivating compassion, empathy, and tolerance… humans demonstrate their *inner* prowess.

Some humans arrive on Earth with an inborn ability to direct their own energies. To motivate themselves. To choose how they are going to show up. Deciding their responses to Life's upsets and challenges. For others, developing "self-control"… self-management… is an acquired skill. At times requiring a series of incarnations. And herculean effort.

In humans of Earth… emotion and mind work together to self-direct. In some people… they self-*deflect*. This mind-emoto collaboration is actually similar to the senses of taste and smell… as they coordinate harmoniously in the process of fuel acquisition. Harmonious self-cooperation = always a good thing. Altho playing very different parts… taste and smell… feelings and thinkery… these 2 collaborations show… mutual effort improves the outcome. Making both better. More congruent. More functional. Making Life work good.

As a patience scout in the Land of Humankind… I traveled as an observer… deep within the fraught and fray. In myriad different situations and relationships… I noticed and noted: What effects does patience have? When is it best utilized? How is patience received in human interactions? Does it improve a situation? Does it detract? How does a human build their patience muscles? How healthy is a patient person? How do they feel about their Life?

How effective is impatience? Is impatience a useful strategy? Is it helpful? How is impatience received? When applied… does it improve the situation or interaction? Does it detract? How does an impatient person feel about the living of their Life?

One of my consistent observations… the person on the *receiving* end of the snap of an impatient reaction feels put down. Belittled and unworthy. Less than. Definitely not valued. Not heard. Mistreated. Impatience breeds impatience. And emotional hurt.

Please take note: There is much truth in "impatience breeds impatience." In my research it became very clear... humans find it hard not to react to someone else's impatience with their own impulsive irritation. A knee-jerk reaction, as they say. Jerk indeed. Snappish. Condescending. Patronizing. Can lead to yelling and name-calling.

Spiraling out of control. Feeding the forces of impatience. Allowing the forces of impatience to consume you and your interactions. You become their minion. A sycophant of the snappish. An action figure of annoyance. Stirring up more drama. And trauma.

Patience itself is an acolyte of kindness. You choose emotionally to be patient. Just as you choose to be kind. Attentive. Uplifting. Fun. Exercising your upbeat emotional muscles.

Impatience is selfish. "You're doing that wrong!" "This is really irritating." "I am so over this!" "Get me outta this joint!" Impatience is punitive... looking to punish. On a mission to... "make you feel bad!" Making you feel bad because I feel tweaked. I would rather blame you for my tweak... than take any sort of response ability for my own tweaked self.

Patience is a practice in selflessness. Calming down. Not grabbing on and wielding your upset. Letting the twang slide by. Taking in the goings-ons and who you're with. The context of the moment. Choosing a measured response. Deciding to be centered and respectful as you live your Life.

Points of clarification to consider as you practice being patient while human:

You don't think about patience or impatience.

You *feel* patience or impatience.

You practice patience in your responses to Life.

This is similar to the difference between thinking about meditation and meditating. Thinking about meditating and actually meditating are 2 very different things. Ditto... thinking about being patient and being patient are 2 *very* different things.

Your thinkery may remind you, "You could be patient." But, patience is a competence developed within the emotional nature. A competency to exercise because you care. About Life.

Humans have a fascination with both "contrast and compare" and with making lists. Here are 2 lists contrasting and comparing the qualities of patience and impatience:

Patience	Impatience
Calm	Anxious
Persevering	Hasty
Tolerant	Complaining
Understanding	Judgmental
Compassionate	Impulsive

| Mindful | Frantic |
| Hopeful | Pessimistic |

Patience is the ability to endure… difficult circumstances… a challenging person… an unmet expectation. Hopefully, meeting the moment with a fairly good attitude.

Patience is the Big Kahuna of A Kind Heart. An expert at gentle awareness. Always your ally in relationship. With children… lovers… friends. Elders. Associates. Accomplices.

With your self.

Patience is the capacity to be met with delay, difficulty, or distress… and not totally fritz out about it.

Patience is a function of awareness. It's what you *choose* to do with Life input.

As you are human… external stimuli comes your way and you react or respond to it inside yourself. You decide… "What's this?" "What does it mean?" "What am I going to do about it?"

This epoch you are incarnating into prides itself for being "fast paced." The forces of impatience find plenty of action figures to play The Game… suited up with annoyance and irritation. "Go faster!" "You're wasting time!" "Get out of my way!" Irritability and impatience are miffed, shortsighted tools of interaction. Careless. Callous.

Note to self: These are not the allies they pretend to be.

In many situations and relationships, patience is a healing balm. Tolerance. Kindness. Especially in the face of "not getting."

It doesn't really work to "be patient" with the expectation the other person will "be patient" back.

As you are being human… practice patience and tolerance because it makes no sense to pollute your inner Life by flying to rage. Leaping to judgment. Frying your own circuits as you spew antagonism and hostility. Yet that is exactly where many humans of Earth jump to first. Usually because they have a sorely inadequate emotional tool kit.

Impatience is like having an emotional cramp. A spasm of limited response options.

We've spoken of taking parenting classes to move beyond the mistreatment, neglect, or abuse of your own childhood. As you are being human… it is also beyond brilliant to take classes or get yourself some therapy (always a smart move) to develop more useful emotional tools to deal with your self and your world.

Humans need more ways to *be*. More ways to respond to Life's circumstances… obstacles and opportunities. More tools… to counteract that mad dash to anger. Short-temper. Anxiety. Grudgment.

Every cognent being heading into incarnation is required to have one goodly dose of patience stirred into their incarnate equipment. Their personal porridge. At one point… even before taking on my karmic assignment… it occurred to me, "I wonder what 2 doses of patience would do?" I sure found out! It's a genius move.

I noticed a difference… a distinct upgrade… in my ability to hold on to my patience in irritating or frustrating circumstances. In my human Life… I was noticeably able to be more tolerant… and, interestingly, more attentive… with my children. At the time, this was a pleasant and unexpected bonus.

In my experimenting… I didn't rush right to 3 doses. Over the course of several human incarnations, I continued to experiment with 2 doses. And take notes. One facet became very clear with the additional dose… I had more patience within me from an early age. And, boy have I learned… from my own experience and thru observation… it takes effort for a human to train themselves in the ways of patience. Especially being able to have patience pop up in reaction as the moment calls for it.

You *can* build your patience muscles while in incarnation. But, whew! That patience-building involves both exertion and determination. So many full-press reps! It is *so* much easier to come in to your incarnate Life with your inclination to patience already installed and fortified. However… if you're in incarnation and detect a lack of patience within yourself and your interactions… worry not. You *can* reconfigure your equipment. You *can* become more patient. You can train yourself to exercise those particular emotional muscles. It's totally worth the effort.

Continuing my exploration of patient while human… the time came… I walked into the Pre-Incarnate Prepwork Zone… turned right around and headed back to the Install Your Patience Here kiosk a 3rd time. I just had to know. In that moment, I did the best I could to manage my expectations. But, sure as shootin'… it *works*! I have never looked back.

Infused with this 3rd dose… responding with patience became the very nature of my incarnate vehicle. Life's challenges… the tweakables… lubricated. Soothed. Smoothed.

A lot of fuss and fray is in the mix on Planet Earth. Pustules of frustration. As we are here now… there is still time for you to receive more than the required single dose of patience. Your choice.

I gotta tell you… the way some humans are so short-fused… you would think they stood behind the door as patience was being handed out, pre-incarnation.

The punchline to my Patience Thesis is this: Infuse your human instrument with a triple dose of patience before diving into the drama and trauma of your upcoming incarnation. You'll be glad you did.

I'm sure many of you here… in your previous incarnations… have also been on a quest to explore The Art of Being Patient While Human. I wish you Life's Very Best as you continue to deepen into patience in your upcoming incarnation.

Patience… don't leave home without it.

Many times… due to karmic combinations of nature and nurture… you are absorbed completely and absolutely deep within your humanness. Your struggles and conflicts are so real. Your opinions and beliefs so solid… beyond question. The requirements… the maintenance… the tasks of daily living… keep you entirely entangled in your wild-eyed whoop-dee-do. There is really no room… no inclination… no interest… in looking around beyond yourself. Or within yourself. To gain perhaps a wider perspective. Evolving from panic to panorama. Altering the viewpoint from which you perceive your world. A different way of looking at your self. And your Life. It doesn't even cross your field of possibility.

As mentioned earlier… it almost always takes a hard whack… a devastating loss… an upsetting failure… a major disappointment… for a human to startle out of their profound complacency. Jangled to the point they actually sit down and begin looking around in this Life they are living. Looking *at* this Life they are living. Looking beyond their narrow scope. To see… "Is there more to Life?" Room for change? Other possible paths? Diversions. Potentialities.

Finding a foothold along their Path.

The Spiritual Truth of your nature is not even a question as we are here in this light-filled, cognent reality. The story will be different while you are in human form. On Earth, your appetites and addictions… your worries and fears… your striving for success, fortune and fame… general survival… keep you deeply identified *as* the vehicle you're cruising around in. The driver believes they *are* their car.

You will believe you *are* your feelings… your thoughts… your work… your obstacles… your achievements. Until a certain point… the arrival of a whack perhaps… you'll be *all* tied up in the game, Boo. Identified as what you are doing… rather than who you are being.

Yes, this was discussed in Orientation. I know as we are here in the steady, illuminating glow… it seems koo-koo to spend time clarifying The Truth of Spiritual Identity. But this distinctive mis-identification is *such* a large misconception… a mighty delusion… for humans of Earth.

As you prepare to incarnate… it is truly worthwhile to engage your Magic Decoder Ring… especially your Recall + Retain button… to imbed this Quest For Clarity within your comprehension unit. For easy access while human.

When you are being human… it will take some reorganizing of realization for you to recognize… *you* are not your thoughts. Your human instrument is equipt with a mental body… it thinks. It perceives. It ideates. This mental activity equipment is yours to use. It should not use you.

This will be an even bigger, fatter deal when it comes to your emotional apparatus. Your instrument comes appointed with razzamatazz emotional paraphernalia. For you to operate and utilize. Your emotions will feel sooooooo real. You will believe… "I am my anger." "I am my frustration." "I am my self-doubt." "I am my anxiety and confusion." "I can't help the way I am." Yes… you can.

You are not your physical body… even tho it sure "looks like" you are. Speaking of "looks"… you are not your appearance. You are not your physical fitness… nor your flab. This physical apparatus is the state-of-the-art vehicle you'll use to navigate your physical plane reality. It's a neato-keen piece of ambulatory equipment. It is not who you *are*.

Each human incarnate is animated by the spark of Spirit. Your essence of conscious awareness enlivens your vehicles. You utilize your physical, emotional, mental instrument… as you cruise around being human in the physical, emotional, mental environments of Planet Earth.

I know here in spacious, cognent reality, you're thinking… "Why is she even talking about all this? Who in the world would not know that the driver is not their car? That the tea is not its pot? That the human instrument is just a convenient way for individualized Spirit to move around in those physical, emotional, mental atmospheres of Planet Earth? Who would think they *are* their gear shift? Their brakes? Their rear windshield wipers? How does this great confusion even occur?"

Ahhh... excellent question.

Basically... as you head from our spatial reality here... on your way into your human incarnation... prepare to be blindsided. Yes, pre-incarnation, you are asked to state your desired preferences, intentions and outcomes. However, as you travel thru the astral veils and etheric architecture... that's not exactly how the myriad aspects and nuances of your Life will show up when you arrive on Earth. There you will encounter some enigmas and more than a few mysteries. Along the lines of "What am I doing here?" "Who *are* these people?" "Am I even equipt for this endeavor?"

Your incarnant Life comes equipt with quite a compilation of perplexities. There will be a puzzlement or 2. Or 2,222. The Great Wonder Wheel of Life has a few tricks up its sleeve. What can I say? Just to keep things "interesting?" Amusing? Stupid? Koo-koo?

Earth is not called The Planet of Paradox because that has a snazzy ring to it. Paradox... absurdity... contradiction and conundrum... rocks the very core of Earthtone existence.

Heading into incarnation, enrobed within Your Etheric Sconce... you travel thru those astral veils, that etheric architecture... karmic and dharmic impact fields... which collide with and tweak your best intentions and motivations. One way I've heard this described in human lingo... "you fall into your reflection." Losing sight of your goals and identity... your deep, centered knowing. Your clear Light vision.

You wake up human.

This "losing sight of"... this spiritual amnesia... is not a requirement. It doesn't happen in every planetary system. But it sure does happen on Earth. Crazy as it may sound... this spiritual amnesia is one of Earth's big attractions. Say *what?*

It's true. Beings are drawn to this Planet of Paradox exactly so they *can* fall in so deep. The fog... thick and perplexing. The quizzical curiosities seeming so real. It takes serious conscious effort to resurface from the muddle of this thick pea soup trance.

You have to resurface. You have to remember. You *want to* consciously place your feet upon your path.

So many cognent beings in this expansive Light realm we're currently in... get all twitterpated by the prospect of falling so deeply asleep... then struggling back to awakened awareness. Thinking... "I'll ace it!" "It'll be so fun!" Yeah well, maybe sometimes it will be fun. But I gotta tell you...

speaking with transparency and all… if you were to interview humans currently incarnate about how "fun" their Life is… you'd get a lot of blank stares. Or great guffaws. "Are you kidding me?" "You're nuts!" "This is a trick question, right?"

Most humans of Earth are not having all that much fun. Especially as you make it to adult Life… you'll slog thru a lot of clutter, confusion, and chaos. Emotionally as well as physically. The majority of times, human Life on Planet Earth doesn't feel fun at all. It has a bite. A sting. It binds. Think mental hand cuffs or emotional straightjacket. There are nettles and thorns. It grates on your sensibilities.

The grind can make you grumpy.

I'd love to tell you… of course you ride the range conscious and aware… delighting in your human instrument… with its trifles and peccadilloes. But truth be told… you'll be miffed. Your human predisposition to identify *as* your thoughts and feelings… and how you look… and what you do or do not do… keeps you thoroughly, painfully entranced. A deep ache. Disappointing.

Self-terrorizing… as you wander around in your Earth-tone human suit and its generated reality.

I know I've mentioned this before… there's a lot of stupid on Planet Earth.

Humans spend much time wandering. And wondering… "Why am I here?" "What *is* going on?" "Is this all there is?"

Moments arise in human time... when poets and visionaries are able to articulate The Love of God. The gifts of conscious Spiritual awareness. One of these gifted incarnants, Hafiz, lived in the land of Persia in the long ago. Hafiz demonstrated a rare talent... crafting uplifting thoughts and phrases into insightful poetry. Speaking the perspective of God... of Lovelight-filled awareness. Hafiz reveals what we in spacious, cognent reality want all humans to know:

"I wish I could show you when you are lonely or
in darkness the astonishing light of your own being."

There are moments in Earthtone reality when that "astonishing light" shines unobstructed. Moments of Grace. More and more incarnant humans are consciously tuning their mechanism... their thoughts, feelings, and choices... to be able to receive and embrace these blessings. Able to know the "light of their own being." Grace, indeed. For themselves. For all concerned.

Shining a light on your human suit's "generated reality" we mentioned a moment ago... here's a bit of tricky business you may notice while ensconced in humanosity. Identified as their beliefs, perceptions, and feelings... humans can't help but emotionally accessorize the moment. Rarely does a person perceive an interaction or situation as what it just *is*. Each moment... each connection or condition... is adorned with judgment. "This is great!" "This sucks." "That's not right." "Looking good!" "This needs to be different." "She's right, cause she thinks just like me." "Their politics are so wrong. I'm insulted."

Within the context of humankind evolving... judgement can be a useful tool. In the way-back, judging was helpful to determine useful food sources and evaluate personal safety. "Am I about to be dinner?" Good to be able to judge the scene and assess suitable safety measures. Situational awareness, as it's called on Earth.

However... in this epoch you are incarnating into... the majority of humankind has evolved beyond immediate "eat" or "be eaten" concerns. I'm sure you recall our earlier conversation about the amygdala and the reptile brain... with its tendency to hijack human emotional reactions. A variation of this hijacking definitely shows up in the form of over-judging. Spiraling madly out of control. "Must fiercely criticize." "Must let my dissatisfaction be known." You will find humans are ready to harshly judge "at the drop of a hat"... as the locals would say. A hat that drops way too often.

Humans judge how other people look. "Look at her! How can she be seen in public like that? I would *never* wear that hideous outfit!" They are particularly critical when another person believes differently than they do. "She's an idiot to think that way." "Don't go near him... he's the wrong political party... the wrong color ... the wrong religion... the wrong caste."

You will hear an Earthtone saying... "You can't tell a book by its cover." Many people shortchange themselves as they only choose to judge Life's various "covers." Missing out on what the story inside the book might have to say. Who the person they're judging might reveal themselves to be. The exploration of Life... beyond short-sighted bias.

Sadly, but truly... the majority of incarnate humans also stress themselves out with harsh *self*-judgement. "I'm too fat." "Too scrawny." "Too short." "I can't stand my bad complexion." "My flabby upper arms." "My nose is too big." "I'll never wear a bathing suit again!" "They won't like me." "I'm not smart enough to apply for that job." "I never do anything right." Sigh. As humans would say... "Egads!"

This raging case of judgment continues as humans busily judge their lives. All the "rights" and all the "wrongs." Seldom is there "enough." Hardly ever are things "fine." "Brilliant." "Perfect." Or even "Nice." To note: Harsh self-judgment does nothing to lift inner well-being or feelings of self-esteem. Zip. Nada.

A lot of human suffering comes from their inclination to judge. This judging fixation is the root of the human tendency to "accessorize the moment." Always with the judging. "This is so good." "This is completely lousy." "A dream come true!" "A total nightmare!" Oh, that crazed, self-limiting accessorizing. When you are being human... it will be a huge step in your personal journey to awakening... as you can see the moment for what it *is*. No rocketing highs. No plummeting lows. No splash of extra sauce. No superfluous drama... trauma... or Dramamine (a popular human anti-nausea medication). Just what *is*. Here. Now.

There are many steps in a human's awakening journey... mini and grande. A person's ascent to their full potential is always a work in progress. Here are a few indicators along your path:

Practice not only what you speak... but also what you realize.

Embrace self-improvement and personal upgrade.

The enhancement of saying "Yes!" to Life.

Step beyond the self-limiting whine of "Oh, why bother?" Or... "This is too hard."

Hey, Honey... you're on your way to being a human of Earth. It's all hard. Like they say... choose your hard. The rest is a lively cha-cha-cha.

Reflecting on is-ness calls to mind another human visionary jewel … akin to the remarkable Hafiz. Offering an opportunity to release yourself from all the fuss. Getting over trying to make something more… or less… than what it is. *Being* in the moment.

Allowing what *is* to be its is-ness.

The following is attributed to Australian playwright, novelist and poet, Harrison Owen (1890-1966).

In some circles of humankind this fine perception is known as:

The 4 Immutable Laws of Spirit

"Whoever is present are the right people.
Whenever it begins is the right time.
Whatever happens is the only thing
that could have happened.
When it's over, it's over."

Let's also add:

"What happens matters."

Because it does.

CHAPTER SEVEN

An Unexpected Bonus

"It's more like a cha-cha."

"It really boils down to this: that all life is interrelated.
We are all caught in an inescapable network of mutuality,
tied into a single garment of destiny."
~ Dr. Martin Luther King

Completely absorbed within the on-going toil and
turmoil of all things... rarely do we humans take a
step back to consider this interwoven fabric of destiny we
are each a part of.

We miss or deny the truth "that all Life is interrelated."
Our perceptions of "myself and others" / "us and them" are

psychological constructs. Used to divide. And often to feel superior. "We're so much better than *they* are."

Do these contrived constructs make us feel safe? Special? Chosen? Within our human family... we fabricate boundaries between ourselves... just like the lines between countries we draw on a map. Viewing our planet from space... those lines... those borders... do not exist.

As King T'Challa, of the advanced African nation of Wakanda, observed:

> "The illusions of our division
> threaten our very existence."

He makes an astute point.

We are each carbon-based Life forms... with hearts pumping red and white blood cells thru-out our bodies. Our lungs draw in the same sweet breath of Life. We eat and digest food. We tell stories and build shelter. We each want security and well-being. A better Life for our children. There is more the same about us than there is different.

As mentioned earlier in this volume... each and all... we are water molecules within the ocean of Life.

There is more to us than you may think. Together, we are a great body of human Life essence traveling thru time. Weaving into... affecting... influenced by and influencing...

the generations of human Life who have lived before us and particularly the generations who will live after us.

Just as we are affected by and have built upon all who have gone before us... the choices and actions we each make... our decisions and activities... what we do and what we don't do... further the weaving of our Life tapestry. We craft the framework future generations will build, live, and, hopefully, thrive upon.

Being as we are... living as we do now... we are creating history as we pass thru it. We influence those who will arrive on the planet after us. We are their ancestors. These future generations will look back on our achievements, conflicts and impact just as we look back on the accomplishments of the Greeks and Romans... ancient Islamic mathematics, art, and architecture... the artists and thinkers of the Renaissance.

We humans are absolutely identified within the structures... the constraints... of temporal spatial reality. This shackles our ability to see and appreciate... we are The Flow of Awakened Awareness traveling thru all time.

As similar as we all are as humans of Earth... our thinkery... our philosophies and religions... our beliefs and politics... create the world's divisions and discord. Literally within the 6 inches between our ears. Conflict generator *extraordinaire*. Fussing. Keeping the world small.

Finding more to be upset about and criticize... than to be supportive of and embrace.

Another Truth of Life we all have in common... recognized since before the time of Plato:

> Everyone you meet is fighting a great battle.
> Be kind.

Every human being is in the midst of their own struggle.

Recognizing that truth is the best reason I can think of to be kind. All hail compassion! Empathy rides again. You never know the burden another person is carrying. There is no good reason to make their load heavier.

As the Dalai Lama reminds us:

> "Compassion is the radicalism of our time."

Speaking of the 6 inches between our ears... oh, that illustrious brain. The human command post. Hardware and software. A little over 3 pounds (1.5 kg) of gray and white matter... controlling all body functions. From hormones to walking. From neuron pathways to digestion to toenail growth.

Thru our 5 senses... our brain interprets information from the outside world. Within ourselves... we give this information meaning and context. Formulating what's going on... we assemble external output. We react... expressing ourselves accordingly.

The brain then stores this interpreted info, these interactions and realizations in memory.

Ground central for the very essence of mind and soul. The brain is where our physical, emotional, and mental bodies congregate and collide. Our scramble of thoughts and attitudes... creating their resulting habits... have a strong, daily effect on our physical bodies and our emotional well-being.

The brain and its resident intellect... thinking, deciding, believing... is where we get ourselves in trouble. By thinking, deciding, believing... someone else is lesser than... or "not like me." Being afraid a person I don't understand is going to harm me. Many times, our *reactions* to our own thoughts and beliefs are blown way out of proportion.

Human thoughts and beliefs lay the foundation for... political disagreement and strife... racist opinions and actions... disapproving religious judgment. The proudly pious. The arrogantly rude and callous. Deepening partisan and cultural divides. Bringing hard truth to... "it's all in your head."

In early 2021, I was astounded by the clarity of this statement from political commentator, author, and actor, D.L. Hughley:

> "The most dangerous place for black people to live
> is in white people's imaginations."

Wow.

Upset or fear is generally not about the black guy you actually know. Hughley points out… "It's the black guy in Chicago. It's the black guy they saw on the news. It's the black guy on the video. It's more the *idea* of the black man than the actual black man." He goes on to say… "*I'm* scared of the black guy in their imagination. I hope I never meet him. The *idea* of us is much more impactful and fearful than the reality of us."

These *ideas*… these imaginings… *are* powerful. They are cruel and spiteful ideas. Hurtful ideas. These notions and beliefs do not allow black people, or brown people, or Asian people be who they *are*. These attitudes and made-up stories about who "these people" are only embolden biased stereotypes. Convincing us to be afraid of one another. Inventing distance. Walls.

This is also true of gay and lesbian people within the imagination of homophobes. What are people imagining about gay men or lesbian women or transvestites that makes them so disgusted and enraged? A person who is gay, lesbian or transvestite is a human being. Their Life path is their own. Different than yours. In some people's minds… they are fornicating non-stop. That is inaccurate. Gay, lesbian, and transvestite people make breakfast. They have jobs. They grocery shop. They buy houses. They become educated. They love their families. They help other people.

If you are uncomfortable or infuriated by homosexual people... what are you telling yourself about them? What are the stories about them you're making up in your own head? What are you believing from what you heard somebody else say?

It's who we imagine the "bad guys" to be that solidifies their status as bad guys. Their status as "those" people. "I can't stand them!" The version of them you make up and hold onto in your own head is what's generating your contempt.

Many media outlets and commentators make a lot of money exploiting people's resentments and fears. They focus their listeners on... "They're out to get you!" Whoever "they" may be. Evidently there's a long list. "They're getting your jobs!" "Your women!" "Your neighborhood!" "Your privilege!"

These commentators shout and spray ... "Be afraid. Be very afraid." Of your neighbors... "those" people... other sects and religions... liberals. Stirring up antagonism and bitterness. Generating hate and hostility. This is not community-building activity. This is not bringing us together to build a viable future. This is tearing the fabric of humankind apart. The carefully constructed framework of democracy is rent asunder. Ripping apart what generations have honored and sacrificed to build.

Let's be perfectly clear... fear-mongering commentators are well paid. Many of these pundits of negativity actually stand in contempt of their listening audiences. Deliberately arousing public alarm about particular issues. Many do not even believe what they're spouting. They fling their abysmal vitriol… their venom and bitterness out there… only interested in generating money for themselves and their advertisers.

Looking beyond self-terrorizing and division… it's obvious… we're all on this same Planet Earth spaceship hurtling thru time and space. We are each a woven strand in our "single garment of destiny."

The rapid social and cultural changes of the 1960s terrified a lot of folks. Startling them out of their complacency. They now hope to wake up in the era they fell asleep in. Forgetting "the good ol' days" were rife with their own difficulty, discord, and chaos. Fondly looking back… cherry-picking what we choose to remember. Our human tendency is to only remember the perceived "good parts"… better than today. And long for them.

Neither the present… nor our future… are well-served when we long for the past.

Looking back to "learn from history" is a good thing. Sadly, seldom is that "learning" component retrieved or applied. On a personal level… and as a society… we rarely allow ourselves to actually learn from past occurrences or experiences. Remembering "better times" we wistfully look back. Thus sheltering ourselves from the pressures… and the opportunities… of current reality.

As they say… "Don't look back. That's not the way we're going."

We speak of the social and cultural changes of the '60s… it would appear, as we move thru the 2020s… we are in another spin cycle of dynamic change:

The corona virus global pandemic has spawned enormous disarray on nearly every level of human interaction… personal… families… societal… workforce… education… economic.

Politicians have lost sight of the fact they are elected to serve the people and the common good. Fanning the flames of partisan divide… bashing the other party. They focus on fund-raising… and getting reelected.

The administration of the most recent past president… defeated in 2020… upended the status and standing of the United States on the world stage. Gutting international norms and agreements. Eviscerating social justice.

Race relations ignited in many different countries. Black lives do matter. Human rights are human rights. Whites are no longer in the majority. The crises immigrants face affect us all.

Altho warned for more than half a century...
ignoring humanity's effect on the global environment is catching up with daily reality as... floods and
fires... sea levels rising... unusually hot temperatures
on land and in the ocean... cause death and disarray.

There's a whole lot of shakin' going on.

Just because we don't want to see it or deal with it...
does not mean it isn't here. Choose from the above long
list of "it."

Another remarkably clear observation I read in this
past year:

> "To those accustomed to privilege,
>   equality feels like oppression."

As I checked with Auntie Google to make sure I quoted
accurately... I discovered this was a quote from Ruth Bader
Ginsburg... The Notorious RBG. An illustrious human
being... dedicated to women's rights... to human rights...
to the general well-being of others.

Privilege is defined as a special right, advantage, or
immunity granted or available only to a particular person
or group of people.

Interestingly, in the 21st century, this fascination with privilege led to the legal defense of "affluenza"... a psychological

malaise supposedly affecting wealthy young people. Symptoms include a lack of motivation and the inability to feel guilt for their actions which hurt and/or kill others.

Affluenza can be regarded as the opposite pole of damaging racial profiling. Rather than immediately suspecting a person of a crime based on their race or ethnicity… affluenza seems to be a case of… "Oh, your family is rich and well-connected? Never mind. We're sure you didn't mean to do it." Rather than harmful… this variation on profiling proves to be advantageous to the accused. The case made for affluenza states that the accused person's elite social position afflicted them… causing them to not understand the consequences of their actions. Basically… a wealthy person is not criminally liable for what they do.

Sound mostly whacky? Grossly unfair? Yep… it is.

People who live lives of privilege view the world thru an elitist lens… tossing their privilege around. Theirs is the complete expectation others will respond to them with the indulgence they assume from Life.

Many other people who do not see themselves as privileged… are way more privileged than they realize. Having grown up with food on the table… clean water to drink and bathe in… a comfortable home… access to good education = more privileged than a multitude of other humans on the planet.

Facing the world's staggering struggles and injustice… privilege allows many people to think, "Oh, that's not a problem." Because the issue or circumstance is not a problem for *them*.

Since its beginning, the United States has been a white majority country. Cruising thru the 21st century… the white majority in the U.S. is losing its majority status. Some people are becoming very uncomfortable.

As equality is sought… wanted… for people of different racial, ethnic and economic groups… many white people are upset. Even demoralized. This persecuted feeling of theirs… is the perceived discomfort of losing a little bit of their familiar, everyday privilege.

Developing and supporting racial equality is hard. Living in a world without racial equality is hard. Choose your hard.

I first became aware of "choose your hard" thru a friend's post on my Facebook page. Here, I paraphrase:

Marriage is hard. Divorce is hard.
Choose your hard.
Obesity is hard. Being fit is hard.
Choose your hard.
Being in debt is hard.
Being financially disciplined is hard.
Choose your hard.

Communication is hard. Not communicating is hard.

Choose your hard.

Life will never be easy. It will always be hard.

But we can choose our hard.

As I first read this, I was struck by its profound clarity. I thought… "So true." I'm sure you can think of a couple of these comparisons related to your own Life. I consulted Auntie Google to find out who to attribute this wise outlook to. All I found was "Unknown." Congratulations to "Unknown" for wisdom well-spoke.

Cruising and perusing online… I came across a few blog posts whose authors certainly read "Choose your hard" differently than I did. Whereas, I thought, "How refreshing"… others were enraged. Defensive. They seemed to interpret the concept of "choose your hard" as an assault on the way their lives are showing up.

Which again brings us to… different folks respond to the same thing differently. Boy Howdy! I'll say.

No matter how clearly you… feel… think… are… expressing yourself… as soon as 2 or more are gathered… the possibility for conflict and misunderstanding is right there, too. As you convey your clearly intended statement or observation… you immediately activate the other person's fully complicated inner response mechanism. "Are you insulting me?" "How rude!" "Why would you even think that about me?" Uhh... no, wait. "That's not what I meant!"

Occasionally... "This is very insightful. Thank you for sharing"... shows up. Yes, that response does happen, too... now and again.

Remember, other people in their... reactions... criticism... complaint... are only revealing themselves. We each take on Life thru our own filter system. Our own particular rose-colored glasses. Or distorted, divisive defensiveness. A distinct... finicky... dislocated world view. It seems humans can't help it. Wired as we are... we're just being ourselves. Even tho others may mistakenly be calling their misinterpretation *you*.

Interacting with other people is hard.
Not interacting with other people is hard.
Choose your hard.

Many times, the person we are hardest on is ourselves. Sigh. Our self-conversation... our inner narrator... our commentator... rampant with self-criticism and caustic remarks. You know one of The Best Things you can do for yourself?

Stop picking on your fine self.
Give it a rest.
Let yourself off the hook.

The process of personal transformation begins as we loosen the grip of our negative self-talk. Not always falling for our hurtful, limiting self-beliefs. Moving thru Life... before we begin our own process of self-renovation... our fears, anxiety and self-inflicted limitations have the loudest voice. Are the most convincing. Most real. Upon examination, however... these cynical voices are not the most true.

In my early 20s, I rode in the back seat of a friend's car... traveling north on Hwy 101 from West Hollywood to San Francisco... where we shot a film about the Life and work of the artist, Jesse Allen. I remember the amber glow of afternoon light casting a tawny flush on the gently sloping hills... like the flank of a lioness. Riding along, enjoying the beauty rolling by... a voice in my head decided it was time to let me know:

"You are the only person who can hurt yourself.

You are the only person who can help yourself.

You are the only person who can make yourself grow."

Alrighty then. Clear spoke. Those words... that concept... definitely made an impression.

Hurting yourself. Helping yourself. Making yourself grow.

Grow how? Help how? Hurt how?

One of the ouchiest ways we hurt ourselves is our inclination to revisit past emotional pain. Ripping the scabs off.

Rehashing. Slights. Embarrassments. Shame. Poor choices. Feeling awkward. Our wounds... self-inflicted and otherwise. Scraping off emotional scabs... infection sets in. We re-infect our tender feelings with misery and despair. Poking at them... these wounds hurt fresh. Even tho they happened years ago. Digging at your tender emotional wounds. So tender, it feels like it's all happening again right now. Ow.

This rehashing is suffering we do not have to endure. We bring it on ourselves.

"You are the only person who can help yourself." You help yourself as you release your habitual stinkin' thinkin'... a lot of which is kvetching about yourself and your Life. Our struggle as humans is redeeming ourselves from our own neglect and self-abuse. Self-condemnation. Rescuing ourselves from self-hatred and harsh self-criticism. You help yourself by figuring out ways to be compassionate and kind... to yourself.

As you exercise self-kindness... your relationship with yourself changes. You relate to your self without badgering... without harshness. You begin to develop a simple and direct affiliation with the way you are. Rather than habitual self-harassment... you begin accepting yourself. As you are.

You see your self-limiting patterns... and realize you can change them. Or just plain let them go. Aspects of yourself you want to change become clear. Without the drama and distraction of self-judgment... you figure out the steps leading to change. You take those steps.

Do you know what tangling with self-criticism and self-belittling really does? It keeps you engaged in distraction. That wily foe. Distraction thrives on you getting upset and ragging on yourself... losing your centered well-being. Furthering the forces of distraction... reminding yourself what a loser you are. Distraction lives to keep you engaged in anything but inner peace.

Stinkin' thinkin' gets you nowhere. This internal commotion keeps you engaged with everything but the truth about yourself. The truth of your own goodness.

Here's a helpful tool you can use to disrupt negative thinking. To change channels. This is you... developing your ability to eject the harsh clang of negative, self-limiting chatter... to consciously put in its place positive, productive verbal cues. A more uplifting brand of chatter. Clarifying your inner resilience. Taking yourself from wallowing in the self-perturbed... to where you want to be.

This is no joke. In this world we live in... energy *does* follow thought. What you think... what you chatter about in your head... has an effect on your general well-being. Your thoughts... your self-conversations... may be stinkin' or uplifting... either way, they impact the way you are in your Life. Your beliefs, and the way you show up.

In a quiet, centered moment… become aware of what you'd like to be telling yourself inside your own head. Inner chatter is part of the human circuitry. You're going to be talking to yourself anyway. Rather than tearing yourself down… your self-conversation might as well lift you up.

Give your inner chatter an opportunity to work *for* you. You get to decide what you want to be telling yourself about yourself. About your Life.

Create your own affirmation, mantra, or word phrase… emphasizing constructive, encouraging aspects of your Life. Or a positive facet you would like to be true about your Life… and the health and well-being of your inner terrain. This mantra or word phrase is for you to put in place of your hurtful self-talk. The only trick here is you *hearing* your negative self-talk as its talking. As you catch yourself berating or picking on yourself… you have this positive word phrase or mantra ready… to put in the place of your harsh inner narrative. Loaded with self-supportive assurance.

Just like ejecting a tape from a cassette player. Take the snarling, poopy tape out and replace it with words… a phrase… mantra… even a song… that lifts your inner dynamic. Run with it.

My cousin, Hal, the talented flute-player on several of my guided meditation CDs, calls this "thinkus interruptus."

As you exercise your "thinkus interruptus"... your ability to derail and move beyond your negative self-talk... it is crucial you have something positive to put in its place. As your thoughts are ragging on you... you can't just say, "Oh stop it!" Sure, the negative chatter might stop for 5 seconds... maybe 12. But then it comes blaring right back... totally disregarding your demand to stop. Sometimes your brain will actually talk back to you... "Well, if I don't think about that, what *am* I going to think about?" Ah ha! You're ready! You've got something uplifting to put in its place. Giving the ol' thinkery something new to chatter about!

Here are some examples:

"My Life is full of grace."

"Blessings and prosperity are part of my Life."

"I am grateful every day."

"I live a happy, fulfilling Life."

"I live an amazing Life."

"I am grateful for the many blessings in my Life."

"I am healthy and confident."

"Life is good to me. I am good to Life."

Obviously, these are generalizations. You can start with using 1 or more of them... to get the hang of it. Ultimately... create your own, custom-made affirmations... worded for you... suited to your Life. You can choose lyrics from a favorite song… a line of poetry… a phrase from a book. Whatever speaks to you.

This is exercise. Practice. Re-programming. Another good opportunity to be patient with yourself.

I'd love to tell you… you only have to do this once = stinkin' thinkin' be gone! Never to show up again. Wellll… that's not how our ol' habit-oriented thinkery works.

I suggest… choose one positive word phrase and work with just that one… daily, regularly… for at least a week. 2 weeks. Maybe even a month. Give this affirmative phrase time to really sink in. It's best not to jump around. Focus on one. Then… when you're inspired… move on to another.

I realize "eject"… my cassette-player analogy… is definitely old school. But that is exactly what happens. Eject the poopy, self-discouraging tape. Insert your lifting, affirming phrase or mantra = the positive tunes you want to be listening to.

This is your personal choice. Your conscious choice. Grabbing the reins of your inner narration. Making the terrain within you a friendlier place. Choosing who you'll be. Who you show up as. Who you are… inside yourself and outside.

In earlier volumes of Holy Wow!… I write about my "3 Steps to Greater Awareness:"

Listen To Your Thoughts: What does your mental dialogue sound like? What "tone of voice" do you use with yourself? What are you telling yourself day in and day out? You develop your awareness as you change your caustic thoughts and pessimistic attitudes.

Self-Kindness: A *stunningly effective* Life Strategy. *This healing balm transforms and uplifts your awareness.* Release yourself from inner neglect and abuse... from self-imposed shame and inner conflict. Note to self: Self-exploration without a healthy dose of self-kindness becomes self-abuse.

Appreciation: A Life-transforming force. Focus on what *is* rather than fixating on what is not. With appreciation... you call the wisdom of the moment out to meet you. You say "Yes!" to The Great Possibility. When you know you are blessed, you are doubly blessed. Gratitude Lubricates the Miracle.

A "being human" observation:
If you're not in Gratitude... you're whining.

What percentage of your thinking is complaint? How much of your thought activity is self-judgment?

As you actively choose to be more aware of your thoughts…
you become more aware of your feelings. You begin to see
your knee-jerk reactions. You become more aware of how
you are showing up in your Life.

With this increased personal awareness… you bring about
healthy change within your self. You can't evolve aspects of
yourself if you don't see them… when you're not aware of
them. Until you do see them… they've got you. Once you
actually *see* your reactions, habits, and patterns… what you're
doing… or not doing… you've got them. Now something
can be done.

Your emotional blisters… your unconscious reactions to
others, to input and circumstances… blind you to your own
transformation. As you become aware of what you're doing…
how you're being… you can change your beliefs and behavior to
outpicture who you are now. Rather than who you were then.

Be gentle with yourself. I know… this sounds like a foreign
concept. When you've spent decades berating yourself… it
feels kind of unusual… odd, even… to consciously be nice
to yourself. And yet… as you look at The Great Planetary
Repository of All Things… who deserves your kindness more
than you?

The more accepting you are of yourself… the more
accepting you are of others. The more tolerant you are of
yourself… the more tolerant you are of others.

The more you value yourself... and your Life... the more you value others. And the glory of Life itself.

Your emotional nature is where the work of consciously transforming your Life truly takes place. Transforming your relationship with your self. With your work... your family... your friendships... your inner terrain. The landscape of what is real for you. This is not drudge work. This is not pain-in-the-patoot work. This is you becoming happier and healthier work. This is you becoming more of your true self work.

Think of this process as inner remodeling. Refurbishing. Renovation.

Lasting transformation occurs as you honor yourself.

As you transform your self-limiting thoughts and harsh emotional reactions... you are converting your inner terrain. From a landscape of distress, anxiety, and self-hatred... to a more tolerant, accepting, compassionate self-outlook.

You "make yourself grow" as you realize... consciousness is always consciousness. It is not your consciousness changing or becoming "more"... it is your awareness of yourself *as* consciousness that awakens and grows.

Just as the sun is always shining... you are always consciousness. Even if it's overcast where you may be... or dark from your perspective... in fact, the sun is *always* shining. Even if you are having a tough time... or your awareness is not yet awakening... you are still always consciousness.

Have you noticed... as you are playing a game... like solitaire, checkers, or chess... the very first move you make affects the whole development of the game? And most likely the outcome. Your choices make a difference. Much like "choose your hard"... you choose your Life. Even when it doesn't seem that way.

Within the context and parameters of your Life... the situations, obstacles, and opportunities... you are creating your own adventure. Do I go to college after high school... or do I get a job? Do I go on a date with that new guy tonight... or do I stay home to finish my project that's due soon? Do I take the job at the bank... or the one at the real estate office? Every choice you make affects the trajectory and development of your unfolding Life. It all looks so happenstance... should I turn left or should I turn right? And yet... in the midst of it all... you are scripting the flight plan and choosing the particulars as your path unfolds before you.

Participating in your unfolding Life trajectory... is a good reason to become more awake and aware within yourself and your Life. Taming the wild stallion of your mind. Living with less of the stinkin' thinkin' gafuffle. Less emotional raking yourself over hot coals. Fewer useless distractions. Less tying your shoelaces together at the beginning of the race. Fewer obstacle illusions.

Your inner resilience plays a mighty role in the way... and how... your Life unfolds. Consciously choose to tune your inner response mechanism to be exhilarated by what is working in your Life. Rather than demoralized by what isn't.

It's all an inside job.

Decide to be optimistic and grateful... rather than bummed and defeated.

> Rather than... I *have* to do this.
> Grump. Grump. Grump.
> Decide... I *get* to do this.
> Appreciating this moment in time.

An outstanding definition of an optimist: A person who reckons taking a step backward... after taking a step forward... is not a disaster. It's more like a cha-cha.

Here is an unexpected bonus: As you awaken... you begin to see the beauty... the holiness... in everyday Life. Ordinary life becomes extraordinary. Magical. The little things... the challenges... your realizations and daily knowings... the very process of Life itself... begins to nourish your soul. You start to relax within yourself. You feel better inside. Dare I say... peaceful. Centered. Okay.

You are releasing yourself to this glorious, transforming process that *is* Life.

If not you... who? If not now... when?

The Path *Is* The Goal.

❧ ❧ ❧

In earlier volumes of *Holy Wow!...* you read about the "previews of coming attractions" weaving thru-out my current incarnation. "Previews" of things destined to happen in my Life before they actually show up. Along with the voices in my head... telling me things like... "Be kind to yourself, Sister. Be kind." "Remember what this feels like, because you are going to be on the other side of it." And the abovementioned... "You are the only person who can hurt yourself. You are the only person who can help yourself. You are the only person who can make yourself grow."

I also commented earlier... as an only child with a friendly relationship with my parents... regarding their future... the only "preview" I ever got was, "I will help my parents in some ways as they age." A pretty obvious statement. Not all that insightful. I see now... this vague approach reflected my parents' own attitude toward "planning for their golden years." As members of The Greatest Generation... they were not inclined to talk about their plans for when their health declined. They did not seem to be very interested in... or even have... such plans.

As my dad turned 80... I tried to have a "planning conversation" with him. His response... "Let's wait and see what happens." End of conversation. I was well aware... this is not an effective approach. But what are you going to do? This is not a conversation I could have with just myself.

I knew from earlier discussions my father did NOT want to live in a care facility. And he wanted to be cremated. My mother made it clear she wanted to be buried next to her mother in the small North Carolina town where she grew up. This was touching... and completely understandable. My mother's mother died unexpectedly when my mother was 15. A harsh blow to her husband and 7 children. Most especially for my mom. She was the youngest daughter and considered her mother her stalwart defender and best friend. I don't think Mama ever recovered from losing her mother at such a young age.

As my parents made these 3 wishes clear, I took note... tucking this away for future reference.

On one of their visits with us in Oregon... we took my parents to The Maritime Museum in Astoria, Oregon. Scott, the kids, and I had been there before... I knew it was somewhere my dad, a history buff, would enjoy checking out. In one room of the Museum was a big, stand-up, old-time radio... literally a piece of furniture... playing a recording of President Franklin Roosevelt's December 7, 1941, "a day that will live in infamy" speech. Watching as my folks stood looking at that big radio... transfixed as the speech played… I realized, "OMG! They actually heard this speech as it was being delivered." My dad would have been 24 years old… my mother, 19.

I was struck by this moment. That fateful day as Pearl Harbor erupted… and all that followed… was a vibrant, painful piece woven into the fabric of their lives. Listening, they remembered it… not as "history"… but as real Life. Undoubtedly, recalling exactly where they were… as they first heard the shocking news of the attack. And, the next day, listening to FDR's speech. Just as I recall exactly where I was when I first heard JFK had been shot. Watching my folks that day… I thought about how my kids only know the Vietnam War from photos and movies… something they study in a text book. Like them, I had distance from FDR's speech. I read about it. I studied the war that followed. My parents lived it.

It's always been fascinating to me… the ways different countries, races, and societies treat their elders. Some with great reverence… acknowledging the Life understanding that accumulates with the passing of years. Other societies relegate their elders to the dust bin… seeing them as barely viable. Hardly worth spending time with.

In this regard… the United States and much of the Western World… demonstrates its fixation with youth. "Look at her in a bikini at 55! She still looks 25!" Rather than respect for the accumulation of years… with its wrinkles, sagging skin, and gray hair… the focus is all "youth, youth, youth!" And more youth. Old folks are just so… old.

Youth is a gift of nature.
Age is a work of art.

In Portland in the mid-'90s, I worked for a friend of ours who was a guardian conservator for the elderly frail. Altho technically this was not my usual "preview of coming attractions"… in many ways, it turned out to be very much like one. Metaphorically… this job took me to an elevated vantage point to look out over the broad plateau of eldercare matters and concerns. I learned about powers of attorney… trusts and wills… the B vitamin shots that address some aspects of dementia… funeral planning and expenses… advanced care directives, death certificates, and other pertinent documentation. My parents were in their 70s at the time and in relatively good health. I figured, "I'll stash this info away for later."

"Later" came much sooner than I could have imagined.

I went on a road trip to Oregon in September, 1972… 3 weeks after my 23rd birthday. I ended up living in Oregon for 26 years. My parents continued living in the house I grew up in near Burbank, California. We spoke on the phone a couple times a week. Especially after Isaiah and

Lyla were born… we all got together at least once a year. Either they would travel to Oregon or we'd go visit them. My dad worked off and on for Walt Disney thru the '50s, '60s and '70s… including the last 10 years of his work Life before he retired. Thru her job at the Toluca Lake branch of Bank of America… my mother had several friendly business connections at Disney. This meant there were always free passes to take the kids to Disneyland. A terrific family perk.

My parents came to visit us in Portland the month after I left my job at the guardian conservator's office. They had not been to the house we were currently living in. As I took them on a tour… my mother asked what we were doing for dinner. I gave her a detailed overview of our evening plans. We were taking them to our favorite restaurant… where they did a great job making one of my dad's favorite meals. After dinner, we'd all stroll along the riverfront. About 10 minutes later she again asked what we were doing for dinner (?). I filled her in again. Five minutes later she asked again. Uh-oh. I responded with fewer details.

This was the first I became aware of my mother's slipping mentation.

As time passed, I came to see… Mama presented very well over the phone. As her memory declined… unconsciously, she developed a most useful coping strategy… in conversation, she agreed with everything you said. "This and that happened." "Oh yes, I see." "Then she said that." "Uh huh." As she responded this way... you thought you were carrying on a conversation.

This visit was the last time they came to Oregon. After their visit... and what it revealed... the saga began. A long-distance daughter concerned about her mother's well-being.

I got their doctor's name and phone number from my dad. I called the doctor's office asking for their address. This was the mid-late '90s... before the Internet was even a thing. I wrote 2 detailed letters to their doctor expressing my concerns about my mother's mentation. I offered a few suggestions I'd learned from my job experience... including injections of vitamin B6 to improve memory decline. I never heard back from him.

The next month... I flew to Southern California specifically to go to their doctor's appointment with them. Their doctor was part of a clinic. He was in the room with us for not even 10 minutes. He asked a few questions... "How are you feeling? Everything okay?" There was a stethoscope involved... and a blood pressure cuff. He made notes. As he headed for the door... I mentioned I was concerned about my mother and had written him 2 letters. Going out the door he said, "Yes. Your letters are in her file. I've never read them." Oh, great.

Due to the blood-thinning medication they each took… they'd return to their doctor a few days later… when he would read their lab results and adjust their medication. Again, I mentioned my concerns about my mother slipping mentally. "Oh, really?" he said… heading out the door.

That afternoon… knowing my interest in the Dalai Lama and Tibetan Buddhism… my father had arranged for the 3 of us to see the recently released movie, "Kundun"… the Life story of the 14th Dalai Lama… the current spiritual leader of the Tibetan people. In Tibetan, *Kundun* means "The Presence." This was a welcome respite. Appreciated. And noticed. Altho my dad was a nice person… he rarely reached beyond his encompassing self-melancholy to do something fun or thoughtful for Dana. As an adult, I've often thought he would have benefitted from anti-depressants… since the 1950s.

I grew up in an emotional Sahara Desert. Life was pretty doggone dry. A distinct lack of juiciness. Boring. But I was not terrorized. My parents were good people. They were not good parents for me. There was a stark absence of family enthusiasm. I was never hit or berated… for that I am *most* grateful.

As I mentioned earlier… I didn't know abuse in families existed until I read an article in Ladies Home Journal in my late teens. I was floored. Husbands and wives hit each other? Some children were cruelly abused? I could barely wrap my head around the brutality and just plain mean this article revealed. Turns out it was only the tip of the iceberg.

As I've grown older, learning more about how common hurtful family dynamics are… not for a minute do I make light of my good fortune in not being a battered or mistreated child. Benign neglect… yes. Abuse… no.

There were no great highs and no great lows in our home environment. In my adult years, I would occasionally mention to others… it was as if I grew up wrapped in an emotional water heater insulator blanket. Spoken with a bit of complaint. As if I had "missed out" on… something. Stimulation? A better understanding of emotional ways and means? More family interaction and activity? Thinking about it now… I can't quite get my finger on what I felt was… missing. Not right. Worth complaining about.

During the time we were caring for my folks… all of a sudden, I had a whole new realization… a new understanding about my go-to "emotional insulator blanket" analogy.

One afternoon, as Scott and I headed out to run errands… I carried a bottle of cold water wrapped in an insulator sleeve. All of a sudden… looking at the bottle in its insulator sleeve… OMG! Awareness dawned. An insulator blanket helps what's inside it stay *what it is*. Hot or cold. Whoa. This realization brought a whole new spin to my emotional insulator blanket analogy. In that moment I saw... the dynamics of my childhood allowed me to stay myself inside. I now saw this as an opportunity to be thankful... rather than a reason to gripe a little.

This makes me think of... hold on, it appears we're spinning way off-topic here... Daym Drops, YouTube celebrity and #FoodTitan. The first time Scott and I watched Daym's Netflix show... *Fresh, Fried and Crispy*... he headed to SweetArt, a vegan restaurant and bakery in St. Louis, MO. Going in the door, Daym was spouting some trash talk... making it very clear... "I hate vegetables." He was giving owner and chef, Reine Bayoc, some fuss as she prepared a fried apple hand pie for him. Then she cooked up Zora Neale Hurston's Spicy Chicken Sandwich... which is made with no meat. Boy howdy!... did his tune change. Of the 3 restaurants featured in his St. Louis episode... the other 2 were meat eateries... he chose SweetArt as his favorite! There's a reason I'm sharing this #FoodTitan escapade with you. As Daym left the vegan restaurant, he said, "I went in a hater... I came out greater." El Perfecto! I love that!

To me, Daym's culinary epiphany was a variation on my years earlier evolution of my "emotional water heater insulator blanket" gripe. Grousing right up until I realized the insulating sleeve's true function. I found it pretty tricky... the way Life opened my eyes. That "insulator blanket" showed itself to be a gift rather than a grumble. "I went in a whiner... I came out finer."

Turns out... instead of being somehow deprived... I was way fortunate my childhood allowed me to stay what I am inside. "Well, how about that?"

Back to caring for my folks. A couple months went by... finally, on visit number 4 with my parents to their doctor... and me again expressing concern about my mother's slipping mental abilities... he said, exasperated, like I was bugging him... "Alright. I'll give her a test." He made it pretty clear he didn't think this was necessary. He implied, "I see her regularly. She isn't slipping." His assessment was based on the 7 minutes he spent asking both of them yes or no questions about their health.

He invited my mother into his office. Sitting in a chair outside his open office door... I was able to hear him ask her a series of questions.

He began with: "There are 3 items here on my desk... my pen... the clock... this red apple." My mother replied, "Uh huh." He then asked her a few other questions. The ever trusty... "What day is today? Do you know the date?" Now that I'm an older person... not tied to a work schedule... I see how these queries regarding day and date are bogus questions to ask a retired person. Sure, when you're going to work you need to keep track of certain day and date-related details. When your Life mainly takes place at home... today is today. Sure... it's wise to have a calendar around to keep track of the day and date to make it to occasional appointments, golf games, or lunch dates. Exactly which day and what date it is every day... simply does not have the same significance it does when one is active in the workaday world.

The doctor asked my mom 6 different questions... after which he said, "What are those 3 items we talked about on my desk?" My mother drew a complete blank. She did not remember a thing... not even that he had previously pointed any items out to her. As they came out of his office their doctor said to me, "You're right."

Now began certain tests, prescribed medications, and trips to a wonderful neurologist... in an attempt to slow my mother's mental decline as much as possible.

In some elders... vitamin B shots can reverse memory problems... if the older person is vitamin B deficient. My mother's tests showed adequate levels of B vitamins. Altho there are ways to slow cognitive decline... currently there is no way mental decline in elders can be stopped or healed. Hopefully, those days are right around the corner. Scientific researchers are sure working on it.

The doctor's office referred us to an excellent neurologist... a kind and present man. He was almost undoctorly in the way he listened and responded to questions and concerns. We were fortunate to connect with him. He was about to retire... after a 45-year career.

A neurologist is a doctor who specializes in diagnosing, treating and managing disorders of the brain and nervous system. This doctor we were referred to started his career in the late '50s. He mentioned to me one time... if he'd been told early in his career that by the year 2000 we would still know so little about the function and well-being of the brain... he would not have believed it. He also let me know... in his experience, I was unique in the way I cared for my mom and the degree I advocated for her. Sure, I appreciated him taking the time to tell me this. But, truthfully, I was surprised. In many ways... as with raising my children... I was flying by the seat of my pants in this vast, unfamiliar universe of eldercare. I was simply putting one foot in front of the other. One step at a time. Doing what made sense to me. As always, I was more than grateful for all I learned working with the guardian conservator. Appreciating how that information and knowledge helped me take good care of my folks.

I also give Scott a lot of credit. He dove right in to our eldercare duties. As usual, he took care of so many things around their home... as well as giving my parents his kind attention and care.

In October 1998, Scott and I bundled up our Life in Portland, Oregon… and with our 3 old dogs… drove a large U-Haul to Southern California. We moved into my childhood bedroom. Our actual move was a result of my father's first stroke. Even tho my mother was slowly declining mentally… they had been doing pretty well together. Daddy grocery shopped and made dinner. Mama cleaned up after. Yeah, a few things were falling thru the cracks… but, all in all, they were managing to hold their own.

Then came Mama's fateful phone call… "Dana, Daddy's had a stroke. He's in the hospital." In that moment… I could say I was prepared… and not prepared. In a heartbeat… our lives were now under the influence of all that phone call implied. Gears shifted immediately.

It turns out that my dad stroked on a Tuesday… he knew something was definitely wrong. He didn't say anything to my mother. She didn't notice. Unless he was paralyzed on the floor or couldn't get out of bed, in my mother's current mental state she would not have picked up on any clues something was wrong with him. They had a doctor's appointment scheduled on Thursday. Knowing this… rather than calling the doctor right away… he chose to "not make a fuss." This was our family's customary response to most of Life's challenges… including health issues. A resounding "let's wait and see."

My mother drove them to their appointment. As I heard tell… the doctor walked into the room… took one look at my dad and called the hospital. In the flurry of Life as this all unfolded, I am impressed my mom drove herself home. Remembered to call me. And remembered what to say. Again, I was on a plane to Burbank.

While Daddy was in the hospital… I set my folks up with Meals on Wheels and arranged with a recommended agency for a woman to come to the house 3 days a week to clean, cook, and keep an eye on them. This arrangement started after my dad got home from rehab and I had returned to Oregon. I called them in the evening after this woman's first day. "How did things go? Is she going to work out?" My father said, "She was very nice. I don't want her to come again. We'll be okay on our own." I called the agency the next day to cancel her services.

Until the very end… my dad was in complete denial as to my mother's slipping mental abilities. Before I realized what was going on with my mom… in Daddy's occasional notes to me in Oregon, he would write… "Your Mama's getting mighty forgetful." Yet, he thought nothing of sending her driving off somewhere by herself. Fortunately… she did manage to find her way home.

Early in our time as caregivers, I read a book about a woman with diminishing mental capabilities. One time, while driving her car she forgot what the brake was for. Whoa! This was startling to even consider. That particular degree of forgetfulness had not even crossed my mind.

As Scott and I began sharing day-to-day Life with my parents… it was challenging not to respond with hasty irritation to Mama's forgetfulness. In the swirling expectations of any moment, it was easy to forget… she can't help it. She forgets.

As I am sure is true with many families… certainly of my parents' generation… my mother's big social communication blitz was her long list of annual Christmas cards. The first Christmas we lived with them, she and I began working on this holiday project together. Because she knew who she wanted cards to go to… she addressed the envelopes. I signed our names, put the cards in the envelopes, sealed them, and put stamps on.

I began noticing duplicate addressed envelopes coming thru. At first, I didn't say anything. When the 3rd envelope addressed to the same family showed up… I snapped. Showing her the 3rd envelope… I did not hide my irritation… "Mama! This is the 3rd envelope you've addressed to Jean and Johnny! You've addressed several envelopes twice!" In a small voice, she responded… "You didn't have to tell me."

She was right… I didn't.

She was doing her very best. I didn't *have* to make her wrong. It was just an envelope, after all. Getting over myself... I chose to change channels. I become more involved in the addressing part of the project. More patient. She still addressed the envelopes... I just kept an eye out to be sure only one envelope got addressed per family.

With children and with elders, getting "more involved" is a key strategy to lubricating successful interactions.

When Scott and I arrived at my folks', they were like 4-year-olds. With my mom assisting my dad... they could dress themselves... and they played well together.

To smooth the moving parts of their morning ritual... each evening before Scott and I went to bed... we set their breakfast up for them: 2 bowls of fruit in the fridge... 2 muffin halves in the toaster oven... the table set... the coffee maker ready to go. Each morning... after they dressed, Mama wheeled Daddy down the hall to the kitchen. They sat at the breakfast table leisurely sipping coffee... eating their fruit and muffin... reading the L.A. Times.

I've got to hand it to my dad... he was beyond patient with Mama. Many mornings, I sat at the dining room table... catching up on correspondence... or refilling their many pill containers... how much of what to give to whom and when. Morning. Lunchtime. Dinner. Before bed. Wrapping my brain around organizing their pills definitely took some doing when we first got there. Sitting in the dining room, I was within earshot of them at the kitchen table. My mother would read a headline from the front page of the paper... with commentary... sometimes enthusiasm. My dad would respond... "Well, how about that." Three minutes later... she would read the same headline... with the same commentary... the same enthusiasm. He'd say, "Well, what do you know about that?" And on it went... with her reading the same headline 5 or 6 times. He never once said... "You've already read that!" "You told me that already." No annoyance. No irritation. Just a kind, steady presence to her unsteady, repeating absence of awareness.

There were a few episodes when Daddy ended up in the hospital for several days. All he could talk about was wanting to be home... at the kitchen table... eating his muffin and sipping coffee.

One time, Daddy arrived home after a hospital stay. Mama was, of course, glad he was back. She commented out loud, "I don't like when I reach over across the bed at night and Daddy's not there." I heard my dad mutter... "She doesn't reach over like that when I *am* there." Cute.

When I worked for the guardian conservator, we had about 100 clients. Every one of them dealing with some degree of dementia. Most were estranged from their children and had no one looking out for them.

The courts referred new clients to our agency for a variety of reasons. Mainly, when an elderly person needed someone to make safe and sane decisions for them. Handle their finances. Look after their best interests. Most times, this included placing our new client in a care facility.

Fortunately, the man I worked for was highly reputable and kind-hearted. A good guy. Clients would come to us as a result of, say... an elderly person came into a bank or super market saying they could not remember where their car was parked or how to get home. Or where home was. The police would be called... and our office soon after. My boss would appear in court to assume temporary guardianship.

In the office, I handled the phone calls related to incoming clients. I'm sad to tell you... calls from new client's relatives went something like this... "I hear you have my Aunt Mable. She always wanted me to have her dining room set with the 8 chairs and antique sideboard." "My neighbor, Jack, wants me to have his farm. We shook on it. There's no paperwork... but he wants me to have it." "I need to get into my Uncle Ben's house right now to pick up some family heirlooms." Their calls were always about "the stuff." Not once... and I mean literally, not once... did a person calling about a new client say, "I hear you have custody of my Aunt May. Is she alright? Does she need anything? Where can I go to visit her?"

We also received our new clients' forwarded mail. In most cases 90 percent of their mail was a variation on… "I am a professional numerologist, for $149 I'll send you all your lucky, winning numbers. You'll be rich!" "You are so fortunate! I am The Astrologer to The Stars, send me $59.95 and I'll mail you all of your best star signs for prosperity and love." Basically… "Send me your money for something worthless." Wow, guys.

I am a longtime admirer of the prophetic arts… especially astrology. It was deeply disappointing to see these potentially visionary talents used to swindle frail and hapless folks at the most vulnerable time in their lives.

Rather than praying for these ailing elders… many people were preying on them.

I saw another unfortunate scenario play out regularly when siblings were involved… or not involved… with their parent's care. This was not only with our conservatorship clients, but also with families I've known. Invariably, one sibling is doing all the work. Taking care of their parent's activities of daily living… grocery shopping… handling meds… driving their parent to appointments… making Life choices. The other siblings… who are not helping at all… somehow believe it is their job to criticize and belittle the choices and actions of their sibling giving care. It's crazy.

As Scott and I prepared to leave Portland to take care of my folks... a friend asked, "Now don't you wish you had sisters and brothers?" Without skipping a beat, I said, "No!" I was just fine handling everything myself... with Scott's help and later, Isaiah's. Much preferred... over having siblings bickering, complaining, second-guessing... and doing nothing.

Here's a cool story about one of the woman clients in the care of the guardian conservator I worked for. Rather than spending thousands a month for a room in a care facility... this brilliant woman bought herself a stateroom on a cruise ship. Her monthly expenses were less than if she lived in a retirement home. She stayed on the same ship... cruising wherever the ship's itinerary took her. Occasionally, our office received a post card from her. The cruise ship staff all knew her situation and kept an eye on her. She had access to the ship's many amenities. Her room was straightened daily. She had a wide variety of free food and beverage to choose from. A swimming pool and lots of deck space for walks... maybe even shuffleboard. Shows to attend for entertainment. Shops. Folks to mingle with.

There are many possible variations on the theme of elder living arrangements. This woman created a pretty cool solution to what can be a restrictive... often depressing... Life predicament. Well-played. Respect.

I particularly saw with our women clients as their dementia progressed... some became sweet and docile, very agreeable... and others turned into raving, screaming bitches. This did not appear related to how their personality had been before their decline. It seemed to be just where their diminishing mentation took them. Fortunately, Mama took the sweet and agreeable route. During our years caring for my folks... my mother was much easier to be around than she'd been as her full-on, fussier self.

It's true... my mother was a complainer by nature... and easily upset. One day, as we were caring for my folks, she and I were getting lunch ready. Pouring herself a glass of milk... she misjudged the rim... the glass tipped... spilling milk all over the table. She looked at the spilled milk for a moment. I waited for her usual irritated eruption. With a sigh she said, "I could laugh or I could cry. I'm just going to laugh." Whoa... *that's* different. Grabbing a towel to wipe up the milk... chuckling, I said, "Good choice, Mama."

Before my father's stroke, my parents had plane tickets to come to Portland for Lyla's high school graduation. Naturally, those plans changed. Lyla was deciding between Lewis & Clark College in Portland, Oregon and Guilford College in North Carolina to begin her freshman year of college. She was looking specifically for a Peace Studies Program. She chose Guilford. Her decision to attend college on the East Coast opened the door for me and Scott to move to Southern California and help my folks.

In my world... the hardest part of moving to help my folks... was knowing Lyla's childhood was cut short. She no longer had a home to come home to... for Thanksgiving or winter break or during the summer. Sure, she could come to Grandma and Granddaddy's house... but that wasn't the same as coming "home." Where she grew up. With her friends nearby. Interestingly... at the end of her freshman year... after we moved... she transferred to Lewis & Clark.

Our plans to move to SoCal were in full motion. About a half-hour before we were driving away from our Oregon home, my mother called saying, "You better not be bringing those dogs." Oh yeah, like *that* was going to happen. I said, "Mama, Scott and I are coming to take care of you and Daddy. Our dogs are part of our family. They're old dogs. We're bringing them so we can take good care of them, too." By the time we arrived at their home, Mama had forgotten her opposition to our dogs coming with us.

My mother fell prey to those financial con jobs I had become aware of thru my job. We arrived in their home to find many bogus charges on their credit card bills. "Lucky Canadian Lottery Tickets!" "Send us your money to get this free thing!" "Win Big Now!" For decades, my mother was a bank executive... proud of her career... her financial skills and knowledge. One of the peculiarities of Alzheimer's disease... people with Alzheimer's have little or no insight into their developing mental deficits. This puts them at risk.

In my mother's mind, she was still a top-notch banker. When unscrupulous folks called asking for her credit card number... she gave it to them. I was stunned as I began to realize the situation. That was *so* not her! As I quizzed my folks about these credit card charges... my dad said, "Mama gives her credit card number out over the phone." Hearing his words, indignantly she said, "I do not!" He said, "Yes... you do." "I do?"

I asked my dad, "Why didn't you stop her?" "I didn't want her to make a fuss." In my dad's reality... it was better to lose money than to risk imagined conflicts by confronting his wife.

For the most part... a person does not realize they have Alzheimer's. The people around them do.

Of the reported cases of dementia... 60 to 80 percent are diagnosed as Alzheimer's... a disease of progressive memory loss and impaired mental ability. Alzheimer's is caused by biological changes in areas of the brain which control thought, memory, and language.

This mental decline affects the person's ability... to participate in conversation... to perform tasks... to attend to everyday activities. They have trouble paying bills and handling money. As the disease progresses, their daily Life is disrupted by their difficulty making decisions and remembering where things are. Eventually, the person may have trouble walking or even speaking at all.

Alzheimer's definitely brings personality changes. My mother was always a fairly gregarious person… engaged in what was going on… enjoying being part of the conversation. She became much quieter… interacting in conversation less and less. I wondered at the time… was she aware something was "not quite right"… causing her to hold her tongue for fear she would say the wrong thing? Or could it have been she was less and less able to follow the course of the conversation? Easily could be a combination of both.

So, here's a sad piece… my dad was not an emotionally expressive man. I can imagine many people reading that, thinking… you know a man who is? Thru my childhood… it would have meant so much to my mom to hear a loving, acknowledging word from her husband. Having grown up in that scenario… here I am, the adult daughter… sharing day-to-day Life with them in their declining years. This is when Daddy decides to start saying sweet things to my mom. Here's the poignant part… in her dementia, these kind, verbal tidbits did not connect. His acknowledging words made not a ripple in her awareness… sliding by… water off a duck's back. Oh, Mama. So sad. I am the only person aware of their relationship dynamic… or lack of it… in their earlier years together. Now, here I am watching… as my dad's belated efforts to be sweet… prove to be too little, too late. Sigh. Poignant, indeed.

For nearly 50 years my parents had wonderful next-door neighbors, Ken and Irma. The 2 couples enjoyed many outings and adventures together. A few months after Scott and I arrived, Irma told me… a couple years earlier, the 4 of them were out one evening for dinner and a show. Irma and Mama were standing together… waiting while Ken and my dad got the car. My mom turned to her dear friend and said… "Irma, I'm lost."

Ken and Irma definitely noticed something was slipping with my mom. Even tho I lived 1,000 miles away… Irma said to me, "I hoped you would notice." I thought, *I wish you had told me.* Again, an instance of older folks "not wanting to talk about" illness, decline, or difficulty. As I mentioned earlier… my mother presented very well when we spoke over the phone. It was not until they came to visit us that I went… "Uh-oh."

Caring for my mother… I learned there are 3 stages in the progression of Alzheimer's. In the 1ˢᵗ stage memory begins to go awry… demonstrating more forgetfulness "than usual"… difficulty following thru and completing tasks… unable to follow the thread of conversation.

With the 2nd stage memory loss and declining abilities become more pronounced. People fail to recall the names of loved ones and longtime friends... even forgetting what their relationship is to people they have long known.

By the 3rd stage... the person is bedridden... neither talking nor able to get around.

One of Scott's aunts lived in stage 3 for several years. Not really living. Basically vegetating.

People in a persistent vegetative state may open their eyes, make sounds, or move... but they show no signs of awareness... neither of themselves nor of their surroundings. They often wake up and fall asleep at regular intervals... and have basic reflexes... like blinking when startled by a loud noise.

A person can linger in a vegetative state for years. Their cerebrum... the part of the brain controlling thought and behavior... no longer functions. However, their hypothalamus and brain stem... both managers of vital functions... breathing, blood pressure, body temperature, heart rate, sleep cycles... continue to operate. The person is there... and yet, not there. For their friends and family members... this is a distressing, heart wrenching time.

Age is the best-known risk factor for Alzheimer's disease. Altho I am sure you've heard of unfortunate early-onset cases where people are diagnosed in their 40s or 50s. There are studies looking at the risks created by unhealthy lifestyle choices: lack of exercise… a poor or unhealthy diet… drinking too much alcohol… smoking.

Hereditary factors and genetics are suspected to play a role. Having a first-degree relative… a parent or sibling… with Alzheimer's increases the risk of developing symptoms by 10 to 30 percent. However, genes do not determine destiny.

As I mentioned… our neurologist was confounded that after 50 years, still so little was understood about the human brain. With Alzheimer's disease, researchers know *what* is happening in the brain… they still can't figure out *why*.

If you find symptoms of dementia developing… either with yourself or a loved one… make an appointment for an initial evaluation. This will determine the extent of the problem and check for possible contributing factors. Detecting the disease early is helpful in many ways… including planning for the future and creating an effective treatment plan. Slowing the person's mental decline has significant impact on all concerned.

Recognizing there is no cure for Alzheimer's disease… treatment focuses on improving quality of Life. Loved ones or caregivers help the person maintain brain health… manage behavioral symptoms… slow or delay the progressive decline of the disease. Soon, day-to-day assistance will be required.

An absolutely vital consideration for families caring for declining elders:

Don't burn out the caregiver.

With this in mind... at the end of this book, after chapter 9... you will find 2 "Afters." One contains resources and suggestions for the health and well-being of caregivers. The other discusses documents and affairs to have in order to facilitate the legal aspects of caring for the elders in your Life and, ultimately, transfer of their resources.

Because I was living in Oregon and my mother in Southern California... with my dad not inclined to pick up on or identify her symptoms... I have no idea when her indicators of mental decline actually began developing.

My mother was a lifelong solitaire player. In Portland, I came across a new way to play solitaire... Tri-Peaks. Visiting my folks one time in the early '90s... enthused to share this with my mom... I said, "Mama, I want to show you a new way to play solitaire!" I arranged the cards for Tri-Peaks... which looks very different from the traditional solitaire set-up Mama was used to.

Seeing the cards in this new arrangement she said, "Oh Dana, I can't learn that." I heard her response and became defensive... "She just doesn't want to learn this new way to play from me." Years later, in the context of what had become very clear… I realized… her response had nothing to do with me. Unrecognized by me… at the time I showed her Tri-Peaks, her mental abilities were already declining. She wasn't saying, "No, I don't want to learn something new from you." She was saying, literally, "Dana… I *can't*." This did not occur to me at the time.

Going thru my folks' decades-long accumulation of stuff… I came across a 3-ring notebook where my mother kept crossword puzzles she'd done. Evidently, for years. Toward the back of the notebook… it was poignant seeing the squares for words filled out less and less.

Ours was a multi-dimensional eldercare opportunity. Physically, my mother was doing pretty well. Her declining mental abilities definitely limited her day-to-day Life. In the context of his decades-long practice of participating very little in family Life… my dad was in pretty good shape mentally. Years earlier, after a fall, he became blind in his right eye. After his first stroke, he was paralyzed on the left side of his body. He was a big man… over 6 feet tall and big-boned. Our challenge as caregivers was to not hurt ourselves as we helped him… from bed to wheelchair… wheelchair to toilet… in and out of the car.

As our caregiving chapter unfolded… our son, Isaiah, was 24. He flew from Portland to spend Christmas, 2000, with us at Grandma and Granddaddy's. At that time… both of my parents were in wheelchairs. They were both incontinent. After the holidays... Isaiah returned to Portland, buttoned his Life up... and came to join us on the care team. Scott and I are ever-grateful for this choice he made.

My mother died at the end of March, 2001. Her birthday was September 11. On the morning of September 11, 2001, I was the member of our care team who would wake my dad up and get him ready for his day. I imagined waking him up saying, "Today would have been Mama's 79th birthday." About a half hour before I was going in to get him up, Lyla called.

"Have you seen what happened?"

"What do you mean 'what happened'?"

"Turn your TV on."

"Why? What's going on?"

"Airplanes have crashed into the World Trade Center."

"WHAAAT? Are you kidding?"

I turned on the TV.

As that unimaginable day unfolded... I was thankful Mama had passed 6 months earlier. Even in her dementia, my mother's tender feelings would've been hurt that this terrible attack happened on her birthday.

We'd been caring for my folks for several months when a day came decked out with a particularly frustrating series of interactions with my mom. One particular exchange being: "Mama, you need to take a shower." "No, I don't. I just took a shower." "Mama, you haven't showered for days." "How do you know that?" "I live with you."

I came to Scott and said, "*This* is the Patience Olympics!"

Patience tested daily. Sounds just like child-rearing and relationships, doesn't it? In all 3 cases... kids, elders, friends and lovers... you can count on stuff happening. Now what are *you* going to do with it? Let's see... in every moment... it's my personal choice how I'm going to respond. Tweaked and twisted? Spraying my grudgement? Or... as the flow goes... riding along with it. Doing the best I can. Complete with good attitude.

"Row, row, row your boat gently down the stream.
Merrily, merrily, merrily, merrily... Life is but a dream."
Cha cha cha.

Scott and I were so blessed. Yes... there were aggravating incidents in the course of our eldercare saga. Yet, all in all, my parents were pretty easy to get along with and care for. We were fortunate. I mentioned earlier... as my mother declined mentally... she leaned in the direction of sweet and agreeable rather than shouting and raving. As I said... Mama was actually easier to be with in the day-to-day during this period than she was as her full-on, fussing self. Small favors. Actually, that one was pretty large.

Thanks to my mother's decades of working for Bank of America... during the years employees were valued and received excellent benefits... my folks had outstanding health insurance. This was definitely a beneficial lubricant as their health declined... for their many doctor appointments and consultations... their hospitalizations and various therapies.

I am grateful.
With the help of my husband and son...
I kept my parents safe.
We gave them kind, loving care.
At the most vulnerable time in their lives.
Karmic agreement honored.

CHAPTER EIGHT

Age Is A Work of Art

"You'll see… it's a captivating ride."

Thanks, guys… for arriving back "on time." Okay so, right in that sentence, are 2 bits of human colloquial lingo. Males and females on Planet Earth are also known as "guys" and "gals." Somehow "guys" became a catch-all moniker pertaining to both women and men. As in the greeting… "Hey, guys!" Or the query… "What's up, guys?" Just a point of clarification… some women aren't keen on being referred to as "guys."

And "on time"… do you remember? We discussed that phrase in your earlier Orientation. Being "on time" is a human acknowledgment of punctuality. In social interactions, it is considered "good form" to show up for a date or appointment at the agreed upon time. More human-speak... "good form" like "well-played" indicates doing something with style and flair. Classy. Righteous.

One of your Orientation learning modules had you watching watches. I appreciate the way you utilized your newly developed Earthtone time protocols to be here at our agreed-upon time. It could be said... your grasp of that tutorial certainly proved *timely*... another little quip... a play on words there. You will find... some humans love that kind of verbal repartee. Some call it "banter."

Interestingly... as fractious and disjointed as Human-kind can be... the majority of humans on Planet Earth have come to a mutual agreement regarding... "What time is it?" Acknowledging the sun is rising on some areas of the planet while others are just tucking into bed... humans have agreed upon The Time and divided it into "Time Zones." Their current time standard... Coordinated Universal Time... is based on Earth's rotation.

In the Earth year 1884... a group of astronomers and representatives from 25 countries convened in Washington D.C., in the U.S. of A., to devise The International Date Line (IDL). This agreed-upon imaginary line of longitude passes through the mid-Pacific Ocean... exactly halfway around the world from the prime meridian. The prime meridian, in Greenwich, England, is also an agreed-upon, imaginary north/south line establishing 0 degrees longitude. The day begins on the west side of the IDL... starting in Asia... moving on to the Middle East. Europe, Africa. Swooping around the planet in an east to west fashion. The last time zone of a given day... passing thru the Hawaiian Islands... collides with the east side of this Line. Then... zoop! There's that ol' sun... rising again. It's nice the world's humans can agree upon something. I hear it keeps the trains running on time. That's a little historical jest.

On a clock or a watch... as we speak of humans of Earth keeping time... each day begins 1 minute after the stroke of midnight. Having familiarized ourselves with this Earthtone temporal jargon... shall we move on? Let's.

Resuming your Enhancement Upgrade Seminar... our itinerary today has several fascinating components built right in.

I'm sure you recall from Orientation... here in The Interpretorium, your B.E. Suit... the Bio Energy Simulator you are currently installed within... is the healthy 35-year-old model. Today... with an assist from good ol' Realizmotron... you will experience what it is like to be an ageing human of Earth. This process of growing older definitely has its quirks... along with a few qualms and inconveniences. In many places on the planet, you will be eligible for "senior discounts."

Here again, patience lubricates the myriad moving parts… for the elders… and those who care for and about them.

One thing an older human will tell you is glaringly apparent… some days are better than others. This refers to physical well-being, mental agility, and emotional peace. Thru-out your human incarnation in general… you will have good days and bad days. Days when you are feeling good physically. Getting things done. In a fine mood. And the less-than-stellar days. When your little wagon is draggin.' Everything that can go wrong does. You're feeling kinda grumpy. Not nearly as much fun… nor as exhilarating… as the good days.

As you are an ageing human… this whole "good days/bad days" actuality becomes significantly more pronounced. Serious. Noticeable. Your good days will feel especially perky… you're standing straighter… breathing deeper. Getting that drawer cleaned out… or your address book organized. Maybe doing some yoga. These activities feel enjoyable… rather than efforting. These are good days to do something creative… a hobby or project. Writing a few letters… getting them stamped *and* mailed. Maybe having lunch with a friend… or catching up on family phone calls.

Then there are the days when you won't exactly feel like grabbing Life by the reins. You don't feel like grabbing the reins period. You get up later than usual. Energy depleted.

Joints ache. Even easy movement leaves you winded. Mental processes are foggy. Where did I leave my phone? I going to have to take a nap. Did I leave the garage door open? I'm pooped. I'll definitely call and have something delivered for dinner. When I find my phone.

In this case, "pooped" means feeling drained or droopy. Tuckered. Your incarnant vehicle has run out of gas. As you know… I favor tossing in these human vernacular phrases… idioms, euphemisms, expressions… patois/patwa… jargon, lingo… to familiarize your Enhanced Audio Receptor System (E.A.R.S.) and your human conversation buds with local-speak. For when you're on Planet Earth and you want to talk story with your fellow humans.

In the Earthtone time period known as the later 19th century… also identified as the late 1800s… there lived a human incarnant who was famous for talking story. He had much to say… often saying it with humor and flair. Considered the first worldwide celebrity… "Known to everyone ~ Liked by all"… Mark Twain was a towering figure in American literature. I mention him here today to share with you 2 of his wise, insights:

"Kindness is the language which the deaf can hear
and the blind can see."
So true.

And this nugget of clear observation pertaining to today's Enhancement subject matter:

"Do not complain about growing old.
It is a privilege denied to many."

"A privilege denied to many." A privilege, indeed. Death at a young age presents loss of so much. Loss of years of just plain living... lost potential... lost experiences. Lost love. Families grieving the loss of a beloved. Communities... of every kind... suffer the cost of losing colleagues and collaborators... integral participants. Vital influences.

Numerous times... you will hear humans lament... "She died too young." "He had his whole Life ahead of him." "So sad... her kind, helpful ways lifted so many people." "They won't know what to do without her." "He won't get to watch his children grow up."

You may recall the crucial "dying too young" explanation from Orientation. The segment about your human Breath Allotment Packet. The bottom line being... you enter the human realm with a predetermined number of breaths. The span of your Earthtone Life... from your All Access Entry Threshold to crossing your Terminus Threshold. How many days, months, years... moments... you are assigned to live in your human packaging. All determined by the number of breaths commissioned in your pre-incarnation Breath Allotment Packet.

This number is firm. No more... no less. While you are in human form... there is no way to add breaths to... nor subtract breaths from... your current incarnant allotment.

Breaths. An inhale + its accompanying exhale = 1 breath. A yawn... 1 big inhale + 1 big exhale = 1 breath. A gasp... 1 quick intake of breath + 1 exhale = 1 breath. A sigh... 1 inhale + 1 exhale (with or without vocalization) = 1 breath. A sneeze... 1 quick intake of breath + 1 explosive exhale (messy sometimes) = 1 breath.

During Orientation we discussed human breath physiology. A healthy adult, at rest, draws about 16 breaths per minute. This calculates to a little fewer than 1,000 breaths per hour... 23,200 breaths per day. The average human draws more than 8,000,000 breaths in the span of a year. Your Breath Allotment Packet can contain anywhere from 1 breath to 777,777,777 breaths per lifetime. Occasionally, more than 777,777,777 breaths are allotted. This may sound like a swell idea... more time to knock around on Planet Earth. But, I gotta tell ya... by the time you've gotten to nearly 800 million breaths... your Bio Energy Navigation Gear is pretty well spent. Nearly kaput. Your shelf-life is wavering. You're about to drop off-line.

As you incarnate… your breath allotment embeds within Your Etheric Sconce. Your total number of breaths is an item of incarnant information completely veiled from your conscious human awareness. There are incarnants who have dreams or insights about their death… seeing the way they will die. But thinking in terms of the number of breaths you have been allotted… highly unlikely that will ever cross your mind.

Coming to your last breath… you simply drop off-line. This may happen after a long, extended illness. You may be in a coma… you will hardly notice as your venue changes. You may stumble… or fall off your bike… hit your head… and that's it. You may nail your demise thru a chemical overdose. You may choke on a piece of meat… or a crisp rice cake… or a bite of banana. Whenever it comes… even after a long illness… for those left behind, it will be too soon. Too abrupt. Too final.

It is this pre-incarnate allotted number of breaths… that determines whether you are one of the "privileged" humans who gets to experience the value and vagaries of living into your "Golden Years."

While ageing itself is a biological process… what it means to be "young" or "old" is a social construct. There is no inherent cultural meaning in the biological process of ageing. Different cultures imbue youth and age with their own societal concepts, context and meaning... in their space and time.

Humans define ageing in different ways:

"Functional age" measures age by capability... taking into account social, psychological, and physiological "age."

"Chronological age" is based on the calendar... adding up the years from a person's date of birth.

Older people contribute in many ways to their families and communities. A longer Life can bring unanticipated opportunities to an elder. Pursuing new activities. Getting to know their grandchildren. The treasure of further education. A person may finally have time to engage in a passion long-neglected... as the demands and obligations of their younger years played out.

The extent of these opportunities and contributions greatly depends on one factor... Health.

The circulation of blood thru-out the human body is a very basic and essential part of ongoing good health. Yes, this is an involuntary process... a human has no immediate control over the flowing of blood thru their body. Due to assorted biological factors... circulation slows as years accumulate. As poor blood circulation develops... the possibility of blood clots increases. This is particularly true regarding blood flow in the lower extremities... the legs and feet.

Elders slip and fall... breaking bones... scraping or puncturing the skin. The general healing process slows as circulation declines... posing greater possibility for infection and complications.

At the biological level... a wide variety of molecular and cellular damage accumulating over time... brings ageing to the human instrument. The effects of this accumulation lead to gradually decreasing physical activity and mental capacity. Included is the growing risk of disease and disability.

I will be perfectly clear... these organic changes do not operate in a linear fashion... nor are they consistent. They are only loosely associated with a person's age in years. Using the example of humans who have reached their 70th year... some who are this age enjoy good health and are high-functioning. Other 70-year-olds are frail and require significant help from others. These differing reactions to age continue to be true into a person's 80s and 90s. Frailty comes to many ageing humans... but not to all.

Within the ageing processes... there is a lot of both nature and nurture going on:

> the accumulation of time passing
> spins around the sun
> decades of gravity's substantial pull
> family genetics
> previous habits and addictions

healthful choices and mindful awareness
environmental conditions.

These factors all influence the process of how any human ages.

An observation shared in the human realm:

> Along with age comes wisdom.
> Sometimes age comes alone.

Every human instrument ages differently. There are some commonalities, of course. There are common symptoms for stroke or heart disease or breathing limitations. These diseases and ailments can be diagnosed or identified by their symptoms. The ways the physical body is presenting... or the mental body behaving.

Even in the same individual... ageing can show up in diverse ways in the different bodies... mental, emotional, and physical. Due to habits of lifelong fitness... an older person can be strong physically, but their genetic ancestry could deliver slipping mental capabilities. An elder could "have all their marbles"... a euphemism for being mentally functional... yet for various physical reasons, need to use a wheelchair.

Some humans would say... "It's a crap shoot." Meaning... a gamble... a risk. An adventure. Truly... you just never know. Seldom, if ever, do you have any idea what's coming.

This is, of course, true at any age. Especially true... more striking... as human age advances.

I'm sure this is obvious... in their older years, the accumulation of a human's lifelong habits and practices distribute their just reward. The effects of behaviors, compulsions, and addictions mount up.

In your younger years you may have chosen...

— to not be aware of the quality or quantity of the fuel and fluids you ingest

— to not exercise or follow a fitness regimen

— to allow addictions to alcohol, nicotine, or drugs and other substances to govern your Life

— to continually allow angry, resentful thoughts to fill your inner terrain

These choices calcify as the body ages.

Carrying extra weight because of poor food choices or lack of exercise puts undue stress on your internal processes and your bones and joints... particularly your spine, hips, and knees. Oh, them knees! In the middle of the 20th century... several years after the Second Great War... humans developed surgeries to replace ailing hips and knees with artificial joints. These joint replacements bring welcomed relief from constant pain. After rehabilitation and physical therapy... these all-important joints are again quite serviceable.

Your ankles and feet can take the brunt of this extra weight and lack of fitness. They ache and swell. Poor circulation in the lower extremities becomes a troublesome issue.

Of course... if you made healthy, attentive choices thru-out your incarnation... eating whole foods with an eye to reduced fat and sugar... regularly exercising and stretching your physical body... making healthy choices within your thoughts and emotions... your ageing bodies should be more comfortable... easier to be living in. Yes... they should.

I'd love to tell you... "This will definitely be the case!" But, alas... countless are the vagaries... the quirks of Life... that come to a human of Earth.

Yes, it does "make sense"... a human expression for when something seems reasonable... that a human instrument with a healthy background of choices would age "better" or "easier" than a body abused by lack of awareness or discipline. Many times, that *is* the case. Yet, also, some harsh ailments can be woven thru-out a human's older years... which seem to have no interest in nor connection to earlier healthful practices. Or lack thereof.

Just before our session today... I spoke with a Recent Returnee who lived his last Life on the West Coast of the North American continent. In his recent incarnation, he consistently made healthy choices and stayed physically fit. Three times a week he played racquetball... a high-intensity running and whacking game. He was in great shape... which is a human descriptive for a fit, lean person. Playing his usual Wednesday afternoon racquetball game... he had a heart attack and died. Right on the court. In the middle of the game. He was age 52. Many folks said his death didn't "make sense." It certainly did not seem reasonable.

There are ailments installed within human genetic material that can derail your later years... no matter how fit and mindful you may have been thru-out your incarnation. Hardly seems fair.

Oh, I do want to let you know... "That's not fair!"... is a real psycho logical snag for humans of Earth. With much exclaim and commentary. Spoken sharply. With frustration and disappointment. Disappointment is a harsh teacher for the human psyche.

A note to your human self... things are not always "fair."

Disappointment and discouragement generate around many a human situation or circumstance. This is also true in the realm of relationship and human interaction.

Understandably... shock and disappointment are a frequent human emotional response to a difficult Earthtone medical diagnosis. When a doctor or specialist says... "Your lab results have come back. Things do not look good."

There are many therapeutic discoveries still to be made as the world turns. Western medical practices appear fixated on treating symptoms... indicators of disease or disability... rather than finding and treating the deep-rooted cause. As medical science stands right now on Planet Earth... many human ailments can be mitigated... their debilitating symptoms lessened or moderated. But not cured.

There are stealth ailments... especially cancers... which invade the physical body unawares. The mechanics of these diseases can go on for years... grabbing a solid foothold in the physical body... before symptoms display to call attention to their presence. Not even on the lookout for signs of such destructive disorders... the human host is caught off guard. Unprepared. "What do you mean I have cancer?"

Characterized by the development of abnormal cells... cancers divide uncontrollably... with the ability to infiltrate and destroy the body's normal tissue. Building tumors. Tumors are a swelling... a lump... caused by this abnormal growth of cells. Tumors can be benign... non-cancerous... or malignant... with signs of cancer. Many times, the appearance of tumors is an indication cancer is present in the body. Other symptoms include bleeding or unexplained fevers or night sweats. Cancer can drain the body's energy... bringing extreme fatigue or unintentional weight loss.

Cancers have the ability to infiltrate nearly every part of the physical body... brain... breasts... internal organs... bone and skin. Cancer can metastasize... spreading from tissue to organ to bone thru-out the body. Many times, cancer is not discovered until it has been in the body for several years... undetected as it accomplishes its damage. Because of its cell dividing activity... no organs or body parts are spared from the risk of this disease.

It is interesting to note... the human heart... the great physical body pump mechanism... is only exposed to carcinogens... cancer causing agents... if they are present in the blood. Combining this relative lack of exposure + the fact that heart cells do not often replicate = very little cancer of the heart muscle.

The all-important heart can develop its own difficulties and ailments. Diseases of the heart are the #1 cause of human death thru-out Planet Earth. One of the most common complications is failure of the heart. This occurs when the heart loses its strength... its ability to pump enough blood to meet the needs of the physical body.

This declining propulsion ability is frequently caused by narrowing arteries... which have filled with a material called plaque. Plaque consists of minute amounts of fatty substances and cellular waste products building up in the arteries over time. The artery walls become thick and stiff... restricting blood flow. Less oxygen-rich blood is reaching the heart muscle and the rest of the body. Difficulties ensue.

Some humans are born with genetic or inherited heart defects which can have lifelong influence on their health and well-being. Looking at other problems related to the heart... one finds quite an assortment of ailment possibilities. Heart rhythm abnormalities trigger complications... as do heart infections. Valves of the heart can become diseased... disrupting blood flow. Other debilitating conditions include diseased blood vessels... or structural problems causing the heart muscle to harden or grow weak. This weakness causes blood to pool in the chambers of the heart... leading to blood clots... which bring their own unique blockages and problems. Blood clots increase the risk of stroke or pulmonary embolism.

A pulmonary embolism is its own special calamity. A pulmonary embolism occurs when a blood clot gets lodged in an artery of the lung... blocking blood flow to that part of the lung. Most times, these blood clots travel from the legs... rarely from other parts of the body. Tho, yes... that, too, is a possibility. Physical symptoms... shortness of breath, chest pain, cough... lead a person to seek medical intervention.

Prompt treatment to break up the clot is in order. Administering an anticoagulant... a blood thinning medication. Treating with other interventional drugs or therapeutic measures. Sometimes surgery. These procedures improve blood flow and greatly reduce the risk of death. Wearing compression stockings and engaging in physical activity can help prevent clots from forming in the first place.

I don't usually go into such physical mechanism detail. Perhaps while human... some of you will find it useful to be aware of this treatment protocol.

As with so many ailments that come with age... early detection can lead to an easier path of stabilizing wellness. Quality of Life is where it's at.

Another health concern increasing as humans age is termed a "stroke."

In the language called English... "stroke" is a very busy word. It is one of those word sounds with several different meanings. When you row a boat... applying a stroke to the water with your oar moves you along. Playing the game called golf... your score is based on the number of strokes you take hitting the ball with your golf club. Looking at a clock... one might say... "At the stroke of midnight." When drawing or painting... you spread your paint, pastel, or charcoal onto your paper or canvas with a stroke. You hit or smack somebody with a stroke. Or, completely opposite... moving your hand with gentle pressure over fur, hair, or skin... you softly caress with a stroke.

A stroke is also a medical emergency.

This kind of stroke happens when the flow of blood to the brain is suddenly interrupted. Cerebrovascular accident... or CVA... is the medical term for strokes. Brain cells begin to die within minutes.

Stroke is not a one-size-fits-all commodity. Every person's stroke is completely unique. Tho there are different kinds and degrees of stroke... the after-effects show up in common, recognizable ways. The effects of a stroke run the gamut... from instant death... to permanent or temporary paralysis or disability... to a period of garbled words. Sometimes a stroke is barely noticed.

As we established during Orientation... the human brain is an extremely complex organ. Thru numerous diverse physical and biochemical processes... the brain controls the entire body and its many varied functions. Blood carries Life-giving oxygen to organs, tissues, and muscles. As the blood flow blockage of a stroke restricts blood... oxygen is kept from reaching specific regions of the brain controlling particular body processes and activities. That area and its functions are damaged.

The aftereffects of a stroke depend on:

The area of the brain injury.

The location of the obstruction.

The extent of brain tissue affected.

The chemical changes in brain function.

The longer a stroke remains untreated... the greater the possibility of brain tissue damage and resulting disability.

The damage becomes clearly evident as the impaired part of the body does not work the way it once did.

The 2 hemispheres of the human brain each control different processes and activities thru-out the body. Depending on which area of the brain is damaged... a person may have trouble walking, speaking, or comprehending.

Looking at an array of a half dozen objects... when asked, a stroke victim may not know which object is a "hairbrush." But they can identify "which of these objects would you use to style your hair?"

Early treatment with the appropriate medications and therapeutic protocols can minimize brain damage caused by a stroke. Treatments following strokes focus on limiting complications and debility. Emphasis is also on, hopefully, preventing additional strokes.

One of the first post-stroke treatment protocols is assessing the stroked person's ability to swallow. A stroke can cause paralysis, seizures, muscle tightness or stiffness. One of the most basic human abilities... swallowing... is almost always impacted. Leading to choking and other complications... as aspirated liquid gets into the lungs. In this situation... it is easier... causing fewer problems... to swallow a thicker liquid, like a milkshake... than a thin liquid like water. This leads to putting a measured amount of guar gum or xanthan gum thickener in everything the stroked person drinks. Then watching carefully for signs of choking.

The vast complexity of brain function means a stroke can affect a person's ability to:

Move their legs, arms, hands, and fingers.

Speak, recall words, and use them correctly.

See well and remember details.

Read, write, and communicate with others.

There can be emotional and behavioral changes... altering mood and outlook. Stroke survivors often experience great fatigue.

Many times... especially with therapy... pre-stroke skills can improve or even return over time.

I will say again... each person's stroke is completely, uniquely their own. As are their reactions and responses to this Life experience and what is happening to them.

Any cancer survivor... stroke survivor... heart attack survivor... will tell you... it is one thing managing the physical components of their ailment, treatment, and recovery. It is a whole other thing coping with one's own far-ranging emotional and mental reactions to these unexpected ripples in The Force.

Any survivor of any human Life trauma will tell you... mental and emotional issues usually are more of a big deal... more of an attention-grabber... than coping with the actual troubling physical circumstances. What humans tell themselves inside their own heads. What they do to themselves inside their own hearts. Oy vey!

As you are being human… conditions of Life trauma might include:

Physical activity severely limited due to a stroke or heart ailment

Disappointment in losing a job or a project you were counting on

The shock of an unanticipated health diagnosis

The painful end of a relationship…

each a hard hit. Tough to deal with. Psychologically challenging. And yet… here again, they don't call Earth the Planet of Paradox for nothin'.

There is an enigmatic psycho logical precept related to being a human of Earth. If given a chance… if you're willing to entertain the possibility… these tough situations are designed to be the perfect crucible for deepening your spiritual awareness. For developing your psycho logical capabilities. Resilience. Options.

As well as being tough and challenging… these difficulties are also opportunities. I know you remember… earlier in our Orientation Sessions I talked about the "whack." A hard, stiff whack… like the Life traumas just mentioned… can offer you a profound opportunity to learn more about yourself. To do some deep excavating inside. To open to the living of your Life in a whole new way. Making new choices. Deciding which perspective serves you... and whether it's time to move beyond certain views of yourself and your world. Time to let go of doubts and limitations. Becoming more of who you're meant to be... now.

Your upcoming incarnation on Planet Earth is not a lark... a caper... a fling. Especially as a member of this Orientation pod. You have better things to do than wallow in pain and anguish... doubt and fear.

A hard, stiff whack is a wake-up call. Wake up to your self. Your awareness. Your resilience. Who are you... who are you becoming... now that this whack has disrupted your Life? Your activities of daily living... and all the other stuff... are not going to stop so you can wallow in a pit of despair. Wallowing might seem attractive... for about a minute. Truth is... you're going to keep putting one foot in front of the other. Certainly physically. Especially psycho logically. Definitely spiritually.

In potential... as your human Life rolls on... you will come to see the whack for the gift it is. An opportunity to wake up. Waking up to who you are and who you are becoming. To who you are meant to be.

Patience. Patience. And more. Patience.

Now is a good moment to engage your Recall + Retain Button. When you are human... in the aftermath of Life trauma... remind yourself: "I am willing to pick myself up and look around inside." Explore. Let go of self-inflicted limitations.

Find you.

Which sort of attitude are you going to convey... thru your everyday actions and choices... as your Life continues to unfold? How are you going to show up in your world now?

Patience is key. With yourself... as you move thru your own turmoil. Remembering self-kindness. Self-compassion. Self-care. Patience with others... as they move thru the turmoil in their Life. Compassion. Kindness. Caring.

Every human deals with varying degrees of inner and outer turmoil. Every one.

It's a set-up. Don't let the turmoil win. Don't let it define you. Your Life has dignity and purpose. Design. Meaning. Portent. Value.

Whatever age you are when you wake up... consciously reconnecting... realizing your Dharmic Life Intentions... you will only get older. Now is the time to exercise your patience muscle. Patience as you deal with your own ageing and health issues. Patience as you care for and support others thru their travails.

You've heard it before: Love. Serve. Remember.

A short while ago, we welcomed back to The Realm of Clear Light a Planet Earth incarnant who served as a spiritual guide for many humans beginning in the mid-late 20th century. On Earth, he was known as Ram Dass… describing himself as "a sort of spiritual uncle to a consciousness movement bringing the East and West together." The "sort of uncle" with his own fascinating back story.

Before embracing his Life purpose as Ram Dass… he was a go-getter Harvard professor named Richard Alpert. As a cognitive researcher… he was drawn to investigate the psycho logical and physical impacts of psychedelic substances on the human brain and body. His explorations… considered much too radical at the time… got him banned from Harvard.

Still seeking… searching for an approach that would allow him to experience the powerful, mystical states induced by these psychoactive chemicals in a more stable, permanent way. Wondering… were spiritual practices… meditation, yoga, breathwork… a viable answer? His Life's journey… his path… led him to India.

Thru a series of mundane events and magical moments… at age 36… his consciousness… his Life… transformed at the feet of his Hindu guru… Neem Karoli Baba. Fondly… Maharaj-ji.

Upon returning to the country called the U. S. of A… Ram Dass wrote an inspiring and influential book… *Be Here Now*. This book proved to be… and still is… an evolutionary guide for many humans.

One of his famously insightful remarks:

"If you want to see how enlightened you are,
go spend a week with your family."

If that comment is not funny to you now… if it does not bring a knowing grin… it's perceptive meaning will reveal itself to you as you cruise thru your upcoming Earthtone incarnation.

With his Life progressing into his later years… Ram Dass, recognizing his "uncle" status… saw his work evolving to guide Baby Boomers… the generation born right after the 2nd Great War…. to "not to be frightened of ageing."

Teaching them… and generations to follow… not to be terrified of illness, ageing, and death. "That it's okay."

Ram Dass was working on his book… *Still Here: Embracing Ageing, Changing, and Dying*… wondering what he was going to write for the ending.

At age 65, he had a near-fatal stroke.

He was left paralyzed on the right side of his body… which means the left hemisphere of his brain was stroked. As so often happens with left hemisphere strokes… not only was his right side paralyzed… he also experienced expressive aphasia… limiting his ability both to speak… and to find the right words.

He observed… "I now had an ending for my book because I discovered dependency, sickness, and all that. But every new change brings you wisdom." In his usual forthcoming manner, he readily admitted… that wisdom was not apparent at first. "I was depressed."

"There were three sufferings. The suffering of the body. The suffering of my ego, from being an independent person to being dependent. And the spiritual suffering, because up until then, I had led a graced life ever since I met my guru. The stroke didn't look like grace. So I thought I was at the end of a graced life."

Ram Dass lived an additional 23 years after his stroke. Speaking slowly and deliberately… he continued teaching and lecturing. He maintained his spiritual practices.

Thru this difficult period… his decades of spiritual practice allowed conscious awareness to inspire the authentic well-being of his inner Life.

Describing his reality:

> "My stroke pushed me inside.
> And it's so wonderful.
> I don't wish you the stroke.
> I wish you the grace from the stroke."

A significant spark in the igniting of human awareness... the many books and recorded talks Ram Dass generated continue to guide his fellow humans along their path. Onward... developing their spiritual awareness thru the challenging landscape of ageing, illness, and death:

"Death does not have to be treated as an enemy. Death imbues this moment with added richness."

Here is something you will find to be true as you are human yourself: Currently on Planet Earth... as people consider their own decline and mortality... this elevated, embracing, "added richness" outlook of Ram Dass... is not "the norm."

Within the chaotic minutiae... the whirlwind of details... the weaving fabric of daily Life... it does not occur to most humans to become more aware. More reflective. To embrace the vast tapestry of more mindful perception. Taking the time to realize their role... their connected involvement... within The Greater Scheme of All Things. That very realization itself = the "added richness" part.

A note to your soon-to-be incarnating self... considering the vast cauldron of human awareness possibilities... this state of being... this attitude Ram Dass lived within thru such a rough time... is worthy of your exploration.

Most people are psychologically paralyzed as they contemplate their own death. Horrified. The basis of the human term "mortal fright."

Few people cultivate an awareness of what is actually happening... as they draw their last breath and cross their Terminus Threshold. With their next breath they are reborn. Returning into The Vibrant Love Light Energy of The Glorious Away and Beyond. The Great What Is.

Humans of Earth reside within their own astral-etheric kit of distressing psycho logical elements. These Life components keep them absorbed... entrenched and entranced... by the might of their own anguish. Their own intricate entanglement. Their own enchilada of despair.

This entrenched anguish... this entangled distress... is directly related to the karmic B.I.A.S. the humans of Earth steep within. Like a tea bag boiling in scalding water. Their Belief I Am Separate from God... Source. Fundamental True Light Reality. Has them all mixed up. All fired up. Confused. Defensive. Wary of self. Wary of others.

Wary of Life.

Abandonment issues. And all that entails. Suffering. Rejection. The deep emotional pain of being neglected.

Humans believe God has abandoned them.

And they believe God is a "He." Who judges humans oh-so-harshly for their fragility... their failings and missteps.

You want to just shout at Earth's humans... "Give the Big Guy a break!"

"He" is not judging you harshly. YOU are judging you harshly.

For humans of Earth... a principal feature of the aforementioned "astral-etheric kit of distressing psycho logical elements"... is a fear of being alive. "What if I'm not doing it right?" "What if they're out to get me?!"

Every human resides deep within the dilemma of their own personal pain. In a spasm of frightened uncertainty. Convulsions of confusion. Constricted... in quiet, deep, perpetual fear.

As if terrorists are hiding in the kitchen.

Embedded deep within each incarnate human is a core of self-hatred. I'm not clear if this is a result of their B.I.A.S... or a reason for their B.I.A.S.

I know! A core of self-hatred. Who thought *that* was a good idea?

The approach of Earth's esoteric scholars and teachers has long been "don't tell them about it!" Don't let humans know about their unruly core. Let me ask you here and now... doesn't it seem this formative information would be useful for people to know?

Okay, there is this perspective to consider... in centuries past on Planet Earth... the general approach to the evolution of human awareness... metaphysical knowledge and practices... mystical insight... existed in a mantle of deeply shrouded reality.

In this era of Extreme Consciousness Sport... as Human Awareness Upgrade spills thru-out the 21st century... the time is *now* to reveal a greater, more beneficial truth.

Please engage your Recall + Retain paraphernalia for the upcoming.

Here's the deal... that core of self-hatred is a ruse. A trick. Subterfuge. A very convincing ruse. A ruse that gets a lot of harsh psycho logical air time. "Oh, you tricker!"

Here's the real trick! This deceptive core... unreliable in its convincing scam... is not the final gate. Is not the end-all be-all of human awareness. There is so much more.

Here, where we now are, in The Realm of Clear Light... it is easy to grok... to simmer within The Multitudes of broad, vast, Love-Conscious Awareness. Even as you are an incarnate human... individualized... wrapped in your skin package... there are Multitudes within you. Multitudes. So much more than self-hatred and vengeance. So far beyond mistrusting your self and your Life.

This leads us to appreciate a clarifying metaphor. On the side of your desk is a small drawer. See that knob? Pull the knob. The drawer opens. Inside you will find a dried peach pit. Take the peach pit out of the drawer. Do you feel how rough and craggy it is? You will notice… at one end is an intense, piercing point. Sharp as a needle. This rough, coarse pit is an effective representation of the human core of self-hatred. A craggy metaphor for the agony of painful self-abuse.

But wait! Hang on a minute. What if this coarse pit… this core of self-hatred… is not the end of the story? What if this craggy pit with its painful sharp point contains within something unexpected? Something unforeseen.

What if there is a smooth kernel… the seed of self-love… waiting inside the rough, craggy pit?

You want to know something? There *is!*

The rough and hurtful "core of self-hatred" is just the outer shell… a coarse disguise.

Go ahead… pry open this hard pit. You will find… there it is! The kernel of truth nestled within.

Oh, those dear humans. Compelled to react to self and Life as if self-hatred… and the toxic stew it brews… is their only choice. With their harsh inner voice. Their habit of self-neglect. Looking for who to blame. Complaining. Criticizing themselves… their world… and the people in it. Ruthless, judgmental dialogue filling their inner reality.

Now… believing in that core of self-hatred is proven

a mistake. These constrictions are based on a lack of clear vision. Not seeing the whole picture. Falling for the ruse. Not digging deep enough.

Now *there's* a hefty, spicy enchilada for you!

Transformation times.

As a human incarnate… your nature… the very core of your being… is Love. Huge, all-encompassing Love. Not boyfriend-girlfriend love. Not parent-child love. Not "I love you, therefore you will do everything I want you to do" love. Vast and wide Love. Curling your toes… with deep, perceptive, comprehending Love.

The Love That Heals.

Enthralled by their core of self-hatred… humans have whipped themselves hard. Punished themselves. For centuries. Millennia. Humans reside deeply embedded within their continual fear of reprimand. Not trusting themselves. Not trusting their Life. Energy follows thought.

As you are compelled by your fear of a person or situation… your fear of something bad happening… you draw it to you. You make it happen. You create the mental/etheric environment for it to show up.

Humans get very twitchy about this prospect. "I did NOT draw those painful experiences to myself!" Well… you did and you didn't.

Of course, nothing is simple. Humans love simple. A quick sound bite. Alas... when is Life ever simple? Ever just black and white?

Life is ever more vast and multi-layered than it first appears to inadequate human perception. Karmic complexities and deep-rooted implications... whisked into the stew.

Bottom line: What are you going to *do* with it? Whatever "it" is. In this case... "I did NOT draw this to myself!" Are you going to calcify in your personal outrage? Spinning in anger and indignation? Parboiling in that reaction is not the ally it wants you to believe it is.

Will you allow yourself to open to the intricate vapor trails of complexity? The multi-faceted jewel of self-renovation? Will you allow yourself to settle... search... seek? Become?

As mentioned... many times, what first appears as pain or difficulty... frustration or disappointment... darned if... as Life travels, twists and twirls... there is also some unforeseen elaboration available. Enhancing developments. A pleasant surprise, perhaps. Insight. Revelation. Something good.

Note to self: When human... don't always fall for your first grasp... your first read... of a person, event, or situation. Chances are *really* good... there's more. More to learn. More to remember. More to realize.

I know. You've heard this a zillion times before... energy follows thought. It's physics, Babe.

Busy as you will be being human... there is one certainty to be mindful of:

Thoughts are things.

This dynamic is a variation on "What you see is what you get." What you see, perceive, realize... and what you call it... is the story you tell. Your Life as you see it. The "what it is." How it's all playing out for you. What you are telling yourself about it. Whatever "it" is.

As a human... you're thinking. Rambling around inside your own head. That's what humans do. Who knows... maybe you're grousing. Doubting. Anxious. Perturbed. Concerned about your well-being. Or someone else's. Fretful as you contemplate an upcoming event or meeting. As energy tracks thought... etheric substance is activated... calling sub-atomic particles into action. This emergent activity initiates developing pattern, form, and experience... currently known on Planet Earth as "quantum mechanics." This activation continues accumulating cellular substance until form and experience show up right in front of you.

This etheric, sub-atomic excitation does not only develop physical form and experience. It also arranges and configures... pattern, manner, form... in the vibratory field of human emotional and mental bodies. Ideas and realizations emerge. Music, art, and movement coalesce. Emotional constructs... pain and desperation... compassion and joy... align and materialize.

Harsh inner vexation can manifest harsh external happenstance.

Kind, considerate inner dialogue shows up in Life in its own way.

Gratitude is a game-changer.

In human form... awareness of this interplay... perceiving the way thought and energy maneuver and materialize... is a bridge to the infinite. The harmonic chemistry of the ineffable. Playing out thru human emotions, actions, choices, and deeds.

Here is yet another example of Earthtone poles and spectra. Vast and profound. One pole being humans who embrace and understand the etheric interplay of compassion, gratitude, and reality. The opposite pole... those embedded deeply within their human brand. Weighed down. Constricted by limitation... and misinformation. Stuck in the muck of personality... disposition, temperament, and opinion. Need and greed. Like that's all real.

Between those 2 poles... human contradiction and promise loom. And find expression.

The real question: What are you going to do about it? Your choices. Your circumstances. Your character. What are you going to do *with* it?

How will you show up?

Humans get stuck. Paralyzed by doubt and circumstances. Fear of consequences. Of losing out. Succumbing to the safe parameters of making it thru the day. Moving onward in Life calls for too much. "What if it's risky?" "What if I don't like it?"

Life may be dismal. Drenched in pessimism. Saturated in misery and gloom. Stagnant. "So? Nothin' I can do about it." Some fall for the familiar lethargy of cynicism and apathy. "Who cares?" "My Life may suck, but at least I know what to expect." Those parameters. Limitations... self-imposed and otherwise... are not even questioned.

Some humans paralyze themselves, concerned about "doing it right." Or things "looking right." With variations of "I'm not good enough" stirred into the mix. "I can't apply for that new project ... what if I don't do it right?" "I can't ask her to marry me. What if she's not the right one?" "This new philosophy feels so right. What if it's steering me wrong?" "I don't trust myself... how could I ever trust my Life?"

Shoots! Way to tangle yourself up!

Don't let paralysis by analysis win.

Over-analyzing... what's right? When's right? Who's right? Am I right?

So afraid of being wrong. What if I'm wrong? What if my beliefs are wrong? This is all wrong.

Afraid of being thought ill of. Or reprimanded. Inner human dialogue is frequently a litany of defending oneself.

– From whom?   – From what?   – Why?

It's exhausting. Sometimes, excruciating.

Also, we've got to acknowledge... as well as their deep-seated Belief I Am Separate... human fright is a carryover from the hormonal biology of their Animal Kingdom ancestry. Deeply rooted bio-reactive chemicals and instinctual tendencies. Fiercely territorial. Immediately leaping to fight... over perceptions, opinions, stuff... females. Suspicious of others. Starkly apprehensive of the unknown.

Being wary of others and the unknown has its advantages for members of the Animal Kingdom... based on their instinctual inquiry: "Am I dinner?" This leap to suspicion and distrust... is often less advantageous in Human Kingdom interactions.

As humans begin to grok their "fright"... don't you know there will be much whoop-dee-do about whether this is innate or learned. Nature or nurture. Perhaps this reactive process is best described as... osmosis.

Osmosis:
The process of gradual or unconscious assimilation
of ideas... concepts... knowledge... notions.

Nature? Knowledge? Nurture? Notions? Hmmm . . .

362

Does a young human wake up in their crib soon after birth and go... "Holy pudding! I'm separate from God!" Maybe. Maybe not.

More likely... establishing your B.I.A.S... allowing it to incarcerate your awareness... happens thru human societal osmosis. Repeated exposure to the beliefs and attitudes... of dominant older humans... parents, siblings... teachers, coaches. Newscasters. Television hosts. Internet influencers.

Oh, where does the fright begin? And what am I going to do about it? Now there's a worthwhile question.

We could go on and on. And on. For the moment... we'll leave further disclosure to your own situational awareness... paying attention... during your upcoming incarnant explorations as a human of Earth.

Here's a clue worthy of engaging your Recall + Retain button:

It's not how you start...
It's how you finish.

A clue to take to heart.

Now we will again engage good ol' Realizmotron... moving on to our next in-depth segment about your upcoming Earthtone incarnation.

Having considered some of the background on human ageing... I'm going to adjust Realizmotron's whiz knobs to take you and your bio-energy simulator on a jaunt thru The Ageing While Human Chronicles.

Again, I direct you to the drawer on the side of your desk. This time you will open it to find a mirror a little bigger than the palm of your hand. You may recall from past Earthtone incarnations… humans have long used this mirror device to gaze upon their own reflection. "How do I look?"

Those clever, inventive humans have developed many ways to use mirrors far beyond gazing upon their own appearance. Utilizing mirrors… they've devised mechanisms to bring far away objects visually close… telescopes. They put mirrors in microscopes to make teeny tiny organisms visible to the human eye. People install mirrors to view what's going on behind them while driving their automobiles. And at times… I've actually seen this… a mirror is held under an unconscious person's nostrils, just above the top lip… to determine if they are alive. If they are breathing… little puffs of condensation show up on the mirror's reflective surface.

Mirrors = A handy dandy human device.

Take a moment to check it out… this particular mirror is designed to either stand at an angle on the surface of your desk… or, with an easy adjustment… the support stand becomes a handle you can hold. Grip the handle… lift the mirror up to see your face.

In the context of today… you will use your mirror in its "gaze upon your own reflection" mode. You'll be able to observe the changes ageing brings to the human facial features.

Using your mirror… take a good look at your face and hair as it is now. This visual setpoint will allow you to more clearly observe the modifications that age brings to human skin and hair. Also, often seen particularly in male energy units… your nose and ears may grow significantly larger as you age. Why *is* that? I don't know. Could it be the effect of decades spent in the pull of Earth's gravity? Maybe it's genetic. A combination of both? A puzzlement for sure.

Adjusting my whiz knobs… your ageing face is now in its early 60s. For this simulation we are going *"au naturel"*… with no additional make-up or hair dye. Make-up… rouge, lipstick, paint for eyelashes and brows… and hair coloring… "wash the gray away"… are popular human camouflage. "Age-concealers"… in "Western" or "developed" countries.

Watching in your mirror… you will see the skin on your face start to slowly sag. Do you see folds and wrinkles beginning to appear? As human skin ages… it becomes less elastic. Less flexible. Less supple. More fragile. The body's production of natural oils decreases… making skin dry. Fat in the deeper layers of the skin diminishes… causing loose, saggy skin. Lines become more pronounced. Thus… wrinkles.

See those little lines branching from the outer corners of your eyes? Those are called "crow's feet." To clarify that moniker... Realizmotron is projecting onto your mind's eye a photo of a crow's footprint. Clarity achieved. These crow's feet by your eyes are also known as laugh lines... depending on your general persuasion. You can call them what you'd like.

Some humans are just fine with these sags and wrinkles... "I earned them!" Others... in the throes of prevailing youth-fixation... freak out. "Oh my gosh! I look so *old*." You will hear some women comment... "Oh no! I look like my mother!" Sounding like it's not a happy realization.

Humans have cultivated a whole field of "plastic" surgery... for people who insist on having their skin cut, stretched, reshaped, and injected so they can look... not so old.

Do you notice the color of your hair changing?

Human hair color fades with age... becoming various shades of white or gray. Hair texture can become more coarse. The quality of your hair... its "shine"... may dull. If you are in a male simulator with a beard, goatee, or mustache adorning your face... you may notice "salt and pepper" coloration setting in.

For hair, too... humans have developed myriad notions and potions to "hide the gray." Some of those hair coloring potions are really stinky.

Watching your changes of face and hair is pretty fascinating, isn't it?

Moving beyond the mirror... the fascination continues. The majority of this Realizmotron segment today takes place inside your body. You... experiencing the human ageing process. The years *do* accumulate. You will feel the changes... mental and physical. The biological adjustments the body adopts... as it adapts to its many spins around the sun.

Just a note here... not every human remains in their incarnating instrument into old age. As has been observed... it is a privilege denied to many. A large percentage of incarnants meet their breath quota... passing out of incarnation in their younger years... from birth to 50. Here in The Interpretorium... we have no idea which of you will continue drawing The Sweet Breath of Life into your later years... 50 to 100+. We give these ageing-while-human experiences to all of our pre-incarnants. You'll see... it's a captivating ride.

Now... please stand up in your B.E. Suit. Move around the room. Refresh your body memory. Particularly, give your attention to the ease of movement and balance that is you... in your 35-year-old human body simulator. Notice how sharp and clear your vision is. And the keen sound quality of your Enhanced Audio Receptor System. These 2 senses... sight and hearing... can both decline significantly with age.

We have plenty of space here. By now, you are well adjusted to moving in your simulant physical body. There is little concern you and your arm or leg limbs will smash into any other body. You can walk or jog. Dance. Leap. Do jumping jacks. Pirouette. Fire those cylinders! A human mechanical reference. This movement gives you a feel for… the energy level… the breathing and biomechanisms… of a human body in its 30s. A physical body as it is settling into adulthood.

Have at it! That's another human verbal expression. Oh, here's one… Get your groove on! Along with the equally appropriate… Do your own thing!

As your 35-year-old body is moving around… you don't even look at your feet. You're just moving.

Now, Realizmotron has placed a ball on the floor in front of you. Without looking at your feet… kick the ball. Kick it again. And again. Each time without looking.

Now, stand still for a moment. Close your eyes. Feel yourself balanced in space. With your eyes closed… bring an index finger up to touch the tip of your nose. Yep, there it is.

Successfully completing these 2 actions…kicking a ball without looking at your feet and touching the tip of your nose with your eyes closed… means you have good proprioception. Proprio… *what*? Proprioception. I know… 5 syllables. That's a 75-cent word if ever I heard one! In a minute we'll delve into what it means.

Now, as you continue moving around the room… thanks to the marvels of Realizmotron… I will gradually adjust the whiz knobs to engage your ageing-while-human processes.

You will begin to feel some of your joints getting stiffer. You may be feeling some aches. Are your hips, knees, or ankles beginning to complain? Shoulders, elbows, and wrists can squawk, too. Even your thumbs and the joints of your fingers.

As is true in the human tribe… some of you will feel these increasing aches and pains more than others. Ageing is not a one-size-fits-all endeavor.

If you are moving actively right now… you will notice age-related changes in your breathing. Does it feel like you are not getting enough air in your lungs? This is called being "short of breath"… or "winded."

Those of you who are jogging or pirouetting might want to scale back a bit as we continue. Your ageing body's balance… your spatial equilibrium… becomes more of an issue.

Changes in the physical body's ability to maintain its balance creep up on you. As the years go by…the stability slope gets more slippery. There are several possible causes. Many elders experience chronic illness… taking medications which may contribute to unsteadiness. Long-term physical conditions… Alzheimer's disease or Parkinson's… multiple sclerosis... arthritis or heart problems... often affect the human nervous system and the physical body's balance.

Poor mobility and balance... as well as losing strength in legs and feet... generates increased unsteadiness. As I adjust my whiz knobs... are you feeling that? Be mindful. This instability can lead to falls... and breakage. When older humans fall... bones break more readily than in their younger years. Hips, wrist, ribs... a konk on the head... uh oh. The process of recovery is slower. There can be complications. Poor circulation of the blood... and thus, cells deprived of vitalizing oxygen... is often the culprit for both slow recovery and complications.

Note to your older self: You'll be keeping track of where the bathrooms are. Again, due to a variety of issues... weakening control of muscles being top of the list. You'll want to be able to find those bathrooms. You will be using them more often. This can also lead to using special pads and/or adult underwear... being prepared for annoying leakage.

Now... proprioception = the physical body's equilibrium apparatus. The human body's 6th sense. A person's sense of self-movement and position in space. Healthy body balance and stability utilizes a biological message pathway from the feet to the brain. Mechanosensory neurons are located within muscles, tendons, skin, and joints. These are known as proprioceptors. They are *everywhere* thru-out the human physical body. These sensory receptors receive position and movement stimuli… then transmit this information to the brain. In a nanosecond.

In a younger body… this is a nearly unconscious mechanism. As the years accumulate… this physical body balance network begins to falter. A person loses their fluidity steadying in space. The deterioration of this equilibrium lattice also can contribute to falls.

Now I'll adjust Realizmo's whiz knobs… giving you a body experience of a person who has prioritized health and movement… exercise, dance, running, hiking, yoga… thru-out their Life. As you move… your body feels balanced, fluid… at ease. Certain of its place in space and time.

However, because the majority of humans find it challenging to establish an exercise routine… I will now slowly adjust the whiz knobs for you to experience an older physical body that has not "taken good care" of itself. This is a theme with many variations. Usually having to do with "too much." Too much alcoholic beverage. Too much cigarette smoking. Too much eating heavy, greasy food. Too much sugar foods and sugary "pop" fluids. Too little healthful movement and exercise. This ageing body… now overweight and sluggish… feels very different than you felt a minute ago when you were ageing in a fit body.

371

While incarnate, you will find... especially in societal facets of Western or developed countries... people are judgey about other people being "fat." We hold no judgment here in The Interpretorium. We're simply going for a dose of reality. Each human hoes their own row. For a multitude of reasons and choices, each person is fit... or not. Is overweight... or not. We believe it is instructive for you to experience both ways an ageing body can be.

These habits of eating and exercise bring us back to "is it nature or is it nurture?" What do you think? I believe it's definitely some of both. Some people are born in a physical body that tends to be lethargic and low energy. Perhaps they're born to a family that sits around a lot. Other people are born in a physical body that is energetic and invigorated. Maybe they grow up in an "up and at 'em" family... playing tennis, golf, team sports. Each aspect... each choice... proves to be a defining element.

As with every single thing on Planet Earth... here, too, we find poles and spectra. One pole... a sluggish and heavy physical body. The other pole... light on their feet and energetic. With every possible variation... choice... eating, moving, sitting... variating in between.

These experiences in your B.E. Suit... show you there is quite a difference between the ageing physical body and the body at 35. I'm sure you notice... your ageing human body is not as nimble, agile, or strong as it was when we began this Realizmo segment. Lifelong habits and tendencies catch up with you.

Oh wow! Are you feeling those aching joints? And kind of jerky movement? Like you've got "a hitch in your get-along."

This ageing segment is not only about the physical body. Continual behaviors and practices establish effects and consequences in a person's mental and emotional bodies as well. This shines light on our persistence here at The Interpretorium… don't let negative self-talk and toxic emotional reactions calcify in your inner Life. The accumulation of noxious beliefs and behaviors only adds more difficulty to your elder years.

As you are standing or moving in your ageing simulant body… if you find yourself feeling lightheaded or weak… put your hand on the back of a chair or the wall for support.

As cancers, heart disease, or arthritis continue taking their toll on the body… a human can feel a lot of pain and discomfort. Physical and otherwise. As physical age advances, you might experience tremors and shaking. There is also mental concern and emotional anxiety. "What next?" This may lead to isolating. Devolve to grumpiness. Or a short fuse.

Now is a good time to sit back down at your desk.

Take a look in your mirror again. Your reflection might look a little fuzzed. Let's explore vision changes. With age… in this case, as a human accumulates 40 to 50 years… lenses in the eyes become less flexible… making it difficult to focus up-close. Reading a book or newspaper. Looking at a map or text message. Small font becomes indistinguishable. And numbers… "Is that an 8 or a 3? Is it a 5?" Reduced to a blur. "What does that say?" Thus, humans invented "reading glasses."

Again… some people's vision declines more than others.

Adjusting whiz knobs… you are now looking at your reflection thru prescription reading glasses. Ah, yes… looking sharp.

For some of you, my words may sound muffled. You might be having trouble understanding all I'm saying. Age-related hearing loss occurs gradually… you may not have even noticed your hearing diminish as I slowly adjusted the whiz knobs. Oftentimes the people around the hearing-declined person… their family and friends… notice their hearing loss more than the individual does. "What'd you say? Speak up!" Again.

Ageing can bring deterioration to the inner ear and along the nerve pathways to the brain. Prolonged exposure to loud noises… at any age… contribute to hearing loss. Loud noises can damage the teeny-tiny hairs in your inner ear which are instrumental in conducting sound properties to the brain for interpretation. These hairs can be neither repaired nor replaced.

Sometimes the hearing-loss culprit is simply excessive earwax. A build-up of earwax… your ears' equivalent to sweat… can temporarily reduce how well your ears conduct sound. So, flushing out earwax may be a good place to start if your hearing seems to be diminishing.

There is significant concern about humans suffering from age-related hearing loss. As a person deals with… or doesn't deal with… their declining hearing… they may begin isolating themselves. Their hearing difficulty hampers participating in conversation. They avoid socializing due to embarrassment. "What if I say the wrong thing?"

This withdrawal from interacting with others is neither healthy nor helpful for the ageing person's well-being. Isolating is *not* a solution. Rather… it is avoidance of the inevitable. Hearing aids. Yes… humans have created devices that can improve diminishing hearing capacity. Like so many aspects related to ageing… quality of Life improves as a person is able to hear better.

As is often the case with current human healthcare… hearing aids address the symptoms of hearing loss. These aids amplify external sound directly into what is left of the ear's ability to hear. This should not be confused with a cure.

Another intriguing aspect of ear function... many of the tiny mechanisms found inside the ear also affect a person's balance. You'll find *this* intriguing. The canals of the inner ear are filled with fluid and lined with tiny hairs... tiny as in microscopic hair cells... 15,000 of them. Yes... the very same hairs sending audio information to the brain. As a human moves their head... the fluid in the canals sloshes around... moving the hairs. Thru signals in the vestibular (veh STIB you ler) nerve... these hairs send their essential position information to the brain. A microscopic take on proprioception. As these tiny hairs diminish... human steadiness is also affected.

Aren't these human bodies fascinating?!

Using your tongue... feel around inside your mouth. Now that you have fast-forwarded into your 70s... how many teeth do you have left? Teeth fall out... or are pulled out... for a variety of reasons. Many times, decay of the tooth is not the problem. The teeth are just fine. Problems develop in the gums holding the teeth in place. The gums can become infected and swollen... causing serious complications. In many cases... diseased gums recede... shrinking away from the teeth. Teeth are less securely fixed in place. Thus... their falling out or being pulled.

As you will learn while human... chewing and using your teeth is a big deal. Teeth are instrumental in grinding...

masticating... prepping the food you eat to be swallowed and inserted into the digestive system. Teeth are also essential in the clear pronunciation of words when a human is speaking.

Humans have invented many variations on teeth-replacement devices. For centuries... humans, daily, glue into their mouth whole sets of "false" teeth... also called dentures. In the past... sets of dentures have been made from wood, gold, ivory, or lead. They've even been made from other people's teeth. Modern dentures are constructed from porcelain or acrylic resin.

In the 21st century... dental implants are gaining popularity. Rather than a multi-tooth "set" of dentures, implants replace individual teeth. A metal post is drilled thru the gum into the bone, replacing the root portion of the missing tooth. An artificial tooth... a "crown"... is affixed to the metal post. This looks like a real tooth. Works like one, too.

Dental implants offer a more permanent solution to missing teeth than dentures. Even with the daily gluing... dentures can slip around inside the mouth. This causes trouble chewing and clearly forming words. With an implant... a post is fused to your jawbone. That implant isn't going anywhere. Stable and durable... implants are a good long-term solution. Unlike with dentures, eating is easier and your speech is not affected.

In choosing between dentures and implants... a very human consideration comes into play. Currently, implants cost more than dentures.

For these next few minutes... I am going to introduce you to the brain fog associated with different levels of age-induced dementia. Dementia is a group of conditions characterized by impairment of standard brain functions. Symptoms of this diminishing mentation include... memory loss... poor judgment... decreased problem-solving abilities. Personality changes.

Symptoms of impaired mentation include forgetful-ness... as well as limited social skills and interactions. A real tell-tale sign... thinking abilities diminish to the point of interfering with daily functioning. The very basic activities of daily living require assistance. Many times, an elder with declining mentation strongly resists the suggestion they need help. They do.

Hearing myself say, "They do"... I realize in this context, that phrase can indicate 2 different truths. Yes, they *do* need help. And yes, they *do* resist the very idea they need assistance getting thru their day.

I'm adjusting Realizmotron's whiz knobs to advance your age. It has been established that 14 percent of the human population... age 71 and older... are experiencing some form of dementia. The prevalence of dementia increases dramatically with age. This disordered brain Life affects about 5 percent of humans aged 71 to 79. The muddled mental landscape increases to 37.5 percent in those age 90 and older.

Simply allow this mental/emotional fog to wash over you. Don't fight it. Witness. Experience. Behold.

Many of the underpinnings of Life seem to disintegrate. What was once your solid foundation of reality… becomes like shifting sand. Everything seems uncertain. You feel lost. Adrift.

Humans often become fearful and depressed as they consider what their ageing Life may have in store for them. If this concern and discomfort spurs them to develop healthy lifestyle choices… that would be helpful. However… many times, these fears curl in on themselves. These self-projected terrors can become self-fulfilling reality.

As you move into your human incarnation… the moral to the story of ageing human biology = Take good care of yourself from as soon as you realize you have the ability to do so. Pay attention. Situational awareness comes to mind. Then onward. Best you can.

If you're lucky… you may be born into a host family committed to teaching you healthy habits from the get-go. Or conversely… you could be born into a family who doesn't give a flying fig about establishing such healthy behaviors. For many humans, such well-being awareness does not even exist.

Now's a good time to once again engage your Recall + Retain button. Set yourself up to realize at a young age how important it is to establish healthy habits and practices. Take good care of… your teeth… your eyes and ears… your weight and fitness… your digestive tract and gut biome. Your mental and emotional well-being.

It really *is* all up to you.

CHAPTER NINE

Wily Resistance

"Yes, magic does happen sometimes."

"Do not grow old no matter how long you live.
Never cease to stand like curious children
before the Great Mystery into which we were born."
~ Albert Einstein

T hat Albert Einstein! There's a guy who truly had his finger stuck in the electric socket of Life. It's clear to all he was scientifically brilliant… curious about the properties of light and physics… and other such intriguing matters. He certainly challenged and changed the way we view our world.

Perhaps not as widely realized… Einstein was also a deeply philosophical man. Spiritual. Wise. Insightful. Providing fresh, astute perceptions about being human for us to ponder and realize.

"Stand like curious children." As mentioned… one of the major distinctions between adult consciousness and kid consciousness is an awareness of consequences. Another glaring difference is curiosity. Kids leap on out there! "What's *this*?!" Grabbing Life with both arms. Goin' for it! Some adults come equipt… dancing along with Life's happenings. Many more adults stand paralyzed. Their considerations about participating in the moment running to… penalties… significance… cost… results. Outcome. Consequences. I'm not judging. Merely observing.

The wonder of "curious children" = they're all about "This is so cool! I *get* to do this!"

As we age… that glisten… that sparkling captivation with Life… dims. Morphing into "I *have* to do this." Grunt. Complain. Deep sigh.

From "*have* to" to "*get* to"… is a smidge of inner adjustment. Hugely significant. This "adjustment" certainly contributes to how I feel about my Life and what I'm doing.

In every moment we choose inside.

A few years back… my friend, Robin, shared with me… she was feeling kinda grumpy about doing the dishes one night after a little dinner party.. Nobody was coming into the kitchen to help. Kvetching to herself... she realized she was weighed down... feeling the burden of... "I *have* to do this."

Then... because, yes, magic does happen sometimes... her inner chatter took a turn... to "I *get* to do this." Standing with hands in soapy water... her inner dialogue evolved. "I am blessed to have these dishes to wash. I am grateful I have this food... and these friends to share meals with." That's a place to live inside.

Shift happens.

Einstein encourages us "to stand like curious children before the Great Mystery into which we were born." Considering *all* the creative thinking this man demonstrated in the unfolding of human awareness... I am completely charmed that he stands in awe of the "Great Mystery."

I wonder... which Planetary System do you think Einstein came here from?

If you have read Volume I of *Holy Wow!*... you may recall... early in Chapter 1 you find one of Einstein's insightful quotes:

"There are only two ways to live your life.
One is as though nothing is a miracle.
The other is as though everything is a miracle."

He's right about that.

When you stand around kvetching and criticizing... the miracle is not yours to see. Not because it isn't here, but because you're looking in the other direction... fixating on what's wrong. Rather than what's right.

Toward the end of *Holy Wow!* Volume I... I wrote:

> "When you know you are blessed,
> you are doubly blessed."

This phrase describes a realization I came up with decades ago. There's actually more to it:

"When you know you are blessed, you are doubly blessed. When you don't know you are blessed... you're not."

Whether you are blessed... or not... is your call. It's an inside job. It's you... in the midst of a miraculous (or mundane) moment... realizing, "I am so blessed."

You are "doubly blessed" because... there's the blessing... and there's you recognizing... acknowledging... being blown away by... how blessed you are. Blessing times 2.

This was made super clear to me in a Women's Spirit Circle I offered in the early 2000s in Southern California. This was a Circle of about 10 women... most of them mothers of young children. Read that: under siege by the forces of Life. As in... they each had A Lot... details, demands, distractions... going on.

One of the women did not have kids. She was married to a guy who adored her. And financially supported her. She would share with the Circle about delightful vacations they went on together. The culinary classes she was taking. Her housekeeper. Having time and resources to decorate her home. The other women were drooling. Her Life was so different than theirs… so much of her time was her own. Yet, her attitude was complain-y. There was always something "wrong." Not quite "enough." As she talked story… her Circle Sisters would be ooh-ing and aah-ing. She would be cranky. Peevish. Irritated about some little thing that was "not right."

Watching this dynamic… I thought, "Wow. She does not see how blessed she is." Her other Circle Sisters saw it clearly.

I realized… you have to *know* you're blessed to feel blessed. To acknowledge the blessing. This is a call only you can make. When you don't… see… feel… embrace… how blessed you are… you're not.

This is also true with gratitude. Knowing you are grateful. *Feeling* grateful. This realization… mentioned earlier… came from around this same time:

> If you're not in gratitude…
> you're whining.

Take a few moments to listen to your inner chatter. You're either noticing the miracle... or you're bummed about something. Feeling "in the flow"... or complaining. Sure... sometimes your inner conversation can be in "neutral." But, as you give a listen... the foundation of your inner commentary is either "yuck" or "yum."

Also toward the end of *Holy Wow!* Volume I... I included another of Einstein's sage insights. His deep appreciation of The Wonder of Life reveals... he not only had his finger stuck in the "physics aspect" of the electric socket of Life. He also perceived and genuinely valued the rhythms and patterns of relationship within this "Great Mystery into which we were born."

Einstein said:

"Strange is our situation here upon earth. Each of us comes for a short visit, not knowing why, yet sometimes seeming to a divine purpose. From the standpoint of daily life, however, there is one thing we do know: That we are here for the sake of others... above all for those upon whose smile and well-being our own happiness depends, for the countless unknown souls with whose fate we are connected by a bond of sympathy. Many times a day, I realize how much my outer and inner life is built upon the labors of people, both living and dead, and how earnestly I must exert myself in order to give in return as much as I have received and am still receiving."

Go Albert!

"I realize how much my outer and inner life is built upon the labors of people, both living and dead." I appreciate Einstein's nod to this continuity of consciousness we are all a part of. The vibrant flow of Life awareness streaming behind us. Our foundation. Those we come from. Our ancestors. Ancestors of our family lineage. Ancestors of our spiritual or intellectual lineage. Our tribe. The vitality of Life as it streams exuberantly thru and beyond us.

We, today, are setting the stage for those who come after us. The ones our current choices and actions support and encourage… as generations of Life continue unfolding after our time here is done.

In the future… numerous beings of clarity and Light are coming to follow us. What we do now… each individual choice… contributes to and nurtures that Lineage of Good. Encouraging present-day forces which uplift well-being… are in fact fostering the lightworkers of the future. You are an intrinsic strand in this ever-unfolding interweaving of Light.

We live within the fabric of reality… The Tapestry of Life. Each weaving our own threads… perhaps adding seashells or sequins… shiny bits. We choose our colors, our textures. A loose weave, or tight. Coarse or lacey.

Yes, it's true… we weave upon the loom of our circumstances. The warp and woof of our numerous Life factors. Such diversity. Born into poverty. Born with a trust fund. Parents who are supportive and encouraging. Parents who are cruel and hard-hearted… who should have never been parents. Perhaps a good education is readily available. Or our education barely equips us to maintain. We have to fight and struggle for everything we get. We are given advantages we do not recognize. We receive help that seems beyond what we deserve.

When someone tells us "what's wrong with you" we believe them. Or we ignore them.

We fall in line. We dance to the beat of our own drum.

We weave our Life tapestry with every choice and decision. Every belief and intention.

The way we respond to every challenge and obstacle… to every chance and opportunity… or choose to disregard… weaves the ongoing strands of our tapestry. Tangled, tattered, or smooth. Delicate and graceful. Rough and coarse. Burlap or brocade.

Life looks and feels different when… rather than a beleaguered "Why is this happening to me?"… we look at situations and circumstances as… "This is happening for a reason. What can I learn from the way this is playing out? How can I grow and become more aware?" Options.

When your eyes are open to the gift of Life's lessons... you can't unsee it. The gifts... the lessons... the awakenings... are always here. To be recognized by those with eyes to see.

Sometimes we see our Life intellectually... what I *should* do... what I *could* do. But that does not mean we can "make" ourselves do it. "I should study harder." "I should drop 20 pounds." "I could apply for that job." "I could tell her how much I like her." "I could just continue sitting here on the couch."

I was in my early 50s caring for my ailing parents... when The Patience Olympics first occurred to me. "I could write a book." About the practicality of patience in the realms of... relationship, child-rearing, caring for declining elders. At that time... I thought of this "book" as an opportunity to share my thoughts on parenting... and to offer resources to manage the many aspects of eldercare.

Now... 20 years later... as I am actually writing *The Patience Olympics*... I am in my early 70s. I, myself, am now an "elder." Holy pudding! How'd that happen? *Absolutely* mind blowing.

As you can well imagine... this definitely influences what I am inspired to share with you here. Caring for ailing elders...

yes. Caring for *your self* as an elder… now there's a whole new arena to explore. Yet, another fascinating ball of wax.

When I was in my late 20s… married to Lyla and Isaiah's biological father… each winter his parents left Portland for a month or 2. They flew to Palm Springs. There in the sunshine… they enjoyed their own coterie of fellow snow birds and a gay, mad social Life. I used to think older people went "south for the winter" because it was a groovy thing to do.

Then, all of a sudden… what's this?… I am in my mid-60s. Having been a resident of Hawaii for several years… I'm spending late-Dec till early-March living at Lyla's house in Washington DC… caring for our youngest granddaughter. It is *cold*. More snow than usual. Ice storms.

During this time… a whole new understanding about "heading south" dawns upon me. My inner commentary going something like… "OMG!" My joints… especially my ill-fated knees… really felt the cold. And complained about it.

"Ohhh… now I see." It's not just fabulous socializing drawing elders of the north to sunnier climes. It's their creaking bones and aching joints. Got it.

In the latter part of *Holy Wow!* Volume II… I mentioned… in this incarnation I am not a physical exercise girl. This comes to me both by nature and by nurture. I have long said… "If 'sedentary' were an Olympic event…

my parents could coach." We were not a physically active family. Occasionally, we walked the dog. Not very far.

For me, every day, I think, "I should exercise." This is definitely one of those moments of... "Sometimes we can see... what I *should* do... what I *could* do. But that does not mean we can 'make' ourselves do it." Oh golly.

To be accurate... for me, this is way more than a "moment." Hard-core resistance to exercise has woven thru my Life for decades. Now... as I am older... I totally *know*... if, as I say, I want to age gracefully... exercising and stretching my physical body is really what I need to be doing. Do you think I can make myself do it?

Uhh... no.

It's the craziest thing! I *know* what's good for me. I just can't manage to give it to myself.

A few months ago, I came across a thought-provoking article by Lindsay Holmes... the Senior Wellness Editor at HuffPost. It certainly provoked my thoughts. Evidently... for her own reasons... she, too, has lived her Life strongly resisting exercise. In her article... she did an excellent job of sharing some persuasive observations. I took notes.

"Exercise is a celebration of what your body can do." Interesting perspective.

"We often look at fitness as a dreadful obligation rather than a choice." She's got that right.

"Find something that takes you out of the negative mentality you might have toward exercise." That's exactly what I've been looking for. I'm here to admit... I haven't quite found it yet.

After "contemplating" (ignoring) the possibility for a few years... my 55th birthday present to myself was to join Curves. For some reason I was able to actually do this. As in... I drove there and worked the circuit. I liked it. Wonder of wonders... I *did* it! When we moved to Kona, I joined the Curves here. I continued to marvel at the fact I would actually do it... several times a week. Then, a few years ago, the Curves here closed. Fooey. I haven't found anything to replace it.

Stringing a few of Lindsay Holmes' cogent thoughts together... "A healthy cardiovascular system is high on the list of benefits that come from an active lifestyle. You're not just strengthening your heart... you're also supporting a healthy blood and oxygen flow. Keeping blood pressure and cholesterol down... reducing insulin resistance and strengthening the immune system... all of which are vital to increasing longevity."

Yeow! I *know* all of that! I know exercise is the best thing I can do for my ageing body and multi-dimensional well-being. Why am I not doing it?

If I'm the one who wants to exercise more... who is the one making crazy sure I don't? My resistance to exercise is a profound presence... like a one-ton concrete block sitting on my chest. It doesn't move. Neither do I.

My resistance doesn't say anything. Not a word. It just resists. Most successfully.

Lindsey Holmes also says, "We're trained to think exercise is for changing our body... making gains or shrinking ourselves... not honoring how it is right now." Radical. "Turning to exercise when I felt guilty about what I ate or how I looked made fitness a penalty rather than a priority." She's got my number there. I totally relate to exercise as a penalty rather than a priority. "I *have* to do this." Ugh.

Then she hit me with the big guns. In my notes... I even wrote it in caps:

"THINK OF EXERCISE AS A GIFT YOU'VE BEEN GIVEN."

A brilliant idea! A serious rejiggering of my interior physical activity landscape would need to occur.

"Spend time discovering... what movement brings you joy. What works for you?" Oh, if only I knew.

With my own commentary... I texted the link to Lindsay's article to Lyla. I am blessed with a truly remarkable daughter... a loving, magnanimous soul. Lyla and I are crazy about each other. But I'll tell you what! We are 2 *very different* people. Here is just one aspect of our vast differing.

On her workday mornings… Lyla goes for a run on her way to work. She arrives early so she can swim laps before her day in the office begins. She regularly works out to exercise and yoga videos. She *likes* exercise. You can easily see how unalike we are with just this one example. There are *many* more.

In my text to Lyla I wrote… "Truthfully, I would be / have been uncharacteristically stupid… to not change fitness from a penalty, a drudge, a whiney I Don't Want To… to a priority. Obviously, this is a good time in my Life to change my mind (where it all starts) about fitness. Change from I HAVE to do this to I GET to do this. Who's in charge here? My Resistance CANNOT continue to win!"

I texted those words to her a few months ago. Has much changed? Not a lot.

As far as the "Is this my nature or my nurture" query… I come equipt with boatloads of both. My current self-frustration made even more huge… having watched my dad deal with physical therapy after his first stroke, 20+ years ago.

I am a big fan of physical therapy. Physical therapists should get a lot more "Recognition For Awesomeness" than they do. Physical therapists actively transform peoples' lives… from disability to capability. Giving them back the utility of form and function their illness or injury took away.

By the time we were caring for my folks... thanks to my 2 corrective knee surgeries... I'd had my own forays into physical therapy. Working at a Portland massage school in the '90s... also made me aware of the benefit of good physical therapy. I knew several people who had worked their way back from paralysis... either resulting from a stroke or brain trauma. I was very clear... physical therapy would definitely benefit my dad.

A couple of weeks after arriving to care for my folks... working with their doctor... I began a schedule of Monday-Wednesday-Friday physical therapy appointments for my dad. I got diagrams of the exercises from the therapist and began working with my dad at home. Knowing how much this would help him... I was gung ho!

Daddy was not. Not even a little bit.

At the therapist's office... he would put a little juice into his exercises. As if he was showing off for the therapist. The therapist would ask, "How are things going with your exercises at home?" Daddy would answer, "Oh good. Good." He and I both knew that response was more than bit of a stretch.

Working with him at home... I might as well have been exercising a concrete post. He truly did not "get" how beneficial these exercises could be for him. He was defeated. He couldn't have cared less. Truth be told... I was doing all the work. He was just waiting for our exercise session to be over.

We began his 3 day a week physical therapy regimen in mid-October. In mid-December... due to the upcoming holidays... I asked him if he'd like to take a few weeks off. I said, "After Christmas, you let me know when you'd like to go back." We never went back.

Here in Hawaii... I joined the care team assisting my friend's mother. She'd had a stroke in her brain stem. I didn't know you could have a stroke in your brain stem. Evidently, you can.

She, too, juiced up her exercises at the therapist's office. I get it. At home, she was less than interested. I get that, too.

I am not judging these 2 elders. How can I? I'm my own concrete post. I write here about wily resistance... sharing with you my edge in the throes of it. I don't pretend even a little bit to "have it all together" in this Life. Jokingly, I've said... "My application for sainthood came back stamped **HUMAN** a long time ago." I live with few illusions. An assortment of aspirations, yes.

"I can't exercise right now... I'm too full." "I can't exercise right now... I'm too hungry." "I can't exercise right now... I'm too... excuse/good reason *du jour*."

My "who's resisting?" dilemma rekindles my admiration for Ram Dass's insight... amusing, yet true: "If you want to see how enlightened you are, go spend a week with your family." *Touche!*

In light of our current resistance ruminations... my variation on this would be... "If you want to see how enlightened you are... explore how effective your self-awareness tools are in the face of your own mighty resistance." Gack.

Onward.

Asking Auntie Google about "elders and balance" while writing chapter 8... I had my mind properly blown as I came across "proprioception." Wowza! How had I lived a fairly well-educated 70 years and not ever heard of proprioception? Even working at the massage school for several years... you know... anatomy, physiology, muscle alignment. How had I missed proprioception?

Let me just say... I am glad to know about it now.

Researching... I came across a site with exercise videos to build proprioception. An "easy" video along with a more challenging one. I bookmarked the site. I told myself... "I'll do these exercises in the evening while we're watching TV." Have I? A couple times.

I've come to recognize a particularly cunning ploy of resistance... amnesia. I simply forget. That trickster! I don't even have to resist doing the exercises. I just completely forget about them. Not even a nudge... "Was I going to do something this evening?" Nary a thought crosses my mind.

Oohhh... that *is* a wily ploy. Most effective in The Maintaining Inertia Department.

Let's take a broader look at all this. How does habit... inertia... manage to maintain itself?

Habit is the infrastructure of your interior architecture. And, like so many things "in charge"... habit comes equipt with its own obsession: maintaining its dominion... its territory. Its power over you.

The mechanics of habit is neither "good" nor "bad." It depends on what the habit is. Brushing your teeth = good habit. Saving everything that needs to be done till the very last minute = bad habit. Being kind and understanding = good habit. Flying off the handle at the least little thing = bad habit. Stinkin' thinkin' = bad habit. Practicing self-kindness and gratitude = good habit.

When possible... I like to cite the author of works I share. In this case I have to go with "Author Unknown." Thank you, unknown author, for your wise, well-worded insight. Reading the following... you may recall this from *Holy Wow!* Volume I:

I am your constant companion.

I am your greatest helper, or your heaviest burden.

I will push you onward, or drag you down to failure.

I am completely at your command.

Half of the things you do,
you might as well turn over to me,
And I will do them ~ quickly and correctly.
I am easily managed ~ you must be firm with me.
Show me exactly how you want something done
And after a few lessons, I will do it automatically.
I am the servant of great people,
and alas, of all failures as well.
Those who are great, I have made great.
Those who are failures, I have made failures.
I am not a machine,
tho I work with the precision of a machine,
Plus the intelligence of a person.
You may run me for profit, or you may run me
for ruin ~ it makes no difference to me.
Take me, train me, be firm with me,
and I will place the world at your feet.
Be easy with me, and I will destroy you.
Who am I?
I am habit.

Voila!

Here we have clear insight into the strangle-hold habit has on us humans being. "Train me"... decide what you want and how you want your Life to be. Employ the structure of habit to take you there. "Be firm with me"... get over your resistance and self-doubt. Direct the show... "I will place the world at your feet." "Be easy with me"... continue to let self-limitation rule... "and I will destroy you."

In every human realm... change is frightening. "What if I no longer get *my way*?" Especially those in power are resistant to change. Politicians come to mind. Knowing that any change of "how things have always been" could oust them from power. Their position of power being more important to them than the oath they took to serve our country and its people.

Likewise... our internal habits are resistant to change. "Just keep doing what you're doing." "Don't rock the boat." "Stay the way you are." "You're good." "You don't need to change."

You don't just wave your magic wand... or wiggle your nose... and Ta Da!... healthy habits established.

Here's what I've learned as I attempt to confront... change... my resistance to exercise. There's no "reasoning" with habit. You can't "discuss" the situation and have "an intelligent conversation" with it. You just have to grunt. Get in there with the heavy, earth-moving equipment and break yourself free. Make new habits happen. I've done this before with exercise. I've developed and maintained a routine. Then... over time... for a wide, not totally impressive number of reasons... those new habits fell away. My old inertia habit returns.

As established... inertia comes my way via both nature and nurture. My inner demeanor and my upbringing. Synonyms for inertia: lethargy... apathy... sluggishness. Sluggish... some days more than others. I consider myself neither apathetic nor lethargic. Yet here we are.

All of this I mention acknowledging the art of ageing gracefully. 'Cause if you're going to age... which you probably are... you want to accomplish that Life chapter with as much grace and ease as you can gather.

Due to my mother maintaining her 40-year career with Bank of America... and the benefits offered to retirees 20+ years ago... my parents' "golden years" were pretty grace-filled. I'm not sure either of them saw it that way. As their caregiver... it was clear to me. Her retiree's health insurance was a great lubricant for their ongoing well-being.

Together Scott and I make a good home. I was grateful... relieved... to be providing this safety net of "good home" for my parents. As our caregiving chapter played out... Scott was blessedly engaged and supportive. Caring for my parents would not have happened as pleasantly as it did without him. His far-ranging skills... carpenter... plumber... electrician. Chef. Baker. Landscaper. His willingness to be completely involved. Especially... his caring heart... made a challenging situation work the best it possibly could for all concerned.

By Christmas, 2000, Scott and I had been caring for my folks a little over 2 years. Isaiah traveled from Oregon to join us for the holidays. He grokked the situation with both of his grandparents in wheelchairs and declining. Returning to Oregon, he buttoned up his Life there and came to join us as part of the Care Team. He was 24. He had trained as a Licensed Massage Therapist... and was halfway thru college... when he arrived to help us care for Grandma and Granddaddy.

Isaiah's presence was a real boon for all of us.

My father hardly ever spoke to me. He was never one to chat me up. We'd never had easy, flowing conversations. At this point... in his mind... me being in their home somehow *caused* his disabled state. Rather than the other way around... I was there to help him because he was disabled. As I've mentioned... the effects of stoke can alter a person's perceptions. Even tho he was using a wheelchair full-time... he was not convinced he and Mama needed an assist.

Daddy was more inclined to chat with Scott.

When Isaiah arrived, the floodgates of conversation opened. Granddaddy and Isaiah chatted about all sorts of things... sports... politics... the state of the world... the talking heads on TV. Watching news commentators argue on TV was one of my dad's favorite pastimes. He and Isaiah would joke and carry on.

Isaiah joining us... becoming a fully engaged member of the care team... had a positive effect on the whole situation. Plus, I was delighted to again be sharing day-to-day Life with my son.

Coming to care for my folks... put me back in touch with cousins on both sides of our family. Living in Oregon for decades... I had only heard snippets of my cousins' lives from my folks. Seldom was I directly in touch with my generation of family members.

There are many variations on the theme of eldercare. My parents were both the younger children of large families. As my folks and my aunts and uncles aged... my cousins and I all made different choices as to the many assorted eldercare options:

One set of cousins kept their parents in their longtime home... hiring a care team... who did what Scott and I were doing for my parents... housekeeping... driving to appointments... making meals... being available.

One set of cousins admitted their parents to a care facility and visited them regularly.

Another set of cousins admitted their parents to a care facility and seemed to forget about them.

One cousin pretty much ignored the whole situation. She continued borrowing money from her folks… expecting them to take care of her as they always had. A couple of years later, this same cousin… having made no funeral or burial plans… had to deal with last-minute decisions and commotion as she was in the hard grief of her father's passing. I felt for her.

Acknowledging my father's strong preference not to live in a care facility… Scott and I chose to move into their home… caring for them so they could continue living there. This is not a common response. It's what worked best for the 4 of us. I am not saying our way is best. It is one way of many.

The important thing is to be there for your parents. They have never been more vulnerable.

You may find yourself in a situation of giving them the attentive care you always wished they had given you. All families have their own dynamics and undercurrents… sometimes painful… sometimes supportive and kind. It can be challenging to step beyond past difficulties and grievances. You might find yourself thinking… "They don't deserve me caring for them. They did a lousy job caring for me."

Life is calling you to step beyond your gripes.

This brings us back to "choose your hard." Caring for your ailing elders is hard. Not caring for your ailing elders is hard. Choose your hard.

In chapter 7, I shared with you how I grew up in an emotional Sahara Desert... a home environment of benign neglect. I was not keen on this dry emotional distance when I was a child. I promised myself I would raise my children with a lot more juice. However, I will tell you... this emotional distance my parents generated made it a lot easier for me to care for them in their decline. I did not have any great emotional attachment to who they had been... which would have made me dismal and sad being with them as they grew more frail. I was able to just be there with them... taking care of them the way they are now. There wasn't anything to snag me into bemoaning and grief about how great they had once been. Nor suffering the misery of how sad it was that they were now much diminished.

If you were blessed to have a warm, wonderful relationship with your parents... I am very happy for you. You are blessed beyond measure. I also recognize... that deep connexion can kindle your feelings of loss and disruption... grief and sadness... as you experience your parent declining. It's hard not to feel the loss of who they once were. Who you have known them to be.

I know this might not be comfortable to deal with... but, in fact, it is now as if you are the parent and your parents have become your kids. Of course, it depends on your family's dynamic... but it may not be easy to have important conversations with your folks. About their health. About the details of passing their assets to the next generation. About the realities of their day-to-day care. Some adult children become tongue-tied still... as they stand before their parents. Who were once the all-powerful.

You can feel awkward uncertainty. You want to be "reasonable" and allow your parents to have their way. Their "it"... whatever "it" may be. Continuing to drive. Travel. Living independently. Have their Life the way they want it... the "way it's always been." You don't want to be the bad guy. Yet you, more objectively than your folks... see the steps that must be taken. How much assistance they actually require. All that needs to be done. These may not be "reasonable" times.

Ageing parents are rarely able to be objective about their declining health and their increasing care needs. Resistance may raise its defiant head. Especially if what "needs" to be done is not what they "want" to be done. About their care needs... "I don't want anybody coming into my house to look after me!" Financial arrangements... "You're just after my money!" "I don't want to talk with an estate-planning attorney! They charge too much money." Driving... "No, you can't take away my car keys!" Staying in their own home... "I don't want to go look at that care facility. I want to stay here at home! I can take care of myself."

Become clear within yourself as to "the plan" and what needs to be done. Stepping over any inner trepidation... or your personal resistance... move ahead to make helpful arrangements. I didn't do such a great job with this. I mentioned earlier... with my mother slipping into dementia, as my dad turned 80... I tried to have a "planning conversation" with him. His response... "Let's wait and see what happens." End of conversation. I knew this was not the "right answer." Not an effective approach. But what are you going to do? Either continue with the *laissez-faire*... same ol' same ol.' Or begin looking into plans and preparations on your own.

Over the years... of the many different people I have spoken with about caring for their elders... I only know one person whose mother took the initiative herself. She downsized her home. Made sure her financial affairs were in order. Moved herself into an elder care community. If your parents are already doing this... or are looking into the possibilities... Thank Your Lucky Stars!

Most common among ageing elders... ailing or otherwise... is the tendency to do as my dad did. Pretend the whole ageing and declining process is not happening and does not need to be responded to, planned for, or figured out.

Another aspect of caring for ageing parents requiring boatloads of patience is dealing with their stuff. All kinds of stuff... furniture... clothing... photographs. Keepsakes and mementoes. Stuff in the attic... the house, closets, drawers... the basement. The garage.

There's also paperwork stuff. Bank and investments stuff... titles, deeds, documents.

Stuff stuffed everywhere.

Again, perhaps your parents have already gone thru the majority of their stuff. Likelihood of that... minimal. With slipping mentation... dealing with the details, the focus and activity of clearing out drawers, closets, basements... can be nearly impossible.

"What do you want to do with this, Mama?" "I don't know."

Just a note... you may find cash and important papers stashed in odd places... the freezer... between pages of books... the ever-popular beat-up shoebox in the back of the closet.

Many times, elders have a hard time letting go of their stuff. Once, as we were visiting Scott's folks... Scott took on the much-needed project of cleaning out their garage. He filled the back of his dad's pick-up with a huge pile of what looked like useless junk. The plan was to head out early the next morning for the dump, the recycler, the thrift store. After we all went to bed that night... Scott's dad snuck out to the driveway and pulled out all of the "important stuff." He unloaded more than half the junk packed into the back of the truck. Yes, frustrating.

Yes, patience.

In the declining years of your parents' Life... you are not only dealing with the details, decisions, prepping and sorting of your own Life. You're dealing with the details and decisions... the physical plane reality of your folks' Life, too.

At the end of this chapter... you will come to "1st Afters... Caring For Ailing Elders: *A Layperson's Guide To Getting Ducks In A Row*"... offering helpful information about wills, trusts and probate... Powers of Attorney... beneficiaries... your parent's Advance Directive... funeral arrangements. Lots of "ducks."

Another important consideration... again requiring patience and understanding... is deciding what will happen to your ailing parent's pets. This, too, is a conversation to have with your folks... asking their preferences for their pets' care. Again, possibly your parents have already made arrangements for who will care for Fido, Mittens or Pretty Boy.

In case this consideration is left to you... there are many options.

Some elders want their pets euthanized... "put to sleep"... after they die. Concerned their dear pet would not be able to adjust to a new owner. Perhaps a family member, neighbor or friend will agree to adopt the pet(s).

Many times, it is hard for the adult child or person "dealing with" things to see the "being" the pet is... this longtime, treasured companion. Seeing only "an animal"... they may be inclined to drop the pet at a shelter just to get it over with.

These days there are new possibilities to add to these considerations. One is online animal adoption sites. Another... in almost every state there are non-profit groups offering to help pay for medications and veterinary bills for ageing pets... particularly dogs.

With all the questions, sorting, tossing and future planning on the agenda... as you step into this role as your parent's caregiver... do not expect to be met with sunshine, tulips, and open arms. If you are... Great! However, many times, adult children stepping in to help their parents are met with suspicion. Not just from their parents. Other relatives, friends, and neighbors can act as if you're trying to pull something over on your folks. Like you're mooching... freeloading somehow. Messing with them. Sometimes being suspicious and deluded is related to mental decline issues. Sometimes, it's just the elder's generally fearful way of dealing with Life.

Every set of ageing parents and their adult children has their own interpersonal dynamic. All of your plans and helpful suggestions may just sail smoothly along with grateful cooperation from your parents. Or you may confront opposition and suspicion at every turn.

Do not take it personally… if your ageing elders are resistant or mistrusting of your overtures to help. Do what you can to not be put off by their resistance. Much ratzafratz and complication may fall in your caregiving path. Do not lose sight of this fact: Their safety… their well-being… is the issue here.

The hard truth… the upcoming parameters of their Life might not be exactly the way they think they want them.

My dad knew Scott was Handyman Extraordinaire and had been a contractor for decades. Yet, as we talked about fixes around the house and items to install to accommodate my dad's physical limitations… his reflexive reaction was mistrust. "Guys like that always rip you off! They never do a good job!" "How much is this going to cost me?" He seemed to forget completely… he'd known and admired Scott for nearly 20 years, often raving about the good work Scott did.

Daddy was not living in the situation as it actually was. There's a skilled carpenter in the family. A handyman in the house. His knee-jerk reaction was to succumb to the suspicious version of Life he had in his head. Wary. His mistrust ruled his perceptions. Daddy could not help himself.

My father succumbed to his automatic, yet predictable, reaction. Even tho he knew and admired Scott... he was not able to see this situation for what it was. Rather than being grateful and at peace that things would be handled well... he could only see he needed to be apprehensive and suspicious. That being said... there are cases where ageing elders have good reason to be mistrustful of others... even their own children "wanting to help." Unfortunately, there are many people... relatives and strangers... who are only interested in the elder's stuff and resources and the fleecing thereof.

It would not have occurred to me how dire the situation is... of others preying upon elders' frailty simply to get at their stuff. I mentioned in Chapter 7... elders have amassed resources which many others would happily connive them out of. Altho some folks are suspicious... in many cases, elders are unsuspecting. Even mild mental decline can lead to cognitive impairment... leaving them defenseless. Unable to process what's going on. They are "taken" unawares. Victims of the predatory. So unfair.

As your caregiving chapter begins to unfold... the call is for attentive care... quality of Life... fostering your elders' well-being. However that plays out for you and your family.

Becoming more involved in the duties and responsibilities of eldercare... you will immediately realize... "I am in a rich 'learning-curve' experience here." Absolutely a "quickly-educate-myself-as-well-as-I-can-to-step-in-here-and-do-it" situation.

No doubt... The Patience Olympics.

Truthfully... because of your lifelong relationship with your parent(s)... glum or gleeful... and how that infiltrates your present reality... eldercare requires astonishingly more patience than raising children ever did. Plus the fact that eldercare functions in a state of decline. They are not going to "get better" and thrive. Very different from the engaging delight of being with children as they blossom and grow.

My parents each had a completely diverse set of challenges. When Scott and I arrived to care for them... other than high blood pressure and an enlarged heart... my mother was in decent shape physically. She did a good job getting around. However, her mental faculties... her short-term memory... dealing with the day to day... were noticeably declined.

Soon after we arrived at their house... I got Mama a 50-piece puzzle. A gorgeous underwater scene. Vibrant colors. Just enough busyness. She and I would do that puzzle a few times a day. Or I would set it out for her as I was making dinner or balancing their checkbook. She asked me one time, "Have I done this puzzle before?"

My father was in a wheelchair. Still sharp as a tack mentally... his challenges were all physical. A few years earlier he lost the vision in his right eye. Daddy's first stroke... just after his 81st birthday... was "the event" that called me and Scott to pack up and move to help them. This stroke left him hemiplegic... paralyzed on his left side.

The human brain has 2 hemispheres. Each half of the brain controls the opposite side of the body. A stroke on the right side of the brain results in impairment on the left side of the body... along with other right hemisphere functions such as perception and memory. A stroke in the brain's left hemisphere affects the right side of the body... and a person's ability to speak and comprehend words. Frequently following a stroke... a person is hemiplegic. Paralyzed on one side of their body.

Paralysis of the arms and legs happens in several different ways. Usually due to injury or brain trauma... a person can face Life as a quadriplegic or paraplegic.

Quadriplegia results from spinal cord injury in the neck's 8 cervical vertebra. The higher up the neck the injury is... the more extensive the damage will be. All 4 limbs... both arms and both legs... become paralyzed. At times paralysis is so severe... it interferes with the person's ability to breathe on their own.

Paraplegia is characterized by motor or sensory loss in the trunk of the body and the legs… caused by spinal cord injuries below the first thoracic spinal levels (Thoracic 1 to Lumbar 5). Paraplegics have the ability to use their arms and hands. How much they are able to use their legs depends on the severity and location of their injury. Some paraplegics live with complete paralysis from the waist down. Others have minor mobility issues… perhaps tingling in their legs… or decreased sensation in their lower body. Interestingly… the legs of a paraplegic person are usually healthy. Their paralysis lies in either the brain or the spinal cord failing to transmit neural information to move and control their legs.

Caused by injury to parts of the brain controlling movement of the limbs, trunk, and face… hemiplegia affects one whole side of the body. This is spoken of as right or left hemiplegia… depending on which side of the body is affected.

In each of these forms of paralysis of the legs and arms… the degree of paralysis varies depending on:

- The nature of the injury
- The extent of rehabilitative therapy available
- Some factors that are not yet well-understood
- Luck.

Each side of the brain controls so many vital functions. There is not a worse or better side to have a stroke on. The severity of the stroke determines whether there will be mild or amplified after-effects.

Prompt treatment of a stroke is crucial. Early action can reduce brain damage and resulting complications. Tho we will never know… chances are good… had my father sought medical attention right when he realized something was wrong… he might not have set himself up for the physical limitations he dealt with the last years of his Life.

I mentioned earlier… my folks had a scheduled doctor's appointment 2 days after he "knew something was wrong." Daddy waited until their appointment because he didn't want to "make a fuss." He said nothing and did nothing until he arrived at their doctor's office. Then he didn't have to say anything. With one look at him… his doctor could tell there was something seriously wrong and hospitalized him immediately.

Daddy felt betrayed by his body. He was angry and depressed… an understandable response to such profound Life trauma. For a man of his generation… my dad was unusually health conscious. As I grew up… we had no white bread in the house… no processed lunch meats… only the very occasional hot dog. He took various vitamins and supplements… before that became a thing to do. In his mind… he had consistently made healthful choices. How dare his body let him down like this. How dare it stroke.

My dad was a big man… 6'3" and big-boned. He wasn't fat… but definitely sturdy. There was a lot to him. Helping him "transfer"… moving from his bed to his wheelchair… from his wheelchair to the toilet… took some doing. The caregiver has to be aware… don't injure yourself as you assist the person you're caring for.

Being able to safely make these transfers is *the* crucial element in elder care. If the elder is able to continue making their transfers… with help or on their own… they are more likely to continue living in their own home. Once they can no longer make these transfers… things change. The time has come to either admit them to a care facility… or get more home health assistance. Preferably someone big and burly. And kind.

After Scott and I arrived… it did not take long for the 4 of us to establish our rhythm of daily Life. Fortunately, my parents were quite amenable. At times, my father would grumble about us being there… because they did not need care. He'd toy with the idea we were freeloading. Oy!

As I mentioned… either as a result of his general disposition or a neurological effect of the stroke… he was unable to accurately assess how dire their situation was.

It is a significant blessing for my heart that Scott, Isaiah and I were there to give them good care at this precious and vulnerable time. It was important to me to allow them to have their end-of-Life wishes.

As I have mentioned… for many years, my father made clear he wanted to be cremated. And he did *not* want to live in a care facility. The main instigator for the way Scott and I chose to assist my parents by moving in with them… was my father's longtime, strongly stated desire. He also got his wish to be cremated. My mother's sole expressed desire was to be buried next to her mother. She was cremated, also. After Daddy passed… Lyla and I carried their cremains to North Carolina to be buried in the place beside my mother's mother.

There were 4 girls and 3 boys in my mother's family. Standing at my grandparents' grave, it was poignant to see my grandmother's headstone flanked on one side by her eldest daughter and on the other by her youngest… my mom.

Giving my mother her final wish was a promise I knew I would keep. As a kid, riding in the car with my mom… she would tell me about her childhood and being next to the youngest in a large family. My mother felt picked on… mistreated… left out… by her older siblings. Her mother was her solace. A deep, special connexion. Support. Comfort. My mother's mother died unexpectedly when my mom was 15. It brought my mother to her knees. I don't think she ever "got over it." I made sure she was buried next to her mother.

A particularly poignant moment came for me the morning my mother died. She had been declining for a few weeks... obviously the end was near. Blessedly, she passed gently in her sleep. As I came into their room to start their day... Daddy said she had stopped breathing about 20 minutes before.

Standing at the foot of their bed, I recalled... when I was a child... my father's favorite aunt, Sis Ann... my grandmother's baby sister... lived in Southern California. Every month or 2, my parents and I would drive to visit her. Many times, as we drove home... my mother would say, "I don't want to get old. I don't want to be a burden." Sitting in the back seat... I would think, "She must have been a burden in a past Life." It did not once occur to me she might be "a burden" in this Life. Realizing she had passed... I put my hand on her leg, saying aloud... "Mama, you were never a burden. I know you were always doing your very best."

My mother died a year and a half before my dad. When she passed... I was going to do a small memorial service in their home... inviting their longtime neighbors and friends from their church. Sharing this idea with my dad... I was startled at his strong reaction against my suggestion. He made it very clear... he did *not* want us to have a service for her.

Instead, he said... "After I die... you'll take our ashes to North Carolina. You can make a memorial service for us there with your cousins. Maybe they'll say nice things about us."

As Lyla and I arrived in North Carolina with my parents' cremains... we were blessed by the compassionate guidance of my cousin and her husband... who was the area's funeral director. Preparing their memorial... I didn't think about what Daddy had said. As their service played out... lo and behold. He called it. I realized afterward... their service was exactly as he had described it. Including my cousins saying "nice things."

Our companions of sanity thru-out our years of eldercare were our 3 old dogs... Harley, Jammers, and Maizie. For me, their presence was vapor trails... our connexion to our previous Life... when our kids were growing up.

Isaiah and Lyla were both in college when we moved to care for my folks. It did not occur to me until later in our caregiving sojourn... OMG!... there are folks called to care for their parents while their children are still at home... in elementary school, junior high, high school. Whoa. *That's* intense.

You may hear the term "the sandwich generation." That's these very folks! Not only do they have young children or teenagers at home... they are right in the midst of their career. Their livelihood-producing years. They are the generation "sandwiched" between raising their kids and caring for their folks... while also making a living.

When this dawned on me... many other family caregivers also still had children at home... I was floored by the enormity of it. Grasping the reality of the "sandwich generation," I thought... "They're not sandwiched... they're squished!"

This may be you. If so... my hat is off to you. May gentle sanity prevail. May I make a sanity-saving suggestion? Get as much additional help as you can possibly afford or barter for.

As it turned out... our 3 elderly dogs became gentle companions for my folks. Good comic relief. Especially for my dad. As the caregivers... Scott and I found the dogs to be our compadres in the self-care department. They were delightful beings. Our good buds. We had been a pack for over a decade by then. The dogs also offered me and Scott the perfect excuse to get out of the house and walk them thru the neighborhood.

Yes, these were the very dogs which... on our last day buttoning up our Life in Portland... my mother called to say, "Don't you be bringing those dogs." Yeah, right. That's one "wish" we were not going to honor.

It's fascinating… there are "dog people" and there are "cat people." Usually stated with strong preference. I imagine there are some dog *and* cat people. And some folks who want nothing to do with either. Maybe they are gerbil or goldfish people. I have always been a dog person.

I get a chuckle from the online suggestion to "create your porn name"… by putting together the names of your childhood dog and the street you grew up on. My porn name would be Shadow Rutledge. Poetical. Debbie Buena Vista is another possibility.

People who are not dog people have a hard time grokking… "What's the big deal?" Curious… why are people so besotted with their dogs? Well, because they're… dogs. I've loved me a few.

Interestingly… some people only think of the "trouble" dogs are. "I'd have to clean up after it." "I'd have to feed it and keep its water bowl full." "It's too much mess." "I'd be tied down and couldn't travel." "They die so soon. I'd be too sad." Yes… all of those things do occur when you are a dog's person.

And So Much More!

There's a lot to be said for the value of canine companionship. There ain't nothin' like a good dog.

I am going to close this volume sharing with you a moment so special to me. Perfect, even.

As elders decline and it becomes clear the end is coming... you never know exactly when that will be. With both of my parents... I made what was for me a very meaningful experience on what turned out... with each of them... to be their very last day. Altho I did not know that at the time.

As they each drifted in and out of consciousness... I set up a few of my bowl gongs near them on the bed. Gently sounding these peaceful, resonant tones... I chanted OM. I thanked them for being my parent... for the Life they had given me. Then I sang aloud The Blessing Song:

May the blessings of Love rest upon you.
May Love's peace abide with you.
May Love's presence illuminate your heart.
Now and forever more.

As your path unfolds before you, Dear Reader... for your heart, for your being... I wish you such deep and certain peace.

Now and forever more.

Caring For Ailing Elders

A Layperson's Guide To Getting Ducks In A Row

If your parents... or your family... have not delved into "end of Life care"... including the required legal documents... it will be to your advantage to read thru the following and put different items into action. Now. (Or as close to "Now" as possible.)

1st Afters contains 5 sections:

1) My commentary and suggestions from experience

2) A quick reference outline / checklist of items to attend to

3) Probate, Wills and Trusts... a.k.a. Estate Planning and why this is important

4) Additional strategies

5) Thoughts regarding Powers of Attorney

Each state has its own regulations regarding probate... trusts... wills, etc. Educate yourself as to the requirements in your parents' state of residence.

I write the following as if both of your parents are still living... and you can have conversations with them. This may not be true in your case. If your parents have recently died... much of the following will have to be attended to anyway... with you making the various choices and decisions. It's very likely working with an attorney or paralegal... rather than attempting to do it yourself... is the helpful route to take.

A paralegal is an authorized professional who performs supplementary legal matters but is not a fully qualified lawyer. Paralegals do not practice law on their own... they are overseen by a licensed attorney. It can be less expensive to have a paralegal do some of the basic work... then turn the documents over to an attorney.

It may be one or both of your parents are living but lacking in mental capacity... so you're not able to ask them their preferences and where their assets may be. If your parents are unable to make valid decisions for themselves at the time they need to be made... this can lead to some degree of intervention by … lawyers, social workers, courts, conservators, etc. These are professionals who are concerned about your elder's care and well-being. This is a whole other ball of wax for you.

Even if your parents aren't "that old"… or things are "going well" with your ageing elders… now is the perfect time to take care of many of these recommendations and develop some sort of plan for when things begin to decline. Inevitably, they will.

I also write this assuming you are a caring, conscientious person who wants to give your parents good care. There are many people… adult children, other family members, complete strangers… who look at ailing elders with dollar signs in their eyes… only interested in finding ways to fleece that elder's resources.

This is The Moment for you to step up and be the loving adult child… helping your parents and keeping them safe during this vulnerable time in their lives. This might prove to be an opportunity for you to give your parents the quality of care you would like to have gotten from them.

If embraced as such, caring for your parents in their decline can bring you immeasurable personal healing… self-awareness… and release from past pain. Quite likely… your eldercare endeavor will also rub every raw nerve. I am not painting a Pollyanna picture of sweetness and light.

This new level of care and being involved in your parent's Life is strenuous and demanding.

Caring for your elderly parents will call you to your highest and best... or squash you flat. I am not being over-dramatic here. Choose to engage. Pick up the mantle. Take on these responsibilities which have got to happen. Proceed.

Now is the time to assess your parents' current situation... health... safety... mental clarity... financials.

From what I learned working for a Professional Guardian/Conservator for the elderly frail... and my experiences as my husband and I took care of my parents in their decline... as well as other eldercare circumstances I've been in... I am happy to share these eldercare insights with you. I am neither a lawyer nor a healthcare professional. These are things I have learned or figured out along the way. My intention here is to give you pointers... so you don't have to reinvent the wheel.

This is a "rich learning-curve" environment. As I said... The Patience Olympics. Requiring astoundingly more patience than raising children ever did. It really is a quickly-educate-yourself-as-well-as-you-can-and-step-in-here-and-do-it situation. Believe me, when you take the first steps, the process itself... and the choices you make... become your education.

The true gist of it is... it's not going to get any easier from here. This situation will only require more and more of your attention. The sooner you engage and assess the situation… both healthcare and finance… the better.

Be glad you live in the age of Internet research. There is a ton of information available on any of the subjects I cover here. Scott and I were caring for my folks in the late-'90s… information available on the Internet was not *anything* like it is today. If my suggestions here bring up questions for you… investigate online. Or, as we say at our house… ask Auntie Google.

At https://www.everplans.com I found a complete, state-by-state list of health, legal, and end-of-life resources… advance directive forms, digital estate laws, organ donation registries, probate, and more.

Family dynamics being what they are… you must step beyond any "squeamishness" you may have in dealing so directly with your parents. You have to ask them questions to get a clear take on their situation.

> You want to become more actively
> involved in their situation…
> because it is rapidly becoming *your* situation.

For them and for you… you want to give them and their resources the best, most caring attention you possibly can… or, truly, this Life Chapter can spiral out of control and become a grueling struggle.

You may not be welcomed with open arms as you indicate your interest in being more involved in your parents' lives.

In my experience, I have observed… when siblings have ailing elders… there is usually 1 sibling who is actually taking care of the elders… dealing with their daily affairs, doctor's appointments, meds, etc. The other siblings are frequently criticizing, complaining, and not wanting money spent on their elders… fearing it will subtract from their inheritance. I'm willing to give the benefit of the doubt here… if you have siblings… do any (or even, all) appear to be inclined to step in and become increasingly involved in your parents care or financial considerations?

As Scott and I were packing up our Life in Portland, Oregon to move into my childhood home in Southern California to care for my parents… a friend of mine asked, "Now don't you wish you had brothers and sisters?" I said, "No. Not at all." From what I learned working for the Guardian/Conservator… I was grateful it was just me and I could make the decisions guiding my parents' care. Grateful I didn't have to put my choices up for community (sibling) commentary and criticism.

Rarely does an elder have their will or trust drawn up or made any arrangements related to their future care. In the many instances of eldercare I've been involved with… I have known exactly 1 family where the elder got everything pre-arranged = an incredible gift to her adult child. It is almost always left to the adult children to initiate conversations... and following thru to make legal and healthcare appointments.

An important initial step is to have your signature added to their checking and savings accounts. This will make it Much Easier for you in the coming months/years... to write checks to pay their bills... and to recover assets upon their passing. One of your parents may have to go with you to their bank(s) or other financial institution(s) (stock broker, etc.) and be there with you to add your signature. Possibly this can be accomplished with an authorization letter written by your parents, dated, with their signature. Also have your signature added to their credit cards. You may need to use them for their care.

If your signature is not currently on their accounts... this should happen as soon as possible.

Ask your folks if they have made a will or any trust-related plans. Find out if they have a particular lawyer, banker. or financial person they work with... and how to get in touch with that person. These professionals can help you be aware of assets that need to be... or already are... put into a trust.

There are attorneys who specialize in the field of "elder law" and dealing with inheritance... wills, trusts, probate... and the passing of generational resources.

Go with your parents to their doctor's appointments... to get necessary information about their medications and an understanding of how your folks are doing health-wise. Don't simply assume their doctor is "taking care of things" and everything is "okay." Early in our time as my parents' caregivers... in the middle of a medical emergency... Scott and I found out my mother had been prescribed basically the same drug, to address the same condition, by 3 different doctors. Her body was getting much more of this medication than it could deal with. My parents... who were of "the doctor is always right" generation... did not know enough, medically, to be aware of this. Her 3 doctors had no interactions with each other... and no idea she had received multiple prescriptions of basically the same drug.

Ask their doctors questions. Get your finger on the pulsebeat of your parents' medical reality.

If one or both of your parents is dealing with memory issues and disorientation... there are drugs to slow their mental decline... usually with few side-effects. When we were taking care of my folks in the late '90s... that drug was Aricept. Taking it slowed, gentled, my mother's mental decline. I am sure there are new generations of these drugs... which you can ask their doctor about. Worth noting: after taking Aricept for months or years... if for some reason your parent stopped taking it... mentally, they would rapidly decline to where they would have been if they had never taken the drug. This proved to definitely be true in my mother's case. I imagine this would also be the case with new generations of any "children of Aricept" drugs. These meds are definitely worth looking into… for your parents' care and well-being… and for your own. The slower their mental decline… the better.

You want to find out if your parents have long-term care insurance to help pay for an eldercare facility, if that is where they end up living.

Contact your folks' insurance agent(s)… either by phone or in person… to introduce yourself. It is good for them to know who you are, in case any future changes in policies need to take place.

The Determining Factor as to whether either or both of your parents can continue living in their home… or will have to move to a care facility… is their ability to "transfer." That means using their own mobility… with perhaps a little assistance… to transfer from bed to wheelchair. Transfer from wheelchair to toilet. Transfer from wheelchair to seat in car. As they lose their strength and ability to make these crucial transfers… a greater level of care is required. Keeping them safe and healthy once they lose this ability involves more effort… more exertion… than can safely be provided in the family home.

Super important: Either thru online research and/or with the guidance of an attorney... establish Powers of Attorney (POA) for both finance and healthcare. These are 2 separate documents... which your parents will sign... to give this authority to you or whoever they designate. While your parents are still competent... these are "transparent" documents... meaning the POA only takes effect upon your parents' inability to make healthcare or financial decisions for themselves.

As I mentioned... as any of these legal documents are being prepared... if it appears either or both of your parents are showing signs of incompetence... this can lead to a whole different set of complexities as legal professionals, social workers, and possibly the courts become involved.

As is true with so many aspects of these end-of-Life documents... laws about implementing POAs vary from state to state.

If it turns out your parents have already created Powers of Attorney... you want to find out who currently is assigned these powers. Many times, a couple will set each other up in these 2 Powers of Attorney... but as they get older, this isn't such a good idea. The person with their Powers of Attorney should be someone younger... and trusted.

As your elders decline... having Powers of Attorney allows you to be the one who decides and acts upon what will happen in their healthcare and financial matters. Make several photocopies of each document. You may need to provide copies to doctors, banks, etc. Without Powers of Attorney in place, each of these important aspects of Life can get really tangled and frustratingly complicated.

Many times, families choose to have one sibling with Power of Attorney for finance and another sibling with Power of Attorney for healthcare. Set up these Powers of Attorney according to your parent's wishes and whatever works best for your family.

It is A Very Good Idea to acquaint yourself with your parents' health insurance and Medicare situation. Also find out whether they are up to date paying their bills. Many times in a family, paying the bills is one parent's longtime job. Is that parent still able to manage this? In my family's case… bill-paying was always my mother's job. When she began to slip mentally… evidently it did not occur to my father to take over those responsibilities. The fact that he was in denial as to her diminishing mental capacity did not help him have an accurate understanding of their situation.

In her dementia… my mother began giving out their credit card numbers over the phone, for things like "Win The Canadian Lottery." Unscrupulous people have no problem preying on declining elders. My folks were assessed thousands of dollars in bogus charges before I became involved and was able to take control... stop it... and get a small amount of their money back. Credit card companies will only refund charges made in the most recent month or 2. It is worthwhile for you to look over your parents' credit card statements for any questionable charges.

I can say to you from the clarity of experience... if your parent's legal considerations and their day-to-day care needs are not adequately dealt with Now... either or both can turn into a quagmire of epic proportion. I know I've already mentioned variations on this assertion a few times. I only say this... repeat this... because it's true!

In many ways, your elders needing more attentive care is barely something you can plan for. You don't actually know when or how this is going to play out. In my case... even with all I learned working for a Professional Guardian/Conservator... I could say I was prepared... and not prepared... when the call to action came.

In a perfect world... you'll have pleasant conversations with your parents about... lawyers, bankers, wills, trusts, doctors, and day-to-day needs. Rarely is this a perfect world. Some parents will be suspicious of your interest and intentions. Even in our case... which was more amicable than most... my father would go off about "not getting ripped off by *them*." Even tho "them" was me and Scott, people he knew and trusted (as much as he was able to).

Many times, elders have an unrealistic grasp of their current ... and future... situation. They do not realize the dire circumstances they are slipping toward or already in. And they do not believe they need assistance.

Other older folks might chime in with their concerns that you are "taking over." Not just your parents but older neighbors, friends, aunts, and uncles might say this... because they are in denial as to just how much aid and support we humans need as we age.

Especially where money and resources are involved... your folks may be wary and guarded. Even if you've always had a cordial, friendly relationship with your folks... that does not mean they will be forthcoming, responsive, or comfortable with these conversations... as you attempt to assess their current situation.

Are your parents still driving? Should they be? Are they safe drivers? This is an issue you should evaluate and address immediately. This, particularly, is not an easy conversation or course of action... as your elders struggle with losing their independence and might resent you for "taking it."

When it is no longer wise or safe for them to drive, there are several different transportation services available for seniors.

Do your parents have Life Insurance? If so, check to see whom they have named as their life insurance beneficiary(s). Should they already have a will, trust, or other financial or legal documents... as I just mentioned... they might have chosen each other as beneficiary, or Power of Attorney, or executor of their estate. As they advance in age... this should all be changed to designate you... or another adult child, or an adult grandchild... or a trusted family friend or a legal professional... in these roles.

During the time I worked for the Professional Guardian/ Conservator... I would think, "This information might come in handy sometime." Little did I know "sometime" was just around the corner. As it all played out, I was deeply grateful to that job... to my Life... for giving me a glimpse of the terrain... aspects to be aware of, questions to ask... before Scott and I were tossed headlong into the situation you find yourself in now.

I know this may not be a comfortable thing to deal with... but, in fact, it is as if now, you are the parent and your parents have, in effect, become your kids. It is a fine line to walk between allowing your parents to have it the way they want it (whatever "it" may be)... and you seeing more objectively what needs to be done. About their healthcare or legal aspects or not driving or whether they are able to stay in their home. Then doing it... whether it is exactly what your folks want, or not. Yes, you might meet with some resistance... but at the same time, you need to make some difficult... yet, hopefully, beneficial... choices

As you discuss division of assets with your parents... DO NOT let a situation be set up where you and your siblings or other family members will be expected to share... or divide assets and decide who gets what... at a future time after your parents pass. There is no good reason to set yourself up for the squabbling and ill feelings this could easily lead to.

Discourage your folks from saying, "Our daughter and son will both inherit the house." Of course, the distribution of assets should be fair and equitable... but who gets what is something to be determined NOW. Don't anticipate that adult children will amicably divide assets... sell the house, etc. ... between themselves "later." If there are grandchildren, they may also be part of this equation. It is best for your parents to make these determinations and decide who gets what now... and put their wishes into legal documents... to prevent future bickering and wrangling.

Your 2 most immediate concerns should be: 1) Setting up a trust and/or will (so your folks' assets are not drained thru the probate process or by unscrupulous players). A will alone... without a trust... will likely be subjected to probate fees. And... 2) Evaluating your parents' day-to-day care needs. These will both lead to spending money.

You must make a clear-eyed determination of how much money your parents currently have in checking and savings... as well as any investments they might have. And again... what is their health insurance/Medicare situation?

Whether your parents are still in their home or living in a care facility... make sure you have an up-to-date list of ALL their different medications and the dosage of each. Know what they take and when. Some older folks are right on top of taking their meds... perhaps noting on a piece of paper or calendar page that they took them. Others get confused... forgetting completely and not taking them. Or taking them 2 or 3 times in a day... as it crosses their mind. Are your folks each up to the task of managing and taking their meds as prescribed?

Here is a link to Medication Management Tips for Family Caregivers: https://www.agingcare.com/articles/medication-management-tips-for-family-caregivers-245769.htm

If they're still living in their home... print out their list of medications, put it in a well-marked envelope, and stick it on the front of their refrigerator. Include a recent photo for identification by emergency medical personnel. If you are caring for 2 ailing elders... make one of these info packets... with ID photo... for each person. This information is for emergency medical personnel... if it ever happens either of your parents has a health emergency and an ambulance is called. This list is also helpful to you... to have their meds information at your fingertips. Be sure to update this list as their medications change.

These days caregivers can also email or text themselves this information... so it is available on their phone. This is really helpful whether you're right there in the midst of the emergency... or if you are contacted when you are not present.

This list and photo should also include your parent's name, their birthdate, and their doctor's name and contact information. You want to make this info and identification easy for medical responders. Include, with the list of medications they are taking, what illnesses they have. Also include their emergency contact person's name and phone number. Record their normal blood pressure numbers. Do they wear hearing or vision devices? Does your elder speak English? If not English, what language do they speak?

It is also helpful for emergency personnel to know what the person's last EKG looked like. This gives them critical information on any current heart event that might be occurring. Record anything heart-related or otherwise that may seem "unusual"... but may be "usual" for your parent. Medical responders don't want to treat the person incorrectly due to lack of knowledge.

Include your elder's health insurance information on this list, too. If they are taken to the hospital... this will be crucial information to have.

In a similar vein... you might want to check out Vial of Life online. As stated on their website: "Medical personnel can make the best decisions regarding emergency treatment when they know a person's medical conditions, medications, or medical allergies. This can mean the difference between life and death in the 'Golden Hour' immediately following a medical emergency."

Your parents might find themselves in a medical emergency which renders them unconscious... or makes it difficult for them to speak or even think straight. The information in the vial... or the well-marked envelope on your fridge... speaks for them when they cannot speak for themselves. The Vial of Life program is free.

This is a smart way to have your parents' medical information on hand. A copy of their meds list should also be put in your elder's wallet and their car's glove compartment if they're still driving. This list... and keeping it updated... is especially important for seniors due to their constant medical changes and numerous medications. Emergency personnel who are trying to help them need to know as many things as possible about the person(s) they are treating... especially if there is a complex medical history.

It's easy to make this list, put it on the fridge... and forget about it. That's why I say again... be sure to keep this information up to date by reviewing it periodically.

Restating the bottom line... this collection of current medical information might be crucial in an emergency situation... speaking for the ailing elder when they cannot speak for themselves.

Either with an attorney's guidance or thru online, do-it-yourself research... have each of your parents fill out, date, and sign an Advance Directive for end-of-Life care. In this document, they state their preferences for whether they want Life-saving procedures... drugs, surgery, intubation, and resuscitation, and whether they want to be kept on life-support at a crucial moment... or not. Again, here is an opportunity for a conversation with each parent as to what they want to have happen. This can be a vital document to have in the future. Make copies of their Advance Directive. File a copy with their doctor(s). A copy should be put in their chart any time they go to the hospital. Have a copy on hand for yourself... to show to a medical professional, should you need to.

Years ago... this document of end-of-Life care preferences was often ignored by doctors who were determined to use every machine, surgery, and drug possible to keep their patient alive. Now, it seems these expressed wishes are more likely to be followed.

Early in 2018… I read an article written by a doctor bemoaning the fact that even with an Advanced Directive or the patient's expressed wishes on file… there is still no consistent system for making this information available to attending physicians. This is especially true with emergency medical professionals.

Generally speaking… nurses and doctors are up to their eyeballs dealing with patients and paperwork. The elderly patient's Advance Directive may, indeed, be in their file… but buried in an inefficient manner. Being in the middle of an emergency situation does not lend itself to digging thru the patient's file to see if a Directive can be found.

Here is where you having their Power of Attorney for healthcare benefits you, your parents, and the situation. You are your parent's healthcare advocate. It's a good idea for you to take it upon yourself to be as proactive as possible when it comes to your parent's care and end-of-Life wishes. Speak up. Don't be shy. You are the one who will express your parents' care decisions when they are not able to.

Get burial services in order sooner rather than later. Yes, this can possibly lead to more difficult conversations. You'll want to discuss with your folks any funeral or burial arrangements they may already have in place.

Do one or both of your parents want to be cremated? If so, in their own handwriting… have them write, date, and sign a statement stating "I want to be cremated." Have they already made... and paid for... arrangements? Burial plots, headstones, caskets, funeral services, cremation? If they don't already have these arrangements in place... it is much to your advantage to find and contact a funeral home to set things up as soon as possible. Here again, we are talking about possibly spending several thousand dollars—but you will pay "today's prices." The costs involved will only continue going up.

My parents each passed at home, in their own bed. Because I had pre-arrangements with a funeral home... I made 1 phone call. People from the funeral home came to pick up the body... began the cremation process... and contacted the county to set in motion the procedure for the death certificate. When you receive your parent's death certificate... make copies of that, too.

Be aware you have choices. Of course, a funeral home would want to sell you a big, top-of-the-line casket or fancy urn for their cremains. And if that is what you're looking for... great. But, you do have options. It is up to you and your family how much you want to spend on a casket, urn, burial plot or funeral/memorial service.

A big plus for making these prearrangements is, you will not have to make these decisions and arrangements in the emotionally difficult hours and days immediately following your parent's passing. That alone makes it worth dealing with now.

One of my cousins was in denial as to her father's declining condition. She was devastated when he died... in her mind, "unexpectedly." Casting about to make funeral and burial arrangements... she assumed her father would be buried in a family plot some of my other cousins had set up. The cousin in charge of this family plot made it very clear there was no room for this uncle there. Which sent my bereaved cousin into a spin... trying to secure somewhere for her father to be buried... at a raw and tender time.

Focusing on Legal Considerations: Make an appointment with their attorney to go over their will/trust documents... for your own knowledge and to see if the names or roles should be updated as mentioned above. If your parents have not written a will or a trust... go with them to their attorney... or thru their attorney's referral, to an attorney who specializes in trusts and passing assets from one generation to the next. Set this in motion. Establishing the trust and other necessary documents will run a few thousand dollars. In late 1997, we paid $1,500. I'm sure costs and fees have only gone up. (Perhaps "skyrocketed" is a more accurate term.)

Realizing "now's the time" to get more involved in my parents' Life... my folks and I went to an attorney and listened as he discussed different items to educate us (me).

This gave me an understanding of the steps I needed to take to get our family's pertinent affairs in order. The process of establishing a trust and putting all of your folks' assets into the trust can take weeks or months… depending on how focused you are. I recommend… focus on getting it all done as soon as possible.

This is literally a "no time like the present" situation.

If you have siblings… the timeline of this process might be affected by how much they want to be involved in any or all of this. The person with Powers of Attorney will have the final say.

Remember… each state has its own probate requirements and inheritance laws. You're interested in the statutes of the state your parents live in. It is much to your advantage to educate yourself. Because of the vast informative resources of the Internet… this can be done online, with or without the guidance of an attorney. In the late '90s… I chose to go straight to an attorney we were referred to. You may find it easier or safer to go that route, too. Safer in the sense of, hopefully, getting accurate information from an estate-planning professional. If you do-it-yourself… you don't want to set yourself up for any unexpected rude surprises down the road.

Once the trust document is created… based on conversations with the attorney re: how your folks want to divide their assets, determine an executor, etc.... the attorney's office will draw up the will and/or trust documents and your parents will sign them. All of their assets must be "put into" the trust. Our attorney's office made the arrangements for my parents' house to be put into the trust. With my Power of Attorney for Finance in hand... I went to all of my folks' different accounts and assets and filed paperwork to have them each put into the trust. The lawyer's office may do this for you... for an additional fee. Whichever assets are not actively "put into" the trust will not be covered by the trust document. Thus, they will be subject to probate fees and possible future haggling with your siblings or other family members.

Whatever your parent's day-to-day life is like right now... undoubtedly, they will soon need more help with their "activities of daily living." There are many choices. You can hire a person to come into their home. How many days a week... how many hours a day... and what the person is expected to do while they're there... are determined by you and your folks. This caregiver can be a family member(s) or someone you hire.

You can have a person come in to cook, clean, grocery shop, or run errands... or for companionship. There are aides who will give elders baths/showers or help them dress. And others... usually nurses, at a higher hourly rate ... who give shots, draw blood, change wound dressing, etc.

If you choose to hire a person... I suggest working with an agency rather than an individual. The thought being... an agency's workers are usually vetted (bonded, insured) in some way and perhaps even given some degree of training. Important to you... if something happens and the caregiver can't come... the agency would have someone else they could send to take their place. As opposed to the absent caregiver saying, "Oops, sorry"... which would send you scrambling to cover your folks' care needs.

As you interview an agency... be clear... does the agency recognize the need for a substitute and make all the arrangements... or is their expectation that *you* would call them, saying the caregiver didn't show... and then they send another caregiver?

Either way, this is not a foolproof system. Two mornings a week, Scott and I had a caregiver come... from an agency... to get my parents up, help them dress, set out their breakfast, and be with them for a few hours while we attended meetings and ran errands. It was raining one day, and our caregiver decided she didn't want to wait for her bus in the rain... so she didn't come. Scott and I had already left the house... we had no idea she didn't show up. She did not inform her agency... so they did not know a substitute needed to be sent. So much for best-laid plans.

To be perfectly honest… some, not all, of these care-givers go thru their client's home and steal jewelry or other valuables. This did not occur to me… especially as we found our caregiver thru an agency whose owner was someone I knew and respected. However, this did happen in our case. So, it's a good idea to be aware of this possibility and lock away valuable items… especially small ones.

In this same vein… be sure your elder is not wearing jewelry if they are taken to the hospital or end up living in a care facility. Do not send anything of value with them to the hospital or a care facility.

For a caregiver to come to your parents' home… expect to pay $30 an hour or more. For many caregivers, English is a 2nd language… sometimes making their speech chal-lenging to understand. This may or may not be a problem for your parents.

Does your parents' state of residence have a program that helps pay for in-home healthcare workers?

Many times, after an elder's hospital stay… the hospital sends in-home care aides to your house a few times a week for a month or so after your parent gets home. Each time one of my parents came home from the hospital, these arrangements were "automatically" made by the hospital. Social workers or healthcare aides came to the house… to bathe them, check on their well-being, take blood pressure, monitor meds, etc.

An elder program at a local Community Center can be a good resource for a lot of factors related to your parents' care. Your folks might love participating in these programs… but other times, they'll refuse to have anything to do with it. My mother would say, "Dana, they're all *old* people." (Uh, yeah.) These elder center programs can be very helpful for you to find out about eldercare resources and transportation services available—and possibly even a trust attorney referral.

Contact local eldercare facilities to find out what care options are available… according to your family's needs and assets. It could be your parents have no trouble seeing themselves residing in a care home. Or… as was the case with my father… they might have very strong feelings about *not* wanting to live in a care facility. Sometimes, your parents' "strong feelings" have to be overridden by the reality of the situation.

There are agencies that will help you with either finding someone to come into the home… or finding the right care facility for your folks. Some care facilities have 3 different levels of housing and care options. The elder would start out in their own small apartment… with cleaning services provided and usually dining room meals available to them. As they continue to decline… the next tier of care would have them move into a room in the facility building, but they're still free to move around… go to classes, sing-alongs, etc. Again, with dining room access. Lastly, as their care needs increase… they would move into a room very much like a hospital room where they would be in bed most of the time, having their needs attended to, with meals served to them in their room.

Choosing for them to live in a facility leads to many other considerations. If they own a home… will it now be sold… either to pay for their care… or for the proceeds to be divided among beneficiaries? Will a family member move into their home and live there? Will their house be rented or leased? If it is to be inherited… make sure that intent is clearly spelled out in the will or trust document. Is the house free and clear? Do your parents have a mortgage(s)? Or a reverse mortgage? These are things you want to know.

If your parents have pets who are likely to outlive them… ask your folks if they have plans for them. If not, begin to make arrangements. Ask family members, friends, neighbors if they will care for them after your parents' passing. Find out if there are online pet adoption sites in the area. Taking them to an animal shelter is also an option.

You will need to deal with your folks' furnishings… heirlooms… clothes… cars… knick-knacks and paddy-whacks. *Many* different approaches here. There are businesses which will… for a fee… go thru your parents' house… either after they have passed or moved to a care facility. Sorting out any valuables or resale items. Getting rid of trash.

Setting up and running an estate sale. They frequently have professional connections which smooth this process. You can, of course, do this all yourself… hopefully with the help of family and friends.

I imagine you've heard… as we age, we go "backward"… becoming "younger" and "younger." This is so true. When Scott and I arrived to care for my folks… I say this affectionately… they were like 4-year-olds. They could dress themselves and they played well together.

Unless your parents go quickly… all the more reason to put in place the trust, POA for finance and for healthcare, their Advance Directive and other documents. You will watch them physically, and possibly, mentally, decline… until they require the same level of care as small children. Then, infants.

I wish you well as you navigate
the vast universe of eldercare.

May The Force Be With You.

OUTLINE / CHECKLIST

Now is the time to have conversations with your parents about the following and act upon what you learn.
Each state has its own laws regarding eldercare issues.
What are the laws in your parents' state of residence?
Make several photocopies of each legal document.

HEALTHCARE
Things to find out

Acquaint yourself with your parent's health insurance and Medicare situation.

Have they created and signed an Advance Directive? Where is it? Is a copy on file with their doctor? May be a good idea to take a picture of it and store it on your phone.

Do your parents have long-term care insurance?

What are their day-to-day care needs?

What are their preferences for the future… as their ability to function independently declines?

Are they still driving? Are they safe drivers?

Are there local eldercare programs? Are your folks interested in attending?

Things to do

Attend medical appointments with them. Meet their doctor(s). Understand their current health situation.

Familiarize yourself with and organize your parents' medications. Become involved with administering them, if need be.

Make sure there is an up-to-date list of your elder's meds… what they take and when. Include on this list of meds… medical conditions, average blood pressure reading, EKG, allergies, a photo… as well as a contact person's name and phone number, and their health insurance information. Print this list out and stick it to the front of the refrigerator… should emergency personnel ever need to know. Take a photo of this information for your phone.

FINANCE
Things to find out

Find out about the laws, fees, procedures, and regulations regarding transfer of assets in your parents' state of residence.

Do your parents have a lawyer, banker, or stockbroker?

What and where are their assets? How do they want them divided?

Have your parents established a will or trust? Do they have Life insurance? Who are their beneficiaries?

Have they paid for arrangements with a funeral home? Do they want to be buried or cremated? Do they want a funeral? A memorial service? Do they have a burial plot?

Things to do

Have your signature added to your parents' checking and savings accounts… credit cards… and other investment accounts. Possibly also add your signature to the deed on their house, condo, or investment property.

Establish Powers of Attorney for Finance and Healthcare. And an Advance Directive.

Create a trust or a will. If your parents already have these documents… familiarize yourself with them.

If establishing a trust… be sure all assets and resources are legally placed into the trust.

Be sure beneficiaries, the person(s) with Powers of Attorney, and your parents' executor… are all up to date. Regarding Powers of Attorney and estate executor, find out… are the people designated still healthy and alive? Do they still want to fulfill these legal roles?

If your parents do not have end-of-Life arrangements with a funeral home… contact a funeral home and pay for their funeral or memorial service… burial plot… cremation… NOW.

Probate, Wills and Trusts… a.k.a. Estate Planning and why this is important

This section is to help clarify what these different documents and procedures are. I know I've said this before and here it is again… each state has its own laws, statutes, and fees regarding probate and inheritance. Check out the laws and fees in your parents' state of residence.

I found this information on different online sites. Should you be interested in greater clarification… here are links to 4 helpful sites:

A state-by-state guide to the most common fees:
https://trustandwill.com/learn/probate-fees
https://www.investopedia.com

Free legal documents, forms, and contracts:

https://www.lawdepot.com

https://ez-probate.com/

Estate planning is often viewed as a concern for older people with substantial means. In fact, it is a subject that almost everyone needs to address. Even if your parents' assets are limited to a house or condo, bank accounts, and perhaps an IRA or 401(k) account, you want to be sure that the people they wish to receive these assets upon their death, do indeed receive them… and that their plans are executed with efficiency and the least expense possible. In families with complicated personal relationships… such as children from more than one marriage, a dependent parent or relative, or offspring whose financial resources vary greatly… having clearly expressed directions and a clear explanation of circumstances (in a will or trust) makes distributing your parents' assets easier and may prevent potential disputes among their heirs.

If a person dies without a will, a trust, or any other estate planning provisions… the distribution of their assets and probate fees (how much money the state gets from the estate) will be determined by their state's laws.

A rule of thumb: A will almost always ends up in probate. A trust does not.

Probate

Probate is the legal process... a court-supervised proceeding... to settle an estate after the owner has passed away. Assets of the deceased are reviewed and inheritors determined. A probate court provides the final ruling on the division and distribution of assets to beneficiaries.

Not all estates need to go thru probate. One of the main downsides of probate is the cost. The more it costs, the less beneficiaries inherit. Total probate costs vary widely... depending on certain factors, such as... the state your parents live in... the size of their estate... how complicated their Estate Plan is... and whether someone disputes any part of their plan.

These and other fees are part of the probate process:

- The cost of a probate attorney
- Accounting fees
- Court and notary fees
- Appraisal and business valuation fees
- Estate sale preparation fees.

The probate court process can take weeks or months to complete. Probate can be a nightmare for the recipients. It is often time-consuming, expensive, and just plain stressful for the ones left to navigate it.

If your parents have done end-of-Life financial planning... depending on the legal instruments they chose to use... you and other heirs might end up dealing with probate.

Altho probate proceedings focus on the existence and authenticity of a will... probate can be initiated with or without a will. Thru probate procedures, the estate first pays any debts and taxes... then makes distributions to beneficiaries according to instructions left by the deceased.

Exorbitant probate costs and complexities can be lessened or avoided by having an easily authenticated will or by using investment vehicles that do not require probate.

There are smart, strategic ways to make probate easier or eliminate it completely.

A Will

A will is a legal document detailing how a person wants their affairs handled and assets distributed after they die. A will must be signed, dated, and witnessed as required by state law. Implementing a will requires a legal process... including filing with the probate court in the deceased person's jurisdiction. The will document is publicly available in the records of the probate court.

A Trust

A trust is a legal agreement providing for the transfer of assets from their owner... called the *grantor* or *trustor*...

to a trustee or inheritor. The trustee may be a fiduciary... a person who is obligated to act in a way benefitting someone else, usually financially... who handles the trust assets in accordance with the terms of the trust document and solely in the best interests of the beneficiaries. The trust sets the terms for management of the assets... for distributions to one or more designated beneficiaries... and for the final disposition of the assets.

There are different types of trusts:

- A revocable trust
- An irrevocable trust
- A special purpose trust
- A charitable trust
- A special needs trust.

A trust avoids probate... making the process of settling an estate simpler and cheaper.

Most important to some people... a trust is private. Trusts are not public at all... whereas probate is a public proceeding and the probate records can be viewed by any and all interested parties. If you or your family are concerned about privacy... creating a trust allows your estate to avoid probate fees and probate records... thus keeping your legal affairs private.

Additional Strategies

Payable on Death (POD) or Transfer on Death (TOD) Accounts: Upon death… POD or TOD accounts immediately transfer assets to named beneficiaries without any cost and no need for a court to be involved.

Open Life insurance policies: Similar to a POD or TOD account… life insurance policies have named beneficiaries. (It is suggested to update beneficiaries regularly… in response to a marriage, a death, a birth, or any other major life event.) Life insurance beneficiary payouts can be made with the presentation of a valid death certificate. According to your parents' state's statutes… there may be a nominal fee for the death certificate. This fee will be significantly less than the cost of the probate process.

Jointly titled property: Be sure your name… or whoever has Power of Attorney for Finance or some kind of claim to the property… is on the title to your parents' home and other property they may have before they die. With jointly titled property… upon the owner's death, the property automatically passes to whoever else has their name on the title. Some states are "community property" states… which makes community property with right of survivorship even easier.

EZ Probate: Experts at EZ Probate simplify the probate process… supporting and guiding people thru the procedure… reducing costs and getting beneficiaries access to their money faster. https://ez-probate.com

Thoughts Regarding Powers of Attorney

Having said that the services of an attorney are not required to prepare a Durable Power of Attorney for Asset Management and a Medical Power of Attorney… I want to share with you insightful information I found at https://www.agingcare.com.

K. Gabriel Heiser is an attorney with more than 25 years of experience in elder law and estate planning… and the author of *How to Protect Your Family's Assets from Devastating Nursing Home Costs: Medicaid Secrets*, an annually updated practical guide for the layperson.

From his deep wealth of experience… Mr. Heiser states, "While some online forms are better than others, none of them is worth paying for. Here's why…

"First of all, there is no interview process to determine what type of clauses are appropriate to insert into the document and which clauses to omit or modify. For example, should there be authority to make gifts to certain family members, and if so, how should that be determined and limited? Might some consideration be given to the possibility that the principal (usually the parent) may need to move to a nursing home at some point and need to apply for Medicaid? If so, it is crucial to include very specific Medicaid-planning-related clauses in the POA document.

"Second, there is no one with experience to assist you in determining who should be the agent (typically one of the children), who should be the successor agent, whether the Powers should be 'immediate' or 'springing,' and if so, under what circumstances, etc.

"Third, there is no one witnessing the signing, who can vouch for the mental capacity of the principal (parent), so as to avoid a later claim that the form is invalid. (Yes, sometimes other family members become resentful of the named agent and try to invalidate the POA document.)

"Finally, the online forms vary tremendously in quality and thoroughness, and the lay person (that would be you or me) will have no way to judge good from bad. Merely 'looking official' is not good enough. A POA is a very powerful document; if you sign one, you are giving someone else the power to empty out your bank account, sell your house out from under you, possibly make gifts to people you don't approve of, move you from one residence to another, etc.

"Note that the cost to have a lawyer-prepared POA is usually quite modest, under $200 in many cities. Be sure to find an attorney who does a lot of estate planning and/or elder law work, for the most appropriate advice and forms."

That's definitely useful advice from a guy who's been around that block a time or 10.

Mr. Heiser's article was written years ago… quite likely the "modest" fees for lawyer-prepared POA documents has gone up.

Online, you can find additional helpful information and the particulars for the state your parents reside in at: https://powerofattorney.com/ or https://www.agingcare.com.

Care for The Caregiver

Taking Care of YOU:
Self-Care for Family Caregivers

Best analogy for this situation: Safety instructions on an airplane... when the oxygen mask descends in front of you... put your own oxygen mask on first, before you try to assist anyone else.

Only when we first help ourselves can we effectively help others. Boy! Does *that* get lost in the ongoing concern and busyness of day-to-day eldercare!

Caring for yourself is one of the most important things you can do as a caregiver.

And frequently the most forgotten. When your needs are taken care of, the person you are caring for benefits, also.

If you are a friend or family member who is not the actual primary caregiver… there are ways you can help. Making sure the family caregiver(s) are aware of the following links and services… you will be a true ally in this family's eldercare scenario.

With the caregiver's agreement, you could take it upon yourself to make appointments for the caregiver at a spa, a therapist, or a doctor. Does transportation need to be arranged?

You would also help out in a big way by making the arrangements for yourself… or a family member, neighbor, friend, or a person from an agency… to come be with the elder person while the primary caregiver goes to their appointment or for a walk or has lunch with a friend. Even this "little bit" of helping to organize and make self-care opportunities available… would be a big help to the primary caregiver. Always be sure the caregiver agrees with your plans and suggestions.

This "Afters" offers links to helpful sites online. These can guide you to local self-help services such as… support groups… self-care suggestions… training… relaxation, meditation, yoga, and stress reduction.

A lot of what I'm writing here comes from these websites.

https://www.caregiver.org/resource/
taking-care-you-self-care-family-caregivers/

Connecting caregivers... sometimes it's nice... and it helps... to have someone to talk to.

https://www.caregiver.org/
connecting-caregivers/services-by-state/

This "services by state" tool offered at caregiver.org... helps family caregivers locate public, nonprofit, and private programs and services nearest their loved one... whether they are living at home or in a residential facility. Resources include government health and disability programs, legal resources, disease-specific organizations (heart disease, cancer, Alzheimer's, etc.) and more. Caregiving is challenging, but there are resources to help.

Family caregivers... whatever their age... are less likely than non-caregivers to practice self-care and preventive healthcare. Regardless of age, sex, race, and ethnicity... caregivers report problems attending to their own health and well-being as they manage their caregiving responsibilities.

Many times caregivers report:

- Sleep deprivation
- Poor eating habits
- Failure to exercise
- Failure to stay in bed when ill
- Postponement of, or failure to make, medical appointments for themselves

Caregiving can be an emotional roller coaster. On the one hand, caring for your family member shows your love and commitment. It can be a rewarding personal experience. On the other hand... exhaustion, worry, inadequate resources, and continuous care demands are enormously stressful. Family caregivers are also at increased risk for depression and excessive use of alcohol, tobacco, and other drugs.

If inadequate financial resources is an issue for you and your family... check with the county or state government of the state your parents live in to find out if there are programs or agencies which will pay live-in caregivers (like you) or pay for you to hire a person part-time so you can take a break. Even getting away for a few hours can help you reset emotionally and physically. Getting away for a few days can work wonders. This I share from experience.

Many times, attitudes and beliefs form personal barriers that stand in the way of caring for yourself. Not taking care of yourself might be a lifelong pattern. Taking care of others can seem to be an easier option.

Truthfully... as a family caregiver, you have to ask yourself:

"What good will I be to the person I care
for if I become ill? Or if I die?"
(Or even if I am excessively cranky.)

Breaking old patterns and overcoming obstacles is not an easy proposition, but it can be done. The first task in removing personal barriers to self-care is to identify what is in your way. For example:

- Do you think you are being selfish if you put your needs first?
- Is it frightening to think of your own needs? What is that fear about?
- Do you have trouble asking for what you need? Do you feel inadequate if you ask for help?
- Do you feel you have to prove you are worthy of the affection of the person you're caring for? Do you do too much as a result?

Sometimes, caregivers have misconceptions that increase their stress and get in the way of good self-care. Here are some of the most commonly expressed concerns:

- I am responsible for my parent's health.
- If I don't do it, no one will.
- If I do it right, I will get the love, attention, and respect I deserve.
- Our family always takes care of their own.
- I promised my father I would always take care of my mother.

Candidly... taking good care of yourself is something only you can do. You know what helps you relax. What feels good to you... what feels self-nurturing. It is not likely someone else is going to come along and say... "Wow! You've really been working hard. Let's get you a break and some self-care." Might happen. Not likely.

You have to figure out what works for you... and how to give it to yourself.

What do caregivers need most?
1) Help with caregiving.
2) More financial support.
3) Emotional support.
4) Recognition and understanding.
5) Time to recharge.

Financial limitations can add a lot more stress to the already stressful situation of caregiving. I know from experience... financial limitation can also greatly motivate and encourage creativity. Thinking outside the box... in this case, the box of "I can't afford to set up some time off for myself."

Perhaps there are other family members, friends, or neighbors you can barter with. So many possibilities. They might be interested in spending a few hours with the person you're caring for in exchange for... fresh-baked bread or cookies... a dinner casserole (as you make 1 for your dinner, make another to trade)… caring for their kids for a few hours… singing or playing music for them on your guitar or piano (or whichever instrument you play)… helping with their laundry… giving them a haircut… helping balance their checkbook. I realize bartering may mean extra work for you. But it's *different* work. A change of pace. And creates some time off for yourself.

What I'm saying is… refuse to let limited money win and keep you from getting care you need for yourself.

Here are some additional online links to check out. Some of these sites provide free and confidential telephone counseling, education, support, referrals and resources.

- https://www.mayoclinic.org/healthy-lifestyle/ stress-management/in-depth/caregiver-stress/
- https://careforcaregivers.com/
- https://www.caringbridge.org/resources/ techniques-to-relieve-caregiver-stress/

These are just a few of the helpful sites available online. As I googled "care for caregivers," up came 206,000,000 results in 0.56 seconds. So, there are plenty more sites with worthwhile suggestions and resources for you to look into. I hope you find ideas and recommendations that serve you.

I wish you well as you give yourself good care… while you are taking care of your loved one.

Acknowledgments

With a warm heart, I acknowledge…

My awesome husband, Scott. It's been 40 years, Baby! I am honored to be your wife. Your love still feels like love. Mahalo for your keen insight and your playful laughter. You bless my Life with your loving encouragement and support.

My remarkable Lyla. Thanks for loving me for who I am and forgiving me for who I am not. And for holding and consistently encouraging the vision of *Holy Wow!*... as I moved along doing my best imitation of molasses in January.

Our brilliant, hilarious, intriguing son, Isaiah. Thanks for always being your fine self. And a big thank you for bringing The Lovely Claire Doe to join our family. You and your sweet family grace my Life.

Our talented son-in-law, Michael Bashan. Mahalo, Mike, for being you. And for sharing your talents… recording significant sections and the intros and outros to all of my audiobooks… in your very professional sounding voice.

Our cooleriffic GrandBunnies... Ramona, Lyla Leigh and Abigail Claire. You are each such a treasure to my heart.

Our dear friend, Joy Utz, C.F.o.F. Our very own Certified Facilitator of Fun. Mahalo for you! I am grateful for your kind generosity and attentive, caring ways. This *Holy Wow! Quartet* would not be here without you.

Rita Leiphart, C.C.H. I am forever grateful for your artistry as a hypnotherapist. I hold you responsible for helping me birth *Holy Wow!* after its ridiculously long gestation.

I am blessed beyond measure by the many gifts of insight and connexion which have come my way thanks to the extraordinary friends and fellow humans who have touched my Life. Special appreciation to our longtime friends, Jim and Martha Fish, and their family... and to John Randolph Price and his lovely wife, Jan. A grateful shout-out to Chris Allen... Celiane Milner and her daughter, Amber... Beatrice Rose and her daughter, Sarah... and to Mitch Evans.

From my Unity of Beaverton days... Tori Padellford, Mary Huebner, Bruce and Toni Blue Spruce Rodgers, Rennie Maguire, Grace Muncie-Jarvis, Linda Waltmire, Ruby Gallagher, Anne Morey (a.k.a. Cupcake), Rev. Maureen Haley, and Rev. Ed Townley.

In Southern California... Gilmore Rizzo and Bryan Miller, Ida Smith, Nancy Thompson, Noreen Bernier,

Dianalee and Joan, Patricia Satorie Barnes, Diane Sternbach, Ron Zoboblish, Rev. Dr. Maureen Hoyt, Revs. Michael and Mary Beth Speer, Rev. Shelly Downes, and Rev. Harry Morgan Moses.

Here, in Hawaii… Carolyn and Richard Williams, Bettina Linke and family, Mark Morphew, Cathy Spitzenberger, Robin Bush, Dorothy and Mary Ellen, Maureen and Eric Langberg, Sarah and Jason McCarthy, Barrie Rose, Jude McAnesby, Beth Brandt, Johanna Tilbury, Minoo Elison, Charlie Anderson, Marcia Masters and Rebecca Clancy.

My dear friend, Karen Myer. During my process of writing the original *Holy Wow!* and now *The Patience Olympics*… as you read the drafts… your enthusiasm for its content and your gracious encouragement fortified me more than you could know.

Mahalo to Cheryl Valle of Surf City Images for my headshots and outstanding family portraits. And for being such a pleasure to work with.

You hold this book in your hands right now thanks to the generosity of spirit and skillful coaching of Amy Collins… literally *Holy Wow!*'s fairy godmother. A Big Thanks to Amy. Period. And to Amy's right-hand woman, the Executive Director of New Shelves Books, Keri-Rae Barnum… you have helped me immeasurably. More appreciation to Amy for recommending my ideal editors, Pam Cangioli and

Kim Jace, as well as my very talented graphic artist and cover designer, Mila... Miladinka Milic. Pam Cangioli led me to Ghislain Viau who has done an excellent job as my interior book designer.

To each of you for the part you played in bringing *Holy Wow!* into being... Mahalo Plenty!

Acknowledging that you, kind Reader, might be interested in connecting with any of these talented and very helpful individuals... here are their websites:

Rita Leiphart – www.districthypnosis.com
Keri-Rae Barnum - www.newshelves.com
Pam Cangioli – www.proofedtoperfection.com
Miladinka Milic – www.milagraphicartist.com
Ghislain Viau – www.creativepublishingdesign.com
Cheryl Valle - www.surfcityimages.com

About The Author

Blessed to share the rich gifts of mindfulness, Dana has been teaching others to meditate for 50 years. Recognizing we are Spirit living a human experience, she is fascinated by the rich tapestry of Life… and the many gifts and possibilities available to every human.

Planet Earth is one wild and crazy place. Might as well rise to the occasion.

It is Dana's delight to play the temple gongs, bells, and tingsha that grace her guided meditations. She recognizes this as "a past-Life thing." Dana says… "The resonant tones of the gongs take you places mere words could never find."

She follows her own advice to "choose to be amused" and finds great pleasure in being a wordsmith. As an ordained transdenominational minister, Dana is a Celebrationist, creating Weddings, Memorial Services, and other Life-enhancing ceremony and ritual.

Dana is also A Blessed Momo... standing in wonder of her miraculous GrandBunnies.

Dana and her husband, Scott, live in Kona, Hawaii, ever in awe of the miraculous sunsets.

Dana is totally jazzed that *Holy Wow! Volume IV* is her fourth book.